FIRST THINGS FIRST

HIP-HOP LADIES WHO CHANGED THE GAME

NADIRAH SIMMONS

12

TWELVE

NEW YORK   BOSTON

Twelve
Hachette Book Group
1290 Avenue of the Americas, New York, NY 10104
twelvebooks.com
twitter.com/twelvebooks

First Edition: January 2024

Twelve is an imprint of Grand Central Publishing. The Twelve name and logo
are trademarks of Hachette Book Group, Inc.

The publisher is not responsible for websites (or their content) that are
not owned by the publisher.

The Hachette Speakers Bureau provides a wide range of authors for speaking
events. To find out more, go to hachettespeakersbureau.com or email
HachetteSpeakers@hbgusa.com.

Twelve books may be purchased in bulk for business, educational, or promotional
use. For information, please contact your local bookseller or the Hachette Book
Group Special Markets Department at special.markets@hbgusa.com.

Illustrations by Sara Gilanchi

Print book interior design by Timothy Shaner, NightandDayDesign.biz

Library of Congress Cataloging-in-Publication Data has been applied for.

ISBNs: 978-1-5387-4074-3 (paper over board), 978-1-5387-4075-0 (ebook)

Printed in the United States of America

LSC-C

Printing 1, 2023

THIS BOOK IS FOR
MY FAMILY, FRIENDS,
AND ALL OF THE
COMPUTERS I MESSED UP
DOWNLOADING MUSIC

TRACK LIST

TRACK LIST

"FASHION"

"MUSIC"

"PRINT / RADIO"

"AWARDS / CERTIFICATIONS"

INTRO

I f you knew how many times I rewrote this introduction you wouldn't believe me. In fact, I rewrote it so many times I can't even give you an exact number—somewhere around fifty feels pretty close, though. What I *do know for certain* is that this intro was the very first thing I wrote for this book and the very last thing I edited for this book. Each time I came back to this point I knew I had to make two things clear: 1) just how important women in hip-hop are to me, and 2) just how important women are to hip-hop. So I guess I'll start with that first part.

In 2018 I created *The Gumbo*, a social club and media platform designed to celebrate and center the experiences of Black women in hip-hop. I struggled to come up with a name for the platform for months because hip-hop is not just about the music, it's a culture defined by distinct elements and a myriad of professions, power players and personalities, of which rap is just one component. To me, the fashion designers who dress the rappers are just as important as the rappers themselves, as are the producers, sound engineers, videographers, directors, journalists, editors, actors, comedians, creative directors, graphic designers, staffers at the label, breakdancers, graffiti artists, and whoever else touches this beautiful thing we call hip-hop.

That's how I came up with the name *The Gumbo*. Or better yet, that's how the name came to me one night in a dream. "What's a word that best describes a bunch of different things coming together to make something good?" Gumbo. *Gumbo* was the word. So, I went with that. My decision was affirmed in 2020 when Lil' Kim did an interview with *Genius* and stated, "We always gotta put what each girl does [*sic*] in the pot, and we gotta make gumbo." Exactly, Kim.

Long before the inception of *The Gumbo*, though, I was just a little girl accompanying my parents on their trips to now-extinct music stores like Sam Goody, whose shelves were filled to the brim with CDs by the latest artists to drop and musicians long-battling in the game. I remember purchasing one of my very first CDs, *Afrodisiac* by Brandy, and sitting in the living room for hours with the album playing on loop. I read the album booklet front to back, taking breaks in between pages to practice my dance moves in the mirror.

When I would put my CDs away on my little section of the CD tower that housed all of the discs in our home, I couldn't help but look through the other ones. I was already listening to hip-hop because my parents were. I was born a fan. But there was something about going through the album booklets of Lil Kim's *Hard Core,* Foxy Brown's *Ill Na Na,* and Eve's *Scorpion* that sent my love to another level. Through the photos, liner notes, thank-yous, and sometimes advertisements for merch that serve as memorials for a very specific time in the past, I got to know the artists and understand their process as well as the importance of all the people who helped make it happen. There's that gumbo again.

I also recall joining my dad on trips to different showrooms in New York City, where we would get an up-close and personal look at the latest releases from brands like Rocawear, Baby Phat, Sean John, Mecca, and FUBU, to name a few. He owned a clothing store that sold various hip-hop fashion brands—often referred to as "urban wear" or "streetwear"—and these trips helped him decide which items he wanted to add to his stock. And while I can't remember their names or even their faces, I remember the women in these showrooms and how nice they were. How much they knew. And how much it seemed like they had to do. To put it simply, I thought they were so cool.

Fast-forward to my middle school years, when much of my time was spent seated at the computer chair in my parents' office—or any office I could find, in fact—downloading music from Limewire, and then Frostwire until it burned out the hard drive. And don't get me started on the amount of time I spent discovering new artists and mixtapes on platforms like DatPiff, DD172, 2DopeBoyz, and any other blog site I could access. Funnily enough, I wasn't alone. My parents are music heads too, and my dad and I would exchange a lot of music with one another. Often it was a race with my dad—who was going to hear the new Curren$y tape first. (Spoiler alert: he almost always did, lol.) Now that I think about it, the computer didn't break because of me. My parents were downloading mad music too!

The music that *I* downloaded made it onto this little bean-shaped MP3 player that I had. I don't remember the name of that thing, but it was the first MP3 player I had before my parents upgraded me to an iPod shuffle a few years later. A SHUFFLE! Do you remember that?!

What made the MP3 experience so different from previous years, for me, is that music became just as much of a singular experience as it had been a communal one. Up until then, there was really no way for me to listen to music alone. I couldn't drive yet, so there was no space for loud car rides by myself blasting music that I've grown to love. If I popped a CD into my player, everyone could hear it. I had a Walkman, but I rarely used it, for two reasons. The first is that I never wanted to take my CDs out of the house because I'd be constantly worried about breaking or losing them. The second reason was that CDs were just a lot for me to carry. So the bean-shaped thing was where it was at. I could put my headphones in and listen to music by myself while curating my own listening experience with no one watching me replace a CD on my Walkman or, potentially, making remarks about whether or not they liked the artist or their singles or their project. I even remember the first song I put on my iPod when I got it: "Pussycat" by Missy Elliott. Stop right now and go listen to it. I'll wait.

I know you didn't go listen. Be forreal. Go listen real fast. Then come back to the book. It ain't going nowhere.

When I talk about a singular listening experience, I'm talking about *that*. That song right there. The first time I heard it something clicked. I don't know what kind of kid you were, and if you're the opposite of what I'm about to say then excuse the hell out of me, but up until middle school I wasn't really connecting musical dots like *that*. That's not to say I didn't know my stuff, because I'm almost certain no other kids in my grade school could tell me every single soul song sampled by Jay-Z on *The Black Album*. I knew. But that Missy song in particular lit the lightbulb in my head. Women rappers were building upon and creating a shared legacy. They were setting the tone. They were shaping the genre. They were *reshaping* the genre. They were telling stories deemed too "taboo" to talk about. They were kicking down the doors for *everyone*. And they all knew it. They all saw each other. And they saw me. Still do. Which brings me to that second part I mentioned earlier.

After listening to "Pussycat" I became a full-on nerd when it came to all things women in hip-hop. I wanted, no *needed*, to know everything about every woman in the culture. I needed to know which women produced the songs. I needed to know which women styled the artists. I needed to know which women interviewed rappers when they were making the rounds to promote their album. And I needed to know why, with all that women have contributed to hip-hop, the stories celebrating their accomplishments were few and far between.

The answer is space. Not outer space, but *space* space.* That thing that *Merriam-Webster* defines as "a boundless three-dimensional extent in which objects and events occur and have relative position and direction." The ability to take up said space and feel like you belong and are being seen and heard is an important part of hip-hop. In his piece "Masculinity and the Mic: Confronting the Uneven Geography of Hip-Hop," Rashad Shabazz says that it is space that has allowed young men and boys in hip-hop "to not only counter their spatial disempowerment, but also to exclude women from these same spaces." So even though women have been a part of hip-hop as rappers, DJs, b-girls, graffiti artists, and more from the jump, most of the origin stories name men as the contributors and distributors. And if the legacy to build upon is one that treats the women like footnotes, afterthoughts, and bystanders, then we run the risk of omitting the history made by those first ladies on the mic, turntables, charts, and beyond. Which stinks if you ask me!

That propensity for omission is what I'm going to combat with this book, specifically by looking at some of the "firsts" achieved by women in hip-hop that should be celebrated and just plain written down somewhere for people to read and come back to. But before we go any further I have to make one thing very very clear: being the first to do something is not simply a measurement of rank or importance, at least not to me. Nah. Being the second, third, or tenth person to achieve something is just as important, especially in hip-hop.

The "firsts" in this book show the way women in hip-hop stretched the limits of what people previously thought was possible and paved the way for those who would come after them. With that in mind, each chapter will talk about a lady's "first" in hip-hop. Some

* This isn't a typo. I wrote this twice for emphasis!

chapters will highlight women who were the first women to get something done, while other chapters will talk about women who were the
first people to get it done, regardless of gender. Some chapters will be
rooted in factual things like RIAA certifications while other chapters
will be strictly figurative. They are all connected to some sort of
"first" in some way, and they are all very, very important. And,
because hip-hop is a culture, I'm going to talk about women from all
realms: rappers, writers, designers, stylists, etc.

For example, I am going to talk about Ms. Lauryn Hill being the
first rapper to win the Grammy for Album of the Year. However you
feel about the awards today, you have to understand the sheer amount
of talent it takes to make an album of that magnitude, and for it to be
hailed in that capacity at that awards show, racking up five Grammys
in one night. That's a real quantifiable fact you can find on the Recording Academy's website, and the importance of those wins has to be
discussed.

I am also going to talk about Missy Elliott and how she was the
first woman in rap to go to the future. This is one of those figurative
"firsts" that I can't necessarily *prove* by looking it up, especially since
time machines don't actually exist. But I can make the case that with
her music, production, lyrics, and outfits, Missy Elliott used Afrofuturism to take herself (and us) to another century and beyond. And
how by doing so she created a space for rappers to do the same today.

With all of my memories of those showrooms, you know I have to
get into April Walker too! Terms like *streetwear, urban wear,* and *hip-
hop fashion* are used a lot when we talk about the clothing brands that
outfitted the culture's biggest stars. Whatever word is used, you have
to know that April Walker's Walker Wear made her the first woman
to dominate within the space. So naturally, there's a chapter on her
and her impact. (And yes, we'll get into the different terms too.)

Who would I be if I didn't talk about *Honey* magazine? *Honey*
was the first magazine to speak to young Black women of the hip-hop

generation. Not only did the founders Joicelyn Dingle and Kierna Mayo have some of the biggest names in the journalism game writing for the magazine, but their creation laid the foundation for so much of media we see today, especially when it comes to the ways we talk about Blackness, Black womanhood, and Black women in rap. There's no *Gumbo* without *Honey*. That's a fact.

And I would be remiss if I didn't dive into Queen Latifah being not just the first woman rapper, but the first rapper period, to get a star on the Hollywood Walk of Fame. As someone who loves hip-hop and television just the same, Queen Latifah's domination in both mediums, and then film, and then damn near everything else, is a model for rappers today who want to have and do it all. So, we're going to get into that too.

Now we're *almost* ready to do this, but there are a few more things I have to tell you before we start:

- This book is set up like an album tracklist, which means there are some interludes in here. (I won't tell you what the interludes are about, but I love them a lot because they represent women in hip-hop that I really love.)
- You should read this book in order, the same way I hope you listen to an album in order when it first drops. If you choose to skip around you won't be super lost or confused, but after reading this book a couple of hundred times over the past year I can certainly say doing so in order is the best.
- This is not, and I repeat *not*, an all-encompassing history of women in hip-hop. This is simply a celebration of ladies' "firsts" and the impact that they had on the culture.
- Read that last bullet point again.
- It was impossible to talk about every single woman in hip-hop. So if a woman is not here it does not mean she isn't important to hip-hop or me; it just means that what

I wanted to write about her either didn't come out well or flow nicely with the theme.

- 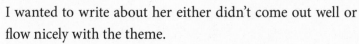 It was also impossible to get in all of the figurative "firsts" that I'm sure exist in your brain. What that means, though, is if you love this book maybe you'll buy it for your friend or cousin or auntie or uncle or mom or dad or whoever you want, and if we sell enough we'll do another volume of "firsts." Deal? (This is where you audibly say, "deal.")

Okay, let's get it.

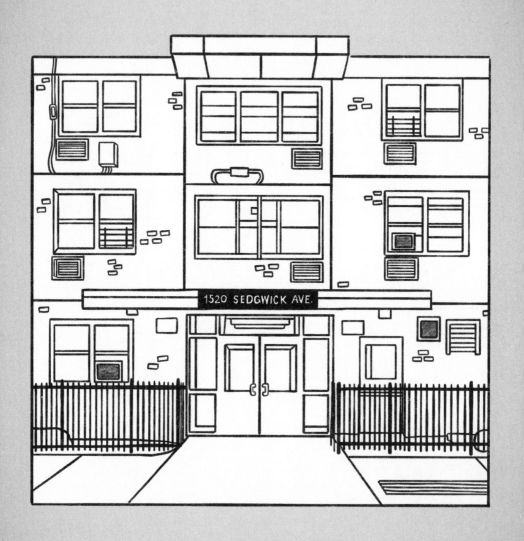

CINDY CAMPBELL PLANNED AND PROMOTED THE FIRST OFFICIAL HIP-HOP PARTY. YUP, THAT ONE.

*Y*ou can't tell the story of hip-hop without mentioning *that* party. You know the one, the "Back to School Jam" thrown at 1520 Sedgwick Avenue in the Bronx on August 11, 1973. Every year around that date, copies of the original flyer flood social media feeds, people share stories about the first time they heard the music—as well as their favorite albums, artists, songs, and videos, anniversary parties are thrown across the globe, panel discussions are held to reflect on how far hip-hop has come, and people do just about anything else you can think of to celebrate the culture. It was on that day that DJ Kool Herc spun a back-to-school party, emceeing and playing the "breaks" or "B-beats" of songs—the heavily percussive portions that encourage people to dance (or dance longer). DJs built upon Herc's technique, with the late Robert Ford Jr. noting in his 1978 *Billboard* article "B-Beats Bombarding Bronx" that "other Bronx DJs have picked up the practice and now B-Beats are the rage all over the borough and the practice is spreading rapidly."

By the late 1970s, DJs were releasing twelve-inch records that would allow people to rap over the beat. Hip-hop took off, and the cultural movement that emerged during the 1970s—among African American, Caribbean, and Latino kids who lived in the South Bronx—in New York City was on its way to becoming the mainstream, global, multibillion-dollar business we see today in festivals, platinum records, books, movies, fashion, and parties. Hella parties. The first official one,* the anniversary of which we celebrate as hip-hop's birthday, was planned and promoted by Cindy Campbell, Herc's younger sister. Yup, you read that right.

The catalyst for that function is a story pretty much all of us can relate to: back-to-school time. And back-to-school time means back-to-school clothes. And getting back-to-school clothes means having the money to buy them. But as Cindy Campbell recounted to multimedia journalist, DJ, and hip-hop historian Davey D in a 2010 interview, the money she was making working at the Neighborhood Youth Corps wasn't cutting it when the time came to go down to Delancey Street to cop her fits. The solution? Throw a party in the rec room at 1520 Sedgwick Avenue and charge for entry, drinks, and food.

After all, you gotta look fly on the first day of class, right?

Campbell was a teenager and therefore not old enough to rent the room herself, so she put up the twenty-five-dollar rental fee and had her dad sign for it. To cover music, she recruited her brother Clive, famously known as DJ Kool Herc, to DJ the party. Herc already had his own sound system that he kept in his room; he also had experience playing at parties, even helping their dad at events he was booked for. Getting him to spin at the party was a no-brainer.

Food and drinks were purchased from a local wholesale store. Flyers for the function were written on note cards—and during a conversation with MC Debbie D in 2017, Campbell said she was able to get a bunch of the cards because she was on the student council at

---

* The reason I say "official" is that hip-hop and its elements existed long before the party. August 11, 1973, is just the official date attached to it. We'll talk about this more in the next chapter.

her high school. I have no idea how she was able to get into the school during the summertime, but that's just a testament to her determination. As her last order of business, Cindy purchased a bunch of slow-jam records for her brother to play at the party to encourage some dancing between a bunch of her girlfriends and the dudes that they liked at the time.

When August 11 rolled around, ladies paid twenty-five cents and guys paid fifty cents to enter. Inside the rec room were adults from the community, including Cindy's parents, who were not only chill enough to let their daughter throw a party under their supervision but also made sure everyone was safe and taken care of. There were also bathrooms for partygoers to use, a kitchen where Cindy's mom prepared the food, and a separate room where Herc was set up on the ones and twos. There was also a buddy system in place to ensure that nobody walked out by themselves. If you were trying to get some wild stuff off, you had to leave and go down the street to do it. No nonsense was allowed at this function. And when the last song ended and the last person walked out of the rec room at around 4 a.m., the party had seen about three hundred guests.[*]

I imagine myself at this party a lot. Not just because it's history, but also because it sounds extremely fun. The parties I've experienced in my teens and adult years have been lit for sure. But something about being at a party, at *the* party, in the early days of hip-hop and getting to hear Herc cut up on the turntables gives me a lot of FOMO. It checked every single box for having all of the elements of a great party, which I will list below. To be clear, these are the elements of what makes a great party *to me*. If you disagree, we just have a different taste in what makes a great party. And this is perfectly okay. Anywho, here are mine.

---

* Cited from Kathy Iandoli's *God Save the Queens: The Essential History of Women in Hip-Hop.*

The Elements of a Great Party, According to Nadirah

1 I have to feel safe. As a woman who knows going out means having a good time but also having to keep your head on a swivel and your P's on the same level as your Q's at all times, safety is of the utmost importance to me. The whole point of going to a party is to have fun, but the moment I'm more occupied with making sure the person I came with doesn't get lost in the sea of people or that I don't accidentally put my drink down on the counter and pick it back up and drink it without thinking, the party becomes just as much of a job as it is a fun time (if not more than that). There's a level of safety I feel from simply *reading* about a buddy system being in place for partygoers who attended that function in the rec room. I feel doubly safe knowing that there were chaperones from the community who were watching over attendees to make sure any and every guest was okay no matter the circumstance. And I feel triply (did not know that was a word, ha) safe knowing that a "no BS" clause was stated from the jump—if you wanted to get crazy or do something inappropriate, the party was not the place.

2 The music has to be good. This seems like a no-brainer, but it's really not, and you and I both know it's true. We've all been to a party where the music was terrible, all the songs played were the exact same songs we heard at a party the night before, or both. So when I say the music has to be good, I don't mean playing a bunch of popular songs. I'm talking about hearing songs I forgot about, tracks blended into the newer ones that sampled their beats, the "breaks" of songs being played and whatever else it is that DJs do to keep the party jumping. And with Kool Herc DJing, everything I just stated is a given.

3 **Great company.** I don't really feel like this needs an explanation, but I'm going to give you one anyway. In short, I don't want to be around a bunch of people hugging the wall. Like . . . if you want to stand around, you can go wait in a line at your local department store. If I go out, I want to mingle and dance. Cindy made sure that was happening at her party.

BONUS **Food.** If this isn't a part of the party setup, that doesn't mean I'm not going to enjoy myself, but let me tell you something! If there *is* food, my enjoyment level will be off the charts. Simple.

Remember what I said in the intro about space being a crucial element in hip-hop? It is space and the boundaries that confine a place or entity that decide who can be let in and who can lead. This is why men and boys in hip-hop can be named as the sole contributors, despite the fact that women have been there from the jump doing everything. It is this very reality that makes it important that you know, before we go any further into this book, that Cindy Campbell planned and promoted the very first official hip-hop party, thrown in the Bronx on August 11, 1973. Again, CINDY CAMPBELL PLANNED AND PROMOTED THE FIRST OFFICIAL HIP-HOP PARTY, THROWN IN THE BRONX ON AUGUST 11, 1973.

Cindy is hip-hop through and through. A graffiti artist and b-girl, she even helped set up her brother's deal for *Beat Street*, the 1984 Harry Belafonte–produced film set in the South Bronx that followed a young DJ and his friend on their quest to make it big by exposing the world to hip-hop culture. Cindy felt the role they originally wanted Herc to play was too negative, so Cindy met with Belafonte, producer David Picker, and director Stan Lathan by herself. She convinced them to change the part and make it more positive.

When it was all said and done, Belafonte advised her to get an attorney. In his words, "You're dealing with Hollywood." Good advice, indeed.

Fun fact: While Cindy was out here brokering deals for her brother, the parties continued. The money that was made at the door went back into the pot for the next party and toward Herc's equipment. Bringing those events to the community and to her people was so important because they truly represented the essence of hip-hop. As Campbell told MC Debbie D during an interview, "We weren't out there buying clothes or jewelry to be flashy. . . . That's not what it was about. We were giving people something, we were giving people a culture. No dressing up to try and get in the club, no. Just come as yourself. And that's what we're doing today. That's it. Be comfortable. And that's what hip-hop is."

That is what hip-hop is, and who knows what it would look like if it weren't for Cindy Campbell.

Five Parties from Women Rappers' Music Videos (I Think) Cindy Would Love

1.
Lil' Kim's beachfront bash in the video for "Not Tonight (Ladies Night Remix)"

What's happening at the party: When Lil' Kim released the remix to her *Hard Core* track "Not Tonight," she not only created one of the greatest posse cuts in rap music history by enlisting the talents of Da Brat, Missy Elliott, Angie Martinez, and Lisa "Left Eye" Lopes, but also hosted one of the best beach functions I've ever seen recorded.

The ladies on the song party on an illuminated dance floor situated in the middle of the bash, and as the camera travels around the room between different verses you can spot Queen Latifah, SWV, Xscape, and Mary J. Blige turning up as well. There's also a jacuzzi, a bar, fruit, and tiki torches, because what is a party on the beach without tiki torches?

Why (I think) Cindy would love it: There's no nonsense here! Just the partygoers dancing and having a time. As I previously mentioned, shutting down antics and ensuring the party was filled with nothing but music and amusement was a priority to Cindy when she was throwing the "Back to School Jam." That's why I think she would love this one!

2.
The performance that doubled as a party in Queen Pen's video for "Party Ain't a Party"

What's happening at the party: Queen Pen's 1998 single "Party Ain't a Party" was produced and mixed by Teddy Riley, who flipped Earth, Wind & Fire's "On Your Face" and gave her a track on which she rapped about turning parties out with her crew. And with some fun verses from Nutta Butta, Mr. Cheeks, and Markell, every artist takes the stage to perform the track in the song's music video.

The vibe is reminiscent of the Tunnel, the popular New York City nightclub that shut its door in 2001, but in the years prior saw performances from big artists like DMX, Foxy Brown, and the LOX and housed popular parties like the Sunday night hip-hop party, Mecca. Honestly, I hate that I wasn't old enough to experience the Tunnel, a reality that's made even more painful when Queen Pen raps that you can link up with her there on the song. Anywho, in the video the rappers are backed by a band and a DJ, taking turns spitting their verses onstage while the crowd of partygoers go insane as they watch the performance. A good time was had!

Why I think Cindy would love it: The function is hip-hop at its core, and with the elements of live performance, dancing, and community, it has all of the things that made the party at 1520 Sedgwick Avenue a success decades prior. Seems like a no-brainer to me.

3.
MC Lyte's function in the video for "Cold Rock a Party"

What's happening at the party: Only MC Lyte could throw a party in an elevator that looks fun enough to make me forget all about my claustrophobia. That's exactly what she did in the video for "Cold Rock a Party," the Missy Elliott–assisted single from Lyte's fifth studio album, *Bad as I Wanna B*.

Why I think Cindy would love it: When Cindy spoke about her events with MC Debbie D and hip-hop's early days, she made it clear that coming as you are and being comfortable were extremely important. The location of the rec room also made it an easy space for Cindy's dad to secure and for attendees to get to. Lyte choosing to turn up in an accessible spot—surrounded by some comfy people rocking hoodies, jackets, and T-shirts—makes me feel like Cindy would be in the building. Or more specifically, in the elevator.

4.
Rah Digga's "Party & Bullshit" video

What's happening at the party: Rah Digga opens up the track rapping "We gon' take this through the roof," and that's basically what the video for "Party & Bullshit" is for nearly four minutes. Between the DJ—who is the song's producer and New Jersey's very own Just Blaze—getting on the mic and engaging with the crowd and the people actually dancing, it's really, really turnt.

Why I think Cindy would love it: Did you not just read the dancing part? No wall huggers and no nonsense. Seriously, I feel like that's all Cindy would need to hear.

5.
Foxy Brown's banquet hall banger in the video "I'll Be"

What's happening at the party: A single from Foxy Brown's debut album *Ill Na Na*, "I'll Be" is one of those tracks that just makes you want to go out with your friends and move your body. That's the main reason why a dance battle ensues in the banquet hall in between shots of Fox and the song's featured artist Jay-Z rapping.

Why I think Cindy would love it: Yes, I know a rec room and a banquet hall are two very different spaces, but out of all of the videos I talked about, this one's location has the most in common with the location of the "Back to School Jam." Both are the kind of spaces that are specifically designed for celebration and fellowship, which is exactly why I think Cindy would have a great time here too.

MILLIE JACKSON, RAP'S FIRST "MOTHER"

Millie Jackson. If hearing that name doesn't bring a song to your mind maybe playing some of her music will. R&B and soul singer Millie Jackson has been sampled over two hundred times[*] by some of the biggest names in hip-hop. Her track "Cheatin Is" lent its beat to Trick Daddy's second-highest-charting single, "I'm a Thug"; her upbeat song "Now That You Got It" was sampled on Boogie Down Productions' "Original Lyrics"; and the opening of her live performance of "All the Way Lover" can be heard at the top of MC Lyte's "Shut the Eff Up! (Hoe)." Her influence on rap music doesn't stop there. In a 2012 episode of *Unsung,* Da Brat called her an inspiration, while rap pioneer Roxanne Shanté praised her as the "original female rapper." Shanté was referring to Millie's early rap performances on tracks, and what would garner her a bunch of honorific titles that include the "Mother of Rapping." You know when you hop on Twitter[**] and see someone tweet a picture of a woman in music with the word *mother,* and sometimes

---

[*] Cataloging site WhoSampled.com has the number at 235 at the time that I'm writing this. That's a lot of songs.

[**] I know it's X now, but it just hasn't caught on yet. Not for me or 69 percent of the platform's users according to an *Ad Age* article published on September

mutha? Well, there are a bunch of women rappers who have an honorific title that includes the word *mother*, and rightfully so. The thing about Millie Jackson, though, is that her rapping predates the start of all of the other "mother" rappers' careers. So if we're going in chronological order, that technically makes Millie Jackson "mother" first. As I'm sure you've already guessed, this chapter is all about that and her.

I must give some background for Millie. To begin, she was born in Thomson, Georgia. Her father was a sharecropper and her mother passed away when Millie was two years old. When she was growing up, her dad would throw parties at the house on the weekend, buying new records and making corn liquor for each function. It was at these parties that Millie got some of her earliest exposure to music, but at the age of thirteen her dad sent her to live with her mother's deeply religious parents. The reason? She decided to wear a pair of high heels to her junior high school prom and her dad could see that she "was going to be a problem" (*Unsung* interview). Ha, he had no idea.

A couple of years later she moved to Newark, New Jersey, holding down a job during the day and going to school at night. Taking her talents to New York, Millie became a waitress at the popular restaurant Schrafft's while also working part-time as a model for *Sepia*, *JIVE*, and *Help!* magazines.* She was going hard, but it was a night out at Palm Cafe on 125th Street in Harlem in December 1964 that would change her life.

The woman who was singing onstage sounded "terrible" to Millie, and when her friends bet her five dollars to go up there and sing better, she jumped at the chance. Not only did she win the five dollars, but a man in the audience loved her voice so much that he gave her a job singing at the Crystal Ballroom. From there it was on.

~~~~~~~~~~

15, 2023. So throughout this book you'll see Twitter, which means X, which means Twitter. Got it?

* Fun fact: Millie Jackson was the first Black waitress at the Fifth Avenue Schrafft's location.

Traditional rhythm-and-blues tracks filled the catalog of Millie's early discography. For example, her song "Ask Me What You Want" had a Motown flair, and she sings about doing her best to get her man whatever he asks for. On "My Man, a Sweet Man" she praises how great her man is. But the songs weren't authentic to Millie, who wanted to use her music to reflect all aspects of the world around her. That meant talking about injustice, infidelity, sex, and everything in between.

Her 1973 track "It Hurts So Good" set the stage for her authenticity to shine. The song hit No. 3 on what was once called the Billboard R&B Singles chart, but it was also an honest cut about being with someone who is no good for you and wanting to stay. This is the kind of realness that she wasn't singing about before. From there Millie developed her stage presence and style on her records, opening her song "If Loving You Is Wrong I Don't Want to Be Right" with a spoken "rap" to set up the story about a woman who is having an affair with a married man. The track appeared on side 1 of her 1974 album, *Caught Up*, which was told from the perspective of the mistress. Side 2 was told from the perspective of the wife. She wanted to share both sides of the story. Pretty daring and iconic if you ask me.

The song I really want to highlight on *Caught Up*, though, is "The Rap." It was on side 1 of the album when originally pressed on vinyl, which means it's a song from the perspective of the mistress. Outside of the boldness of the theme, what really caught me when I first listened to it was Millie Jackson talking for almost three minutes at the start. Today, when we discuss rap it's often through a modern lens that highlights bars, punch lines, and rhymes. And all of those things are true for sure. But the thing about rap music as we know it today is that the concept existed long before that party on Sedgwick Avenue I told you about in the last chapter.

You can go back a couple of centuries to West Africa and find griots—poets, musicians, and storytellers—telling stories while someone played a drum. There are also early folk, doo-wop, blues, and jazz songs that can be likened to rapping. A track from the 1940s called "The Preacher and the Bear" by the Jubalaires is one of my favorite recorded early examples. On it, group member Caleb Ginyard raps, "Gather 'round boys I don't want ya to miss / None of this here story cuz it goes like this."

Millie Jackson's "The Rap" didn't rhyme and may have been more in line with one of my oldheads telling me "let me rap with you"—which simply means talk to you—but her decision to tell a story by *speaking* it over the beat set a precedent. And when she dropped "I Had to Say It" in 1980, lyrics like "Now I got something to say to you and you might not appreciate It / But I don't give a damn if you like it or not, in fact I don't care if you hate it," the lyrics and rhymes made it even clearer that Millie was rapping. She was building on what she had done on her songs in the preceding years.

Millie started adding new things to her set too, specifically telling jokes and cursing during her performances. Her album art rejected tradition as well, with a lot of the images defying the soft, "wholesome" look often portrayed by women soul and R&B artists at the time. Take the cover art for her 1983 album, *E.S.P. (Extra Sexual Persuasion)*, for example. The image shows Millie standing over a clear crystal ball that is placed right in front of her chest, basically putting a fisheye lens effect on her cleavage. On the back of the album, she wears lingerie, complete with stockings and heels. The art on her 1989 album *Back to the S**t!* might be the most popular, because it shows Millie seated on the toilet with her underwear at her ankles. As Brooklyn White wrote for *The Gumbo* in 2021, when it came to Millie Jackson, "her cover art set her apart. You knew what you were getting into from the visual alone."

What you were getting was a woman who pushed the limits in her lyrics too. "Slow Tongue," a song from *E.S.P.*, was all about a man performing oral sex on her. On the live performance of "Phuck U Symphony," Millie intros the track by addressing the people who call her "dirty" but then play her music in private before she starts harmonizing the words "fuck you" and *only* the words "fuck you," while orchestral music plays behind her. It was bold and brazen, letting listeners know that Millie, and any other woman who wanted to, could talk about sex and curse you out just like the guys. It's something we would see from women rappers in the decades that followed.

In the office she handled her own business, forgoing a manager from the beginning and instead choosing to manage her own career. In her personal life she was divorced and had two kids, and when asked in a 1980 interview why she did not marry either of her kids' fathers, she sharply responded, "I got enough problems taking care of the kids, I got to nurse him too?" Not only did Millie make it clear that she was doing just fine without her ex-husband and the fathers of her children, but she also rebuffed the rigid idea of what a family was supposed to be for Black women and championed the women who held it down on their own.

Yet despite her success and impact, music journalist A. Scott Galloway said in that same *Unsung* interview I mentioned earlier "you don't hear her on the radio today like you hear an Aretha Franklin classic or a Gladys Knight classic. It kind of feels like she got left behind." Which makes it all the more important that we—yes *we*, because you and I are in this together—celebrate Millie. This is one of those moments when I wish I was reading this book in a room full of people, just so we can respond to some of the things I'm about to share like one of those YouTube reaction videos. But alas, I am here and you are wherever you are.*

What I'm still going to do, though, is share some important Millie moments with you. They really just drive home the whole "rap's first mother" thing I was talking about at the beginning of the chapter, because it's clear throughout her career and the rap ladies see it too.

---

* I've always wanted to use the word alas in my writing. It's such a cool, fancy word. I'm going to type it again for good measure. *Alas.*

Important Millie Moments According to Nadirah (and Now You Too)

"Intro" on Da Brat's album *Unrestricted*

Da Brat has spoken about her love for Millie Jackson and the huge impact she had on her, and the love is mutual because Da Brat has hung out with Millie at her house! When Da Brat dropped her third studio album in 2003, she chose the name *Unrestricted*, inspired by Millie's album *Totally Unrestricted! The Millie Jackson Anthology*. And guess who's on the album intro? That's right! Millie Jackson herself.

Millie Jackson kicks off Da Brat's album by giving an audible middle finger to anyone who dares try to make her do something she doesn't want to. My favorite part is when she raps, "Let it all hang loose, never feelin' afflicted! / Go for what you want it's called *Unrestricted*."

The *Unrestricted* "Intro" coming from an unrestricted woman such as Millie Jackson made it the perfect way to open the album. The message of the lyrics themselves can be found in the lyrics of many ladies who rap today, and also is reflected in the lives of women who listen to rap and even the women who don't. Millie made it clear that there were not, and still aren't, limits on what we can do.

Lil' Kim, Pam Grier, and Millie Jackson on *The RuPaul Show*

Whenever I'm searching for old interview clips I'm reminded that so many people in entertainment had a talk show back in the day. RuPaul is no exception, having hosted an eponymous talk show on VH1 from 1996 to 1998.

I've rewatched the particular episode I'm about to talk about more than a few times. It's wildly nostalgic, and also pretty damn cool that Ru got three legends as large as Lil' Kim, Pam Grier, and Millie Jackson on the show. Lil' Kim and Pam Grier are already onstage before Millie Jackson comes out to join them. To introduce her, RuPaul calls her an originator that "none of us would be here without." Okay, Ru!

She gets a standing ovation from the audience before sitting down on the couch next to Lil' Kim. RuPaul starts asking them a bunch of questions about everything from rap music to curse words, but the part that I love more than anything isn't the answers, it's the way Millie and Kim playfully tap, hold, and laugh with one another throughout the entire interview. It's the kind of thing you would expect to see between two best friends or a really tight auntie with her niece. Just love, adoration, and respect.

A few years later Kim sampled Millie's intro from "Phuck U Symphony" on "Durty," a track from her 2005 album, *The Naked Truth*. It's a song all about the haters who judge her in public but when they're home alone play her music. What better way to kick off this song than with Millie Jackson saying "Them same ones that be talkin' 'bout I'm dirty / Be buyin' my shit and hidin' it?" Exactly, there isn't.

Millie Jackson's 1971 song "A Child of God (It's Hard to Believe)"

Millie Jackson detailed the response to her record "A Child of God (It's Hard to Believe)" when she joined the legendary Questlove for an episode of his podcast, *Questlove Supreme*. The song's release angered and confused a bunch of people, including gospel radio stations and fans who thought the song would be about a "child of god," before actually listening to the song or acknowledging the part in parentheses.

"A Child of God (It's Hard to Believe)" is a critique of racism, social injustice, and hypocrisy. With lyrics like "I know some people who go to church on Sunday / And these the same people who wear a sheet on Monday," Millie Jackson calls out racist white people who relish in their Christianity while simultaneously going against Christian values in how they treat Black people. For Millie, it's "hard to believe they're children of God."

Released right at the height of the Black Power movement, the song was an early example of Millie using her voice to address the things she wanted to. To be clear, Millie wasn't the first person to use her music to talk about what was happening in and to her community—that ideal is at the core of so many songs. What Millie did with her song, however, was place herself in a lineage of artists who *did*. And that lineage includes rappers who would use their music to call out injustices years later.

Janette Beckman's Female Rappers, Class of '88 photo

That photo of Salt-N-Pepa standing in front of a white backdrop wearing kente kufis, eight-ball jackets, spandex bodysuits, and thick gold chains? Janette Beckman shot that. The picture of LL Cool J holding a boom box on his shoulder? Janette took that. And that shot of Slick Rick rocking a red crown, diamond rings on almost every finger, and a bunch of gold chains? Yup, Janette took that picture too. And that doesn't even scratch the surface of her great body of work.

London-born documentary photographer Janette Beckman has taken pictures of some of the most important people in hip-hop, many at the very beginning of their careers. One picture in particular epitomizes Janette's proximity to those early days, and it's titled *Female Rappers, Class of '88*. Pictured are Sparky D, Sweet Tee, MC Peaches, Yvette Money, Ms. Melodie, Roxanne Shanté, MC Lyte, Finesse, Synquis, an unidentified woman whose jewelry reads "PAM," and Millie Jackson.

Janette shot the photo for *Paper* magazine, a then-black-and-white print publication started by her friends Kim Hastreiter and David Hershkovits. Kim and David knew that she was taking a lot of pictures of hip-hop artists and wanted to have her do a shoot with some of the ladies who were killing it on the mic.

Everyone arrived at a now-closed Mexican restaurant on West Broadway in New York City. "All the women turned up with their boyfriends, and the editors were like 'Actually, no men are allowed in here, so all you guys are gonna have to find something to do for a couple of hours,'" Janette told *i-D* in 2019. "I thought that was brilliant. So the boys went off, and we got all the women onstage."

The stage was inside the restaurant. All of the ladies got on it to take the picture, some sitting, some crouching, some standing. "They all knew each other because it was a small community," Beckman told *i-D*. "They got Millie Jackson in there—she's kind of like the godmother of women in hip-hop."

I told you earlier that Millie Jackson has racked up a bunch of different honorific titles over the course of her career, and Janette calling her "the godmother" is no exception. For her to be in a picture among some of the pioneering women in rap is a testament to her impact and importance.

In the years since Millie Jackson made her debut as a recording artist she has starred in her very own stage play, hosted a radio show, continued to perform across the country, and of course, inspired a generation. The prolific "Mother of Rap" has done it all and then some, kicking down doors at every stop along the way. She's really *that* girl, or as she perfectly put it at the end of Da Brat's *Unrestricted* intro: "All or nothing, never a fraction / Yeah, you got it . . . mother-fuckin' Millie Jackson."

SOME OF THE FIRST RAP RECORDS
(AND THE LADIES WHO MADE THEM)

I said a hip, hop.

If I was to play the breakbeat from Chic's "Good Times" and ask you to rap the first thing that comes to mind, I would hope those words are what you would say. And if not, that's okay, that's what I'm here for. Those words come from Sugarhill Gang's "Rapper's Delight," the track that put hip-hop on a new stage. The song was produced by Sylvia Robinson. Sylvia sang, produced, wrote, and played the guitar throughout the 1950s and '60s. In 1979, she founded Sugar Hill Records alongside her husband, Joe Robinson. As CEO of the company, she set her sights on hip-hop, a genre she first heard while attending a party at Harlem World, a two-story nightclub on the corner of Lenox and 116th.

Sylvia's place in history doesn't exist without some contention. Well, I should say a lot of contention. Before Sugar Hill Records, Sylvia and her husband founded All Platinum Records, which went bankrupt amid litigation, a tax evasion conviction for Joe, and artists leaving the label. As an executive, she credited herself and her family members on songs they had not contributed to. A further analysis would warrant an entire book, or perhaps the documentary on her that's been talked about for years. And that's not happening here. Regardless, Sugarhill Gang's "Rapper's Delight" is just one part of a very long, very important story that should be told on ownership, artists' rights, bad deals, and a whole lot more. Okay, back to the song.

At this party in Harlem, Sylvia heard Lovebug Starski rapping over the "Good Times" breakbeat and an idea was formed. The story, as recounted by Dan Charnas for *Billboard*, goes like this. Sylvia's son rounded up three of his friends—Henry "Big Bank Hank" Jackson, Guy "Master Gee" O'Brien, and Michael "Wonder Mike" Wright, all of whom were inexperienced rappers. At the studio they wrote and performed the rap. But guess what? A bunch of the lyrics were taken from Grandmaster Caz by Sugarhill Gang's Big Bank Hank, who asked to borrow his notebook. (Remember when Jay-Z rapped "I'm overcharging niggas for what they did to the Cold Crush" on "Izzo (H.O.VA.)"? That was the group Grandmaster Caz was in.) The track was fifteen minutes long, with lyrics laid over an interpolation of "Good Times." They had a hit. "Rapper's Delight" landed in the Top 40 in the United States and the rest was history.

It is this history that sometimes gets a bit skewed when we talk about the first rap records. "Rapper's Delight" often gets credited as the first, and that's not true. It did introduce hip-hop to a wider audience, it was the first record released on Sugar Hill Records, and it's without a doubt the first mainstream rap hit. But there was another rap song, "King Tim III (Personality Jock)" by the Fatback Band, that was released a few months prior to "Rapper's Delight." This track is widely considered to be the first rap record. But here's the thing: rapping had been happening years before the songs I just mentioned got released. Somebody out there could very well have a record stashed in their attic that they cut before 1979.

There's another thing to the first rap songs that often gets skewed as well, and that's the involvement of ladies. As I stated before, there's a lot to talk about when it comes to Sylvia's legacy, but there is no denying that a woman had a hand in creating rap's first hit, "Rapper's Delight." In fact, there are a bunch of other early rap records that wouldn't exist without a lady in the room or on the mic. Here are a few more of the first rap records that some ladies contributed to that year.

"Funk You Up": The Sequence

After the release of "Rapper's Delight" on Sugar Hill Records came the label's second rap record, an upbeat, funky jam titled "Funk You Up." The track was performed by an all-woman rap trio from Columbia, South Carolina, by the name of the Sequence: Gwendolyn "Blondy" Chisolm, Cheryl "The Pearl" Cook, and Angela "Angie B" Stone. Angela would go on to have a successful career as a singer under the name Angie Stone, with hits like "No More Rain (In This Cloud)" and "Wish I Didn't Miss You."

When the Sugarhill Gang was slated to perform in their home state at the Township Auditorium, the trio took the opportunity to pull up on them and show the guys that they could rap just as well. A rep with Sugar Hill Records got them backstage to audition, and after a performance of "Funk You Up" for Sylvia Robinson herself, the ladies were on their way. Sylvia flew them up that weekend to record. As Cheryl recounted to Rock the Bells, the ladies recorded the track on Friday, the song was mixed on Saturday, and it was playing on the radio by Sunday. The song went gold three weeks later. The events made the Sequence the first all-woman rap act to release a rap record.

One more thing. You know how a lot of people credit Kurtis Blow as having the first rap song with a hook, in his 1980 single "The Breaks"? Wrong. "Funk You Up" was actually the first. "They had the first hook I had ever heard on 'Funk You Up,'" Kurtis Blow told Kathy

Iandolini in her book *God Save the Queens: The Essential History of Women in Hip-Hop.* "'A lot of people give me the credit for having the first hook—'These are the breaks'—but no, 'Funk You Up' actually came before that. I have to give them their props.'"

"Rappin' and Rocking the House": Funky Four Plus One More

This joint right here is one of my favorites! For starters, the beat interpolates Cheryl Lynn's "Got to Be Real," which is a bona fide classic. Then there's the group itself: Funky Four Plus One More. Their performance on *Saturday Night Live* made history as one of the first nationally televised rap performances, and the group included none other than MC Sha-Rock, who's widely regarded as the first lady emcee. Period.

There are a lot of things that make Sha-Rock so special, but I'll start from the very beginning.

The word *first*, especially in hip-hop, triggers a ton of debate and there are so many ladies who rapped in the 1970s. But as Sha-Rock wrote in her 2010 memoir, *Luminary Icon: The Story of the Beginning and End of Hip Hop's First Female MC*, "Everybody in New York City knew not only was I the first female MC, but I also was the best female MC." She attended a bunch of Kool Herc's parties when she was younger, getting her start in hip-hop as a b-girl. In 1978 she linked up with KK Rockwell, Rahiem, and Keith Keith to form the Funky Four. The group went through a number of lineup changes, which resulted in the addition of "Plus One More" in their name, which represented MC Sha-Rock.

"Rappin' and Rocking the House" was the group's first single. Released in 1979 on Enjoy Records, the song clocks in at a little under sixteen minutes—sheesh!—and finds the crew quite literally rapping about rocking the place. It kicks off with the group members trading lines, during which Sha-Rock proudly proclaims: "They're four fly guys, I'm the best female / I'm tellin' the truth, not a fairytale." It's a simple line, but it's clear, cool, and direct, three things that can make a perfect rap line, in my opinion.

In its entirety, "Rappin' and Rocking the House" perfectly captures the essence surrounding the culture and what was at the time of its release a young genre. The song is fun, fresh, exciting, and long—because who the hell wants that kind of song to end? Not me. Sha-Rock made history in and out of the group, but if anyone around you ever brings up the early rap song that ensures "everybody gonna turn it out," make sure you tell them all about Sha-Rock.

"To the Beat Y'All": Lady B

Lady B has a special place in my heart. I was raised in South Jersey, a little over twenty minutes outside of Philly, and a lot of my family members are from and/or currently reside in the City of Brotherly Love. As a result I spent a lot of time there growing up, and that proximity to the city meant the culture spread into South Jersey. That means I say "jawn," pronounce water like "wooder"—which I didn't even realize until someone in New York mocked me—call Italian ice "water ice," can't put into words what it felt like to watch the 2008 Phillies win the World Series, and grew up listening to Philly radio stations like Power 99, 103.9, 107.9, 105.3, and 100.3. Lady B was on the radio every single time I got into the car growing up, and that's still the case today. She was the voice of my childhood. Full stop. And as a kid who spent a lot of time in the car going to school and then going to practice and then coming home from student government meetings, Lady B was one of the voices I heard the most growing up outside of family, coaches, and teachers. In a way, it was like Lady B was family. So, imagine my surprise and excitement when I found out she wasn't only a cool lady with an impeccable taste in music, but that she also recorded one of the first rap songs with "To the Beat Y'all" in 1979! I was HYPE.

Now, I'm not going to try to tell you a story about when I first dis-covered this news. Because my memory is horrible, lol. And while I want to say it happened when I was doing some *Gumbo* research a few years back, my dad is going to read this and be like, "Come on, Nadirah, I told you that multiple times as a kid." So I won't. And that doesn't really matter anyway. The point is that Lady B is a pioneer, first lady, and GOAT, and occupies multiple spaces in the realm of hip-hop.

There's a lecture that I found on YouTube, courtesy of the *reelblack* channel, where she talks to Michael Coard's Hip-Hop 101 class about traveling to New York and getting a glimpse of the culture of hip-hop right after a local DJ asked her to do a record. The record was "To the Beat Y'all" and there are two things I really love about it. First and foremost, it's super Philly. If you can't tell by simply listening to the beat, it's worth noting that the track was mixed by Nick Martinelli, who was influenced by "The Sound of Philadelphia* and credits legendary Philadelphia musician Dexter Wansel with helping him with his studio training. (Dexter Wansel's song "New Beginning" was sampled on the Lox's 1998 cut "Money, Power & Respect," which features DMX and Lil' Kim. I love little connections like this!)

Secondly, Lady B says something on this song that made me say "ooohhh" the first time I heard it. She raps, "I've been number one all my life / And I've always played the dozens / Said I've got more rhymes in the back of my mind than Alex Haley's got cousins."** That is a bar.

---

* NBC Philadelphia describes "The Sound of Philadelphia" as a genre that emerged in the 1970s and "blended soul, funk and big band styles, and cemented the city in the country's musical landscape with its lush horn ensem-bles and smooth vocals." There's also a song entitled "TSOP (The Sounds of Philadelphia)" that's very good and was the theme for *Soul Train*.

** Alex Haley's bestselling book *Roots: The Saga of an American Family* became the inspiration for the 1977 television miniseries *Roots*, which told the story of Kunta Kinte, an African man captured and sold into slavery in the United

But guess what? Lady B doesn't actually love the song. She told Clover Hope in *The Motherlode: 100+ Women Who Made Hip-Hop* that "it was something that was thrown together. It was kind of a gimmick. It was a one-cut song. I'm proud of it—don't get me wrong. But I'm even more proud of what I did for hip-hop as a genre on the radio."

I'm proud of Lady B. What she did for the genre on the radio cannot be understated. She was one of the first DJs to play hip-hop on the radio, breaking artists like the Furious Five, the Treacherous 3, Public Enemy, Run-DMC, LL COOL J, Queen Latifah, EPMD, UTFO, MC Lyte, Schoolly D, Big Daddy Kane, Rakim, KRS-1, MC Breeze, 3XD, and Heavy D. Couple that with making history with one of the first records in rap? It's no wonder she has a street named after her in Philly.

"Rhymin' and Rappin'": Paulette and Tanya Winley

And all I did is listen to them and dance, then finally I said 'Hey it's my chance'
To rock the mic', to make you high, I'll show you that I'm qualified."

That's how Paulette Winley opens "Rhymin' and Rappin'," a cut by her and her sister Tanya, released on their father's label, Winley Records. This song was also released in 1979, and it's really cool to hear more than one lady rap on an early hip-hop track. TWO TO BE EXACT!

I also really love when Tanya raps that she has rhymes galime[*] and rhymes galore, and when she's finished with those, she's still got

States, and his descendants. The story was based on one of Haley's ancestors and inspired a generation of people in the 1970s to trace their family history.

[*] *Merriam-Webster* defines galore as "in large numbers or amounts," so I'm going to define galime as "excessive." Just know she's got a lot of rhymes.

more. I have no clue what galime is, but I'll be using that word from here on out.

"Lady D": Lady D

If I was a rapper, I'd hope to have a song that's named after me. Lady D's "Lady D" was released in—you guessed it—1979! The song finds Lady D telling us about a man who's trying to date her. The dude is pretty smooth off rip. He sees her, gives her his number, calls her that night, and assures her that he's not like the other guys. Then he takes her to Studio 54 for their first date. I already told y'all I love parties where people are ACTUALLY DANCING, so this is fire to me. After the date he invites her inside, they sit down on the couch, and he starts to kiss her. Lady D is not feeling this, and she proceeds to jump out of her seat, point at the door, and tell him, "Don't try to see me ever no more!" She then closes out the song by rapping,

Now if you straighten out your ways and reach my desire
You just might get a chance to light my fire

In one of the first hip-hop songs ever released, Lady D wanted to make it clear that she was not here for that man making a move without checking with her first. You can never have too many songs that make that clear.

"MC Rock": Jazzy 4 MC's

The 1979 cut "MC Rock" by Jazzy 4 MC's is a little under ten minutes long and features production by DJ Mark the 45 King, who would go on to produce countless other hip-hop songs, including Jay-Z's "Hard Knock Life (Ghetto Anthem)." Already iconic.

Now here's the part that tripped me up. After group members Mercury and Shambu rap, there's a woman that comes onto the track proclaiming, "I said Fly Scha Rock is my name / And I'm going to the Hall of Fame."

Read that again.

She then goes on to say, "I'm not Sha-Rock of Breakout / But I'm here to turn the MCs out." I'm hype that there's yet another woman rapping on one of the first rap songs, but now I have a question! If she's not MC Sha-Rock, who auditioned in DJ Breakout's basement for what would become the Funky Four Plus One More, then was there another lady rapping under the same name?

I did a bunch of digging and researching to try to figure this out. I went through message boards and YouTube comments looking for some sort of insight. I went through a bunch of archives. Nothing. I played it for a few of my oldheads, and they weren't sure either. So I'm sending out a bat signal here. If you, or anyone you know, can help me figure out if these are two different people, please reach out to me. I'll lose sleep over this if not.

MC LYTE, THE FIRST LADY OF RAP VOICES

"**H**ot damn, ho, here we go again"* is what listeners hear at the beginning of MC Lyte's "10% Dis." The track took aim at rapper Antoinette, who she accused of stealing the beat to Audio Two's classic "Top Billin'."** I'll drop some more info about this beef in the footnotes,*** because it's an interesting story that I don't want

---

* Lil' Kim recited this line on her verse on Mobb Deep's "Quiet Storm (Remix)," which is easily one of her best verses period.

** One of my earliest hip-hop memories is of baby me rapping the lyrics to Jay-Z's "Imaginary Players" in the car with my dad? The memory that comes after that is me listening to "Top Billin'" with my family. My dad and uncle really kept that song ON REPEAT. You should listen to it if you've never heard it, and please know that Milk Dee is saying "Suckers that's down with neither one of us, that's how I feel" on the song, and not "Suckers that's down with me" a few years back. This revelation broke a section of hip-hop Twitter a few years back.

*** Here's the story on "10% Dis." MC Lyte recounted what happened in Brian Coleman's book *Check the Technique: Liner Notes for Hip-Hop Junkies*. Basically, Audio Two—Kirk "Milk Dee" Robinson and Nat "Gizmo" Robinson— talked to Hurby "Luv Bug" Azor about getting a woman to do an answer to "Top Billin'" called "Stop Illin'." As Antoinette told Clover Hope in *The Motherlode: 100+ Women Who Made Hip-Hop*, "that's how people got on [the air]—somebody would make a record, and somebody would make a record about their record. Anywho, the whole thing was supposed to be orchestrated

to overtake this particular paragraph. What I love about "10% Dis" is Lyte's voice. It's smooth, it's clear, it's powerful, it's everything. She worked with Lucien George Sr., the father of three of the members of R&B group Full Force,[*] who helped her rehearse and develop her vocals. Lyte told *Vibe* in 2011, ". . . George would coach me on how to make my voice sound strong and how to pronounce the words to where someone else would feel it." And feel it I do, every time I hear her rap. MC Lyte's voice is an instrument in and of itself, and its power as a musical tool is what has helped her record a long list of "firsts" since the release of her debut album, *Lyte as a Rock*, in 1988. These include being the first woman rapper to receive a gold single and the first solo woman rapper to be nominated for a Grammy. In fact, I could write a book on Lyte's firsts that would be just as long as this one if I wanted to! But since I'm going to keep all my MC Lyte love in one chapter, I've decided to talk about her voice, and why I call her the First Lady of Rap Voices.

Before we get to that, though, it's important that you understand how MC Lyte became, well, MC Lyte. Born Lana Michele Moorer in Queens and raised in the East Flatbush section of Brooklyn, Lyte attended Weusi Shule (Black School in Swahili) for elementary school, an educational institution that centered the Black experience, Black history, and Black scholars. There students were well versed in the work of figures like Langston Hughes and practiced jiu jitsu. By the time she got to middle school she zoned in on her love

---

and planned out. But when Audio Two and Lyte heard Antoinette's Hurby-produced track 'I Got an Attitude' and noticed it had the same kicks and snares as Audio Two's 'Top Billin'' they took that as a response to their meeting. And because Audio Two didn't want to come at a female, they asked Lyte to do it. *That's* how we got "10% Dis."

* Full Force produced the UTFO track "Roxanne, Roxanne," and if you read the book in order then you already heard me talk about how Roxanne Shanté's response to UTFO with "Roxanne's Revenge" made history and kicked off a shitload of response records in a war of words known as "The Roxanne Wars."

for music, writing the lyrics to her debut single, "I Cram to Understand U (Sam)."

Lyte's mother told her she danced in her stomach whenever the Jackson 5's "I'll Be There" came on. As a child, the music of artists like Gladys Knight, Al Green, Donna Summer, and Diana Ross filled her home. And when she would head up to Spanish Harlem to hang out with her cousins on weekends in the summer she would get what journalist Michael A. Gonzales called her "first drop of hip-hop" by listening to the Funky Four Plus One More, Grandmaster Flash and the Furious Five, and the Treacherous Three. "They had all those records, so I know I had to be influenced by them," she told Gonzales for *Vibe*'s 2001 anthology *Hip-Hop Divas*.

When "I Cram to Understand U (Sam)" was finally put on wax in 1987, MC Lyte was sixteen years old. Produced by Audio Two, whom Lyte affectionately calls her "brothers," the song became the teenager's debut single and let the world know she was a storyteller who understood the power of her voice right out the gate. On "I Cram to Understand U (Sam)" Lyte provides a commentary on the crack epidemic, rapping about being in love with a man named Sam who appears to be cheating on her with another girl but is actually addicted to crack cocaine. When she raps, "Ju-just like a test / I cram to understand you," the listener can literally feel the distress in her voice as she begins to understand what is *really* going on. No one could write that song like Lyte. And no one could rap it like her either.

Lyte's debut album, *Lyte as a Rock*, would drop in 1988, landing on *The Source* magazine's "100 Best Rap Albums" list ten years after its release. In 1991 she performed at the Sisters in the Name of Rap concert alongside a list of other pioneering women rappers like Salt-N-Pepa and Queen Latifah. In 1993 she released "Ruffneck," the hard-hitting single that would peak at No. 35 on the Billboard Hot 100 and gain Lyte her first gold certification and a nomination for

Best Rap Solo Performance at the 36th Annual Grammy Awards—also the first time a solo woman rapper was nominated, period!

There are a bunch of other album drops, single releases, and new career achievements that would occur over the course of Lyte's career—including the release of one of my favorite songs, the Missy Elliott–assisted "Cold Rock a Party." But we have to talk about the title of this chapter at some point, and that point is now.

I've seen more than a few "greatest rapper voices" lists in my lifetime, and I won't say that any of them are wrong. DMX's raw delivery, growls, and barking are incredible. Busta Rhymes's frenetic delivery is unmatched. And hearing Pimp C's southern drawl transports listeners right to Texas. All of these things are true, but the problem with those lists is that they hardly ever include women, which is a damn shame when you consider Foxy Brown's rough and deep flow, the uniqueness of Amil Whitehead's tone, and, of course, the power, strength, and clarity of MC Lyte's voice.

According to the *Harvard Business Review*, the key to having a voice that is visceral, effective, and commands attention lies in the use of "three linguistic elements": stress (volume), intonation (rising and falling tone), and rhythm (pacing). They note that these elements allow people to color their "words with the meaning and emotion that motivates others to act." That's why she's lent her voice as an announcer for the BET Awards, Grammy Awards, and VH1's Hip-Hop Honors, to national campaigns for Wherehouse Music, Coca-Cola, McDonald's, and Nike, and to the "Tia" doll for the Mattel toy line Diva Starz. All of these things cement Lyte's position as the First Lady of Rap Voices, but I also think she needs to be studied by up-and-coming artists. To this day she raps with the same clarity and power that he had when she first came out. If you watched her performance at the 2023 BET Awards you know what I'm talking about, and if you haven't watched it do that ASAP.

Now, I don't have MC Lyte on speed dial or anything, but if I did, I would do three things: 1) tell her how great she is, 2) ask her if she would host a rap performance class, and 3) pitch her some projects that I think her voice would be perfect for. Her voice is so great and I want to hear it even more than I already do.

Some Random Things I Think MC Lyte's Voice Would Be Perfect For

The Voice of an Animated Superhero

I don't know what the name of this character would be, but as someone who grew up watching the animated superhero television series *Static Shock* and loved watching all of the Black women kick ass in both *Black Panther* films, I *do* know that I really, really, really want to see a Black woman superhero in a cartoon who's voiced by MC Lyte.

In my mind I see Lyte's superhero as a Black woman who lives in a Brooklyn apartment with her three friends who go by the names of Lisa, Sharona, and Destiny, and her dog, Gleam. (I love a good little animal as a sidekick!) During the week she attends graduate school for African American studies, a nod to the rapper's years in elementary at Weusi Shule, and on weekends she throws parties reminiscent of the early days of hip-hop.

It was during one of her many parties that Lyte's superhero first gained her powers. While she was emceeing at the event, a clumsy partygoer got a little too turnt and ended up spilling juice all over the DJ booth. The mic sparks in her hand, releasing electric waves that enhance her five senses and also give her the ability to manipulate her voice and be anyone. Beloved in her neighborhood and across the country, Lyte's superhero works hand in hand with a special task force designed to weed out crime and corruption in different governing bodies and organizations. Somebody call DC or Marvel or whoever else makes these things and tell them to hit me up!

The Narrator of a Motivational Audiobook Titled *Lyte's Limericks*

Whenever I listen to MC Lyte's "Cha Cha Cha" I feel like I can do anything, and that's because Lyte is rapping like she can do anything. The stress, intonation, and rhythm of lines like "I've got the power to spread out and devour / At the same time I'll eat you up with a rhyme" pack a braggadocious punch, making it clear that Lyte means what she says and motivating listeners to be unabashed when it comes to their talents. It's that kind of encouragement that would make MC Lyte the perfect voice for a motivational audiobook titled *Lyte's Limericks*.

In poetry, a limerick is a humorous five with five lines that follows the AABBA rhyme scheme—the "A" lines (lines one, two, and five) rhyme with one another and the "B" lines (lines three and four) rhyme with each other. Having a bunch of MC Lyte's limericks in your phone on your favorite audiobook app to press play on every morning will without a doubt start your day off on the right track.

The New Voice of My GPS System

No shade to the people behind the navigation voices we've grown accustomed to, but I'd love to hear a new voice on one of my many car rides that doesn't sound so robotic. It'd be like having one of my homies in the car with me telling me to "bust this right" or that my "turn is coming up on the left." She's the perfect person for the job, so much so that I'm willing to bet she could even make "recalculating" when you miss a turn sound good.

The Voice of the New York City Subway

Commuting in New York City can be pretty hectic during rush hour, especially when you find yourself packed in a subway car with a bunch of complete strangers and stuck underground with no cell phone service. Hearing Lyte's voice can make those moments a little easier. She has the kind of commanding power in her voice that would make it nearly impossible for you to miss a stop when she announces it. Make it happen, NYC.

And while we're at it, let's update the New Jersey Transit announcements with Lyte's voice too.

My Voice Mail Message

Honestly, I really just want people to call me and hear MC Lyte say, "Sorry, Nadirah, ain't around to chat. Leave a message and she'll hit you back." I'd pay top dollar for that.

MC TROUBLE WAS MOTOWN'S FIRST WOMAN RAPPER

I didn't write this book in chapter order. Some days I would get stuck on a chapter that was really hard to get through so I would watch a bunch of episodes of *Unsung* to get my creative music juices flowing. Other days I would knock out an entire chapter or more. And there were some days where I would go back to the introduction a bunch of times and add in a sentence, a new story, and sometimes a new word. Yes, one single word. All this is to say, some parts of the writing process were easy and some parts were hard. This chapter was the latter. Not because the words wouldn't come, but because it was difficult to talk about someone whose life ended so early. But there was no way I was writing this book and highlighting some "firsts" without talking about MC Trouble, the first woman rapper to sign to Motown Records.

Before I continue this chapter I want to know, what artists came to your mind when I mentioned Motown? You can say them out loud, or write them down somewhere if you're in public and don't want people looking at you wondering why you're randomly saying the names of a bunch of musicians.

I obviously have no way of knowing who you thought of or wrote down, but when I think about Motown I think of Stevie Wonder, the Supremes, the Temptations, Gladys Knight and the Pips, Marvin Gaye, Smokey Robinson,* the Isley Brothers, and of course, the Jackson 5. But what I do know is that every act I just named represents the best of the best in music at one of the most impactful and important labels of all time. In fact, there's a snippet of audio that plays at the top of the 2019 documentary on the label titled *Hitsville: The Making of Motown* that was recorded during one of the label's quality control meetings sometime in the 1960s, where founder and then-president and CEO Berry Gordy is heard telling his staff that "this is serious business because from these meetings come the records that Motown releases to the street. We've got to maintain our high standards. . . ." Motown was the best of the best and they knew it.

So here's the story. In 1988 Berry Gordy sold Motown to MCA Inc. and Boston Ventures Limited Partnerships for $61 million. A lot of things led up to this moment, but two of the biggest factors were that big names like Diana Ross and the Jacksons had left Motown to go to other labels, and sales, which had hit nearly $100 million annually during the best years, had dropped to $20 million.** After the sale, Jheryl Busby,*** who was the president of Black music operations for MCA Records, took over as the president and CEO of Motown and was tasked with reviving the label and returning it to its

---

* Have you seen the video for his song "Gang Banging"? It's a song recorded by Smokey where he sings about people who are wasting their time "drinking that wine," "smoking that smoke," "staying out late," and "preaching that hate," in front of graffiti-sprayed walls. It's really funny and really random and I want you to watch it. Just remember he made "Cruisin'" and "Ooo Baby," so don't laugh too much.

** From a 1988 *Los Angeles Times* story titled "Berry Gordy Sells Motown Records for $61 Million."

*** A fun fact about Jheryl Busby: Busby, Janet Jackson, and Magic Johnson were all shareholders in the nation's first Black-owned national bank, Founders National Bank of Los Angeles.

former glory. That's a big ask and if it were me, I would have been shook.

For some context, Busby was the top dog. The head honcho. Or whatever other phrase you use when you know somebody is running things and running them well. At MCA he promoted established artists like Patti LaBelle and discovered and worked with newer acts like Jody Watley and New Edition. At Motown, Busby set his sights on new jack swing and R&B, bringing acts like Today,* the Boys, and the Good Girls—whom Motown promoted as the new Four Tops, the new Jacksons, and the new Supremes, respectively—to the label. It only made sense to have artists that represented the sounds of what people were listening to. Which meant that Busby needed Motown to stake its claim in another genre as well: rap. Enter LaTasha Sheron Rogers, who rapped under the name MC Trouble.

MC Trouble's deal with the label in 1989 made the teenager the first woman rapper to sign with Motown, setting the stage for what was poised to be a promising career. I mean, imagine being the woman that an entire company is putting their time, money, and energy behind to help them stake their claim in the genre whose rise marked "the single most important event that has shaped the musical structure of the American charts."** Period.

The label hit the ground running with MC Trouble, putting two of her songs—"Can't Get Enough" and "Highroller's Girl"—on the Greg Mack compilation album *What Does It All Mean*. She also toured as part of 1990's *Motortown Revue*, a revival of the traveling

---

* Three things about Today. They're from New Jersey so you know I have to stan. Their song "You Stood Me Up" is a classic in my house. And one of the members, Lee "Big Bub" Drakeford, worked with Mary J. Blige on her *My Life* album and has a pretty great cover of the Commodores' "Zoom," a Motown classic.

** Matthias Mauch, Robert M. MacCallum, Mark Levy, and Armand M. Leroi, "*The Evolution of Popular Music: USA 1960–2010*," *Royal Society Open Science* (May 2015), https://royalsocietypublishing.org/doi/10.1098/rsos.150081.

revue concerts that early Motown artists would go on in the 1960s. There's a not-so-glowing review of this revue that was published in the *Los Angeles Times* that makes me wonder if any of the acts read it and it lit a fire under them. I mean it must have, because what happened next sure made it seem so.

MC Trouble released her first single "(I Wanna) Make You Mine" in 1990, featuring her label mates the Good Girls. She coproduced and cowrote the track alongside LA Jay, and the song peaked at No. 15 on what was then known as *Billboard*'s Hot Rap Singles chart. It's a fun little bop that finds the rapper talking about making a man hers, hence the title of the song, where she confidently raps, "Why lie? For that I'm simply too fly / It takes no time to throw a line." The track would appear on her debut and only album, *Gotta Get a Grip*, and is one of my favorite tracks on the LP along with the title track, a poignant song on race and politics. Like the Sequence did years earlier, she also incorporated singing and rapping on her project.

Less than a year later, while working on her sophomore album, MC Trouble passed away at the age of twenty from an epileptic seizure. The loss was a devastating blow, and tributes came from everywhere. On their 1991 track "Vibes 'n Stuff," A Tribe Called Quest's Phife Dawg paid his respects, rapping, "I'm out like Buster Douglas. Rest in peace to M.C. Trouble."

Rapper Nefertiti released "Trouble in Paradise" as an ode to the young emcee. The Boys lamented the loss of their friend on "You Got Me Cryin'," opening the song by saying, "Man, I was just thinkin' about Trouble and the world. I just can't comprehend. It got me cryin', man." Boyz II Men also dedicated the music video for their hit single "It's So Hard to Say Goodbye" to MC Trouble.

The 1991 concert *Sisters in the Name of Rap* did a tribute to Trouble, with a video highlighting how she "positively touched the lives of millions of people in her short time on earth." That's why whenever I read about or listen to MC Trouble I think about how much was destined for. How she was set to blaze a path for women in rap much like her counterparts at the time. And how she was the first woman to put on for rap at the Motown label. But to be honest, this is one of those chapters that I couldn't end with just my words. So I'll leave you with what the Good Girls' Joyce Tolbert shared with *Urban Bridgez* on what would have been Trouble's fiftieth birthday:

> *She was a beautiful soul and a superstar. . . . Trouble would have created some positive movement within our youth and our communities and schools through music and her voice. Your light in this world was gone too soon, but we will never let your light in this plane go out!*

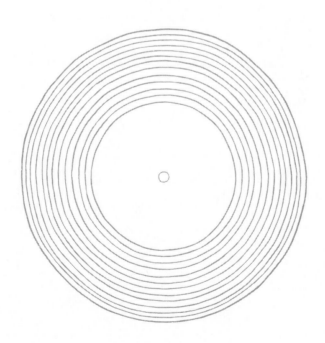

"TV/FILM"

Interlude

CAN COURTNEY SLOANE INTERIOR-DESIGN MY HOUSE?

This book was written in a bunch of different places that include an apartment, the library, my family home, hotels, on the train, and on a plane. None of it was written in a home that I own, an achievement that's on my long-term list of goals. I have no idea when that time will come, but please know when it happens, I'm calling Courtney Sloane first. She's an interior designer who was praised by *Vibe* for her "reputation for understanding the hip-hop aesthetic." That reputation is why Courtney's client list is filled with some of the biggest names in hip-hop, including Queen Latifah, Diddy, and Mary J. Blige.

Hailing from Jersey City, New Jersey, Sloane earned her BS degree in marketing from Rutgers University (my alma mater!) in 1984. The thing about college that I know a lot of people can relate to is that sometimes a person's degree isn't necessarily representative of the direction their career will go in. Courtney developed a love for art and design as a kid that manifested through interior design. In college, Sloane's off-campus apartment was so nice that friends would ask her for help designing theirs. After graduating from Rutgers, she received a full-time job as a retail merchandiser at JCPenney, but she wasn't fulfilled. It was time for Courtney to lean into the work that she loved, and a position at Formica would allow her to do precisely that.

At Formica, a surfacing products design company, Courtney learned a lot from the architects and designers on the team. She also took postgraduate classes in metalworking at Pratt Institute and interior design at the Fashion Institute of Technology. With the experience, passion, and tools handy, she launched her own company, Alternative Design, in 1991. Using materials made by Formica to create furniture, Courtney started hosting events in a Jersey City loft that she shared with friends to showcase the pieces. When a flyer for one of the events caught the eye of Jersey City resident Queen Latifah, the legendary rapper pulled up to the loft and told Courtney she would be back to hire her when she, Latifah, blew up. I don't think I need to tell you that Queen Latifah blew up. So her mom called Courtney to do the interior design on a home they had just purchased. The rest is history!*

Courtney's work for Queen Latifah flung the doors open for her design work in hip-hop. She did *Vibe* magazine's reception area—which was voted "Best Lobby in NYC" by *New York* magazine—and the office of product placement company Da Streetz. Sloane did the interior design for hip-hop fashion brand Enyce's office space. She designed offices for BET too. And when Latifah needed to hook up her Flavor Unit Entertainment space in Jersey City, you know Courtney Sloane was right there to get it done.

If that isn't enough to blow you away, might I add that her resume also includes the Carol's Daughter flagship store, Sony's recording

---

* I've always wanted to say that!

studio in New York, the Rock & Roll Hall of Fame Museum's twentieth anniversary exhibit on hip-hop, and set design for *America's Next Top Model*. No matter the job or request, Courtney Sloane is a design wiz who can make *anything* happen.

For example, when Queen Latifah wanted wheels on her furniture so items could be moved to whatever room she wanted, Courtney was able to do it. When Diddy wanted what Courtney described to the *New York Times* as an "explosive 'breaking the mold' image," Sloane created a wall that looked like a truck drove through it, complete with "torn and twisted steel casings" that enclosed television monitors. And when she was constructing a table for her own showroom loft, she rounded up steel beams from an abandoned subway station to use as a base.

There's really nothing Courtney can't do, and there's a lot that I can't do, especially when it comes to decorating a spot. I know how to make things match, I know how to keep my room open and balanced, and I know how to save a buck! (IKEA and my local dollar store have seen me *a lot* over the years.) But to be quite honest, if it weren't for Pinterest and Tumblr and my penchant for looking up old celebrity living spaces on Getty Images, I would not have a single clue on where to begin when it came to decorating my crib.

That's why I would call Courtney. She's done interior design for the biggest names in hip-hop, knows how to rework materials into new items, can fulfill the most insane requests, *and* she's from Jersey. And I would really like a steel casing like the one she made for Diddy to watch the shows and movies in the next couple of chapters.

Interlude

THE LADIES IN AND AROUND THE FIRST HIP-HOP MOVIE, *WILD STYLE*

Wild Style is one of those movies that you watch and feel like you're really there. Like you're really *in* the Bronx hanging around with people in the early days of hip-hop. It's an obvious result of what the film's director, Charlie Ahearn, told the *New York Times* was "a projection of our dreams." He continued, "There was nothing out there that showed all these artists together in one scene. It was only later that people began to look at it as some sort of documentary. But at first, we were just projecting what we wanted it to be. It was our wildest dream of what could happen." What *did* happen to hip-hop, I'm sure, is bigger than anything anyone could have imagined. That's what makes *Wild Style*, the film credited as the first hip-hop movie, so important. Which means the women who were a part of it remain extremely important too.

For context, *Wild Style* debuted in 1983, the same year as the documentaries *Style Wars* and *Breakin' 'n' Enterin'*, which highlighted the development of hip-hop culture in New York and the b-boy scene in Los Angeles, respectively. In fact, film critic Bilge Ebiri noted in a piece for Vulture that "you could cut about 15 or 20 minutes out of [*Wild Style*] and you'd be left with a literal documentary." It's a fair assessment, especially when you consider in 1984 the films *Breakin'*, its sequel *Breakin' 2: Electric Boogaloo*, and *Beat Street* were released, and each of them used its characters and storytelling to deliver a plot that placed hip-hop at the center. They each may feel more in line with the narrative structure of what we would call a movie today. Nonetheless, *Wild Style* does tell a story, and it's that of South Bronx graffiti artist Zoro—played by Lee Quiñones—who is commissioned to decorate a bandshell for a hip-hop concert. The film is chock full of hip-hop legends and real-life rappers, graffiti artists, and breakdancers.

The important thing to understand about *Wild Style*, which Ebiri also noted in that Vulture piece, is that it

> is credited as the first hip-hop movie, but it didn't introduce rap or hip-hop culture or even the notion that graffiti could be art. There had already been major gallery shows featuring graffiti artists by 1981, and by the time Wild Style *was released in late 1983, bigger productions capitalizing on rap and the break-dancing craze were already underway.* Wild Style *arrived early, but it wasn't so much ahead of the curve as simply well-placed to ride it.*

That last sentence is it! Because, like I said in the introduction, being first is less about actually *being* first and more about creating a pathway for others to travel and build upon. In fact, what *Wild Style* did do was contribute to the movement that spread hip-hop across the world. That's why I've decided to highlight some of the women who were in the movie by way of scenes that they were in.

[0:11:37]
Graffiti artist Rose "Lady Bug," played by Sandra "Lady Pink" Fabara, instructs her crew of dudes on how to write graffiti on a wall.

Born in Ecuador and raised in New York City, Lady Pink got her start writing graffiti in 1979. On her website she notes that she was known as "the only female capable of competing with the boys in the graffiti subculture." From 1979 to 1985, Lady Pink painted subway trains, and in *Wild Style* she played the starring role of Rose "Lady Bug."

Her role in the movie mirrors that of her real-life persona. In this particular scene, Rose is calling the shots and telling the dudes in her crew the Union how to make the artwork on the wall look better. "Don't get drips now" and "You're going to get that filled in more, right?" she says to the guys, as a crowd of onlookers, including Zoro, watch the artwork come together. The pride that I felt seeing Rose lead a team of men the first time I watched *Wild Style* was so large, because naturally I was hype to see a woman running shit! But after doing some research on graffiti artists and street art, my pride tripled.

Chelsea Iversen writes in a piece for the *Bold Italic*, "The socially normalized idea of a graffiti writer or a street artist is gendered male." Dr. Jessica Pabón, a feminist scholar who grew up with graffiti artists, told Iversen that as a result of this genderization, women graffiti artists become invisible. And if the threat of invisibility isn't enough to piss you off, the piece also highlighted the issues of safety that women who graffiti face. Iversen says, "to be a muralist or a street artist, you have to endure these things: being in public spaces for long periods of time, often alone and at night. And for male street artists, it's different. They're less vulnerable."

When asked about her career in an interview with Nijla Mu'min in 2013, Lady Pink said, "I'd like to think I set an example earlier on that no matter what size you are or gender or any-thing, it just takes a lot of dedication and a lot of courage and a lot of heart to get this done, and a lot of women have followed suit. I'm certainly not the very first one." She added that there were women graffiti artists who came before her, like Barbara, Eva, Charmin, and Stony, and a bunch of other ladies who ran in crews and made sure to look out for one another.

Since appearing in *Wild Style*, Lady Pink has gone on to have her art shown in the Whitney Museum, the Metropolitan Museum of Art, the Brooklyn Museum, the Museum of Fine Arts in Boston, and the Groningen Museum of Holland. She's a cult figure in hip-hop whose work is highly sought after by col-lectors and admired by artists. There's no denying her skill and impact, so when she tells you not to get drips, you better listen.

[0:26:47]
Lisa Lee raps during the "Basketball Throwdown" (*PLUS* that deleted scene I wish would have made the cut)

Rapper Lisa Lee, whose role in *Wild Style* reads "Fly Girl" on IMDb, got her start when her father bought Lisa and her broth-ers turntables, a mixer, and a mic. As a member of the Univer-sal Zulu Nation she made her mark as the first (and only) lady in the Soulsonic Force, and would become a member of the Cosmic Force. For Ahearn, Lisa Lee was the perfect fit for the movie.

"MCs at that time, if they were real, had to be able to come out and perform for hours. . . . That meant a strong presence on a stage, and Lisa Lee had that," Ahearn told Clover Hope in *The Motherlode: 100+ Women Who Made Hip-Hop*. "There's no doubt that she was a legend among people that knew hip-hop."

One of my favorite scenes in the movie is when Lisa Lee and her friends pull up to the basketball court where the Cold

Crush Brothers and Fantastic Five are getting ready to verbally battle.[*] One of her friends asks if they're going to the Dixie later that night, prompting Lisa Lee to ask a variation of my favorite question: "Who all gon be there?" When the friend tells them Fantastic and Cold Crush are going to be there, Lisa Lee is shocked. "Oh my god. I think you may have got that wrong," she replies. "You know how Fantastic be talking about Cold Crush."

A few seconds later the Cold Crush Brothers and Fantastic Five step to each other in a scene often called the "Basketball Throwdown," with each member taking turns throwing lyrical jabs about who's going to win the basketball game. The cool thing about this scene is that it's not only really entertaining to watch, but when you think the rhymes are over Lisa Lee appears on the screen and starts rapping, "We have to come to an agreement, who's gonna survive? / The Cold Crush Four or the Fantastic Five?"

I love this scene for two reasons. One, it makes me feel wildly nostalgic. Hip-hop had not yet become the billion-dollar industry that it is today. It was simply a means through which people could express themselves and have fun and I would have loved to witness some of our pioneering emcees just hanging out and rhyming. The second reason is that I really love how Lisa Lee puts on her acting hat to set up what's about to happen and then uses her skills as an emcee to tie it all together. But none of it feels performative or fake. And when I think back to Ebiri saying you can cut out some time and be left with a literal documentary, the realness that was Lisa Lee proves that statement to be more than true.

---

* The Cold Crush Brothers and Fantastic Five battle that went down at New York's Harlem World Club in 1981 is one of the most important battles in rap history. Competing for the thousand-dollar prize, the guys put their best lyrics forward in an effort to win. I won't tell you who took home the cash, but you should check it out when you have some time.

That's actually why I'm sad that Lisa Lee's other big rap scene was cut from the final movie. Everyone is at a party where Busy Bee and Lil' Rodney C are getting busy on the mic, and the scene that was cut features Lisa Lee rapping with them. She introduces herself as "L-I-S-A L-E-E" before rhyming, "I'm always rocking, not stopping / I'm like dessert with cool whip topping." She's skilled, smooth, and commands the crowd perfectly. And *that* is why I wish this scene would have made it in. As one of the first women to rap, period, showing Lisa Lee as an emcee at a party would have been a great way to either teach or remind viewers that women were a part of hip-hop in its earliest days. Thankfully people can watch the clip online, and if you want to see more footage of Lisa Lee rapping watch the 1984 film *Beat Street*.

[0:27:06]
The Rapping Cheerleaders

The other great thing about the "Basketball Throwdown" scene is the trio of ladies I've seen people describe as the "rapping cheerleaders." I'm not quite sure who is who, as the credits listed five names as "Fly Girls" and six different young women (including Lisa Lee) dialogue and rap on camera during that iconic battle scene. Nonetheless, watching the ladies cheer on the game with raps made me really excited the first time I watched *Wild Style*, because I clearly can't get enough of ladies rapping.

[0:47:37]
Virginia, played by Patti Astor, takes Zoro to a fancy function

Patti Astor's role in *Wild Style* mirrors her real-life work. In the movie she's Virginia, a reporter who covers graffiti and street art and introduces the artists to potential buyers. In the real world, she was the cofounder of the Fun Gallery, which show-cased the work of artists like Fab 5 Freddy, Dondi, Lady Pink, Lee Quiñones, Jean-Michel Basquiat, Keith Haring, and Futura 2000.

Raised in Cincinnati, Ohio, Astor first moved to New York City in 1968 to attend Barnard College, dropping out to become active in the antiwar movement. After that she traveled to San Francisco and Paris before returning to New York in 1975. She wanted to be an actress, and soon after her return to the city she was cast in Amos Poe's film *Unmade Beds*. Affectionately referred to as the "Queen of the Downtown Screen," Patti notched more roles in many more underground films before getting a part in *Wild Style*.

Patti is in a lot of scenes in *Wild Style*, but the one I'm choosing to talk about here is when she takes Zoro to a func-tion filled with rich and fancy art buyers and museum owners. Patti acts as an intermediary between Zoro and the art guys who have questions about graffiti and its legitimacy, much like she did for artists off camera.

I chose this scene for two reasons. For one, it shows the ways different people helped spread hip-hop to other areas, in this case from the Bronx to Manhattan. This movement is one of the things that allowed hip-hop artists to show their talent to the world and capitalize off it in music, film, fashion, and gal-leries like Patti's. That word *capitalize* is the other reason I chose this scene. It slightly hints at exploitation that many hip-hop artists would experience from people who wanted to cap-italize on *them*.

What Charlie captured in this scene was inspiring and real, and having Patti play the role was the perfect choice. Patti, both on screen and off, saw the importance of celebrat-ing the work of artists in hip-hop simply because it was the right thing to do.

[?:??:??]
Kara Vallow, executive producer of *Family Guy*, is dancing in here somewhere

There have been many moments when working on this book that I discovered something I was not expecting. This is one of them. As I was reading through the credits for *Wild Style* on IMDb I came across an uncredited dancer by the name of Kara Vallow, and being the researcher I am I decided to find out more. That's how I ended up on her IMDb page and learned she's currently the executive producer of *Family Guy* and a producer on *American Dad!,* and has a long career in television with credits on *Men in Black: The Series*, Eight Crazy Nights, *Johnny Bravo, The Cleveland Show, Dilbert*, and the *Teenage Mutant Ninja Turtles* television series. On top of being in *Wild Style*, she was also an uncredited dancer in other classic hip-hop films like *Breakin'*, Rappin', and *Krush Groove*. I replayed *Wild Style* a bunch of times and could not find Kara, hence the question marks in the time field. But if you can find her, send me a screenshot. You'll be one of my favorite people if you do.

There are a lot of other things that make *Wild Style* really important, but this is a book about the ladies. The first hip-hop film made history by highlighting one of the most impactful cultures ever and paved the way for the movies that followed. What it also did was show that whether they were graffiti artists, emcees, breakdancers, reporters, party attendees, sisters, moms, aunts, cousins, or all of those things at once, women helped create hip-hop and played a crucial role in its development. *Wild Style* is the perfect primary source to remind you of that fact.

ROXANNE SHANTÉ, THE SUBJECT OF THE FIRST WIDELY RELEASED BIOPIC ABOUT A WOMAN RAPPER (AND SOME OF THE OTHER LADIES WE NEED BIOPICS ON!)

"The champ is here! The champ is here!" That's what a young Roxanne Shanté's friend Ranita yells as she walks to the basketball court alongside Roxanne and her mom. Roxanne steps up onto a crate so she can meet her appointment, a boy who's likely twice her age, at eye level. The two are about to battle each other, and whoever has the best bars will take home fifty dollars. Right before she starts rapping, Roxanne turns to her mom—played by Nia Long—and asks her if she can curse. Her mom responds, "I don't care what you do as long as you win that fifty dollars." That's the opening scene of *Roxanne Roxanne*, a biopic that tells the story of pioneering rapper Roxanne Shanté. Released in theaters in New York and Los Angeles and on Netflix in 2018, and screened at the Sundance Film Festival in 2017, *Roxanne Roxanne* was the first widely released biopic about a woman rapper.[*]

---

[*] Cited from Clover Hope's *The Motherlode: 100+ Women Who Made Hip-Hop.*

Born Lolita Shanté Gooden, the Queensbridge rapper who would go by the name Roxanne Shanté discovered her love for rhyming by watching the legendary comedian Nipsey Russell on TV. Nicknamed the "poet laureate of television," Russell would deliver catchy rhymes about any and every thing during his appearances on various shows. "He would sit there and say, like, I'm Nipsey Russell and I don't have to hustle, don't want no tussle, don't like to fussle (ph). And people would ask him questions, and he would answer them in a rhyming form," Shanté told NPR's *All Things Considered* in 2018. "So I sat in front of the TV and was like, I like Nipsey Russell. I like to hustle. So what it did was it started a whole rhyming effect. And I would rhyme the entire day."

In addition to her rhyme skills, Shanté told *Billboard* that she developed her competitive nature from "hearing other people battling from the window and thinking, 'Just wait until my turn comes.'" Her turn would come when her family and friends started taking a young Roxanne Shanté to different housing projects, clubs, and community centers in the city to battle other emcees. Her supporters would put up the money for the entry fee and her mom would give them a commission when she won. And she won a lot. Only in middle school at the time, Shanté was going up against and regularly beating older boys and men. Just like the opening scene in the movie.

Shanté's big break came at the age of fourteen when she recorded "Roxanne's Revenge," a response track to UTFO's hit song "Roxanne, Roxanne." In the song, each member of UTFO raps about trying to get the attention and affection of a fictional woman by the name of Roxanne.

For some context, "Roxanne, Roxanne" became popular because the crew over at legendary radio show *Rap Attack*—with host Mr. Magic, DJ and legendary producer Marley Marl, and coproducer and Marl's manager, Tyrone "Fly Ty" Williams—decided to play it. The song was the B side to UTFO's 1984 single "Hangin' Out," and they preferred it over the single. The guys had the right idea, because

"Roxanne, Roxanne" took off. Which brings me to how Roxanne

Shanté got involved.

On the heels of this song's success, UTFO offered to perform at a concert promoted by Mr. Magic. As *Billboard* detailed in a 2018 article on Shanté:

> *[The concert] promised to be a much-needed financial boon to Magic, Williams and Marley Marl, who were still barely making ends meet. But when the city's other on-air destination for rap, Kool DJ Red Alert's show on the former WRKS (Kiss-FM), added "Roxanne, Roxanne," UTFO backed out—the point at which the story becomes legend.*

In the movie, Marley Marl calls out to Shanté as she walks through Queensbridge Houses and asks her to come to his place. When she gets there, Marl, who lived in the building across from her, tells Shanté he wants her to rhyme over a beat. She lets him know she has laundry to do, but after some quick convincing, agrees to lay down some rhymes dissing UTFO.

How that scene plays out in the movie is how it happened in real life too, with Shanté telling the same story multiple times over the years in various interviews. And I'm going to be honest, I hate that I don't know the date that Roxanne Shanté recorded the track because it's hip-hop history. What I *do* know, however, is that soon after recording the song, "Roxanne's Revenge"—originally titled "Roxanne Speaks Out" but renamed and rerecorded due to licensing issues—was on the radio.* The song was a hit and Shanté became a celebrity practically overnight. It was a first for a woman in rap.

---

* Multiple articles say that UTFO and their label, Select Records, sent a cease-and-desist letter to Shanté and the team for her use of the "Roxanne, Roxanne" beat. If you ever hear the original, consider yourself guaranteed to have five years of good luck!

The biopic shows a bit of what happens next, but if you haven't watched it yet, I got you. UTFO recruited a woman to be "The Real Roxanne"* and put out a track of the same name in response to Shanté. Over in Brooklyn, rapper Doreen "Sparky D" Broadnax heard the song on the radio and decided to fire back with "Sparky's Turn (Roxanne You're Through)." The replies kept coming in, and as Clover Hope noted in her book *The Motherlode: 100+ Women Who Made Hip-Hop*, "there is a Roxanne Wars Wikipedia page, and there's a WordPress blog from 2013 that catalogued about thirty known responses, some available only on cassette tape and vinyl."

Roxanne Shanté told *Vice News* in 2017, "I made one song, and had eighty-three songs made about me, specifically where they said 'Roxanne Shanté.' No other artist has ever had that." Other sources say there are more, to the tune of one hundred tracks in total. Whatever the number, the sheer amount of tracks recorded in response to "Roxanne's Revenge" kicked off a war of words that made hip-hop history and set the stage for more sparring on wax.

That history is on display in the film, with *Roxanne Roxanne* following Shanté through the rest of the early days of her career, depicting an abusive relationship with her older boyfriend and son's father, detailing how she was wronged by different managers and men in the industry, and ending ahead of the release of Shanté's first album.

The thing about movies, though, is that it's literally impossible to fit every single thing in them. The same way I couldn't fit everything into this book. With that in mind, there was only so much the team could include in a one-hundred-minute movie about a figure as

---

* Follow me here. The Real Roxanne on "The Real Roxanne" is a lady by the name of Elease Jack. Adelaida Martinez would rap under the name the Real Roxanne after that, scoring a minor hit in the United Kingdom with "Bang Zoom (Let's Go-Go)." I know, I know. There are so many ladies by the name of Roxanne to keep up with. It's confusing.

important as Roxanne Shanté. Which means there's always more stuff for you to learn.

Like how Roxanne Shanté battled Busy Bee at the legendary MC Battle for World Supremacy in 1985. The panel of judges included Kurtis Blow and DJ Red Alert, and Shanté was certain if anyone was going to sabotage her it would be Red Alert, since he DJ'd for her rival Sparky D.

But that was not the case. It was Kurtis Blow who gave the teenage Roxanne Shanté the low score of 4, which resulted in her losing the competition. It was widely accepted that Shanté bested Bee in the battle, but sexism was at work to stop her from being crowned as the best emcee. Roxanne Shanté talked about the loss with *Vice News* in 2017, remembering Kurtis Blow telling her, "'At that time, rappers had just started getting major deals, they had just started getting accepted into mainstream. For the sake of hip-hop, there was no way that a 15-year-old girl could be the best. There was just no way that we could do that, Shanté.'" She was rattling the boys club in hip-hop long before some of our favorite ladies were even thought of.

There's also the randomness that is Shanté living with Rick James for a period of time. The two connected on James's 1988 cut "Loosey's Rap," to which she contributed two verses. The two performed the song together at the Apollo Theater in Harlem, and I just know somebody out there has the footage!

The movie also doesn't show us the release of Roxanne Shanté's debut album, *Bad Sister*, which peaked at No. 52 on *Billboard*'s Top R&B/Hip-Hop Albums chart. A review by the *New York Times* praised the way the songs "combine humor and raw rhythmic power with Ms. Shante's sturdy sense of identity" and asserted Shanté as "tougher and wittier than the competition."

It's kind of nuts that we have so few biopics that center women in rap. I mean, yes, there have been features that *included* women, like the 2009 theatrically released film *Notorious*, which is based on Biggie. In that film Naturi Naughton plays Lil' Kim, but Kim was not a fan of the portrayal, telling *NME* two days before the movie's release, "The film studio and producers involved were more concerned about painting me as a 'character' to create a more interesting story line instead of a person with talent."

There's also the 2013 VH1 film *CrazySexyCool: The TLC Story,* which talks about TLC's rise to stardom. This right here is one of my favorite biopics, but with so much ground to cover as it relates to the group as a whole, there wasn't much time to tell the life story of the sole rapper in the group, Lisa "Left Eye" Lopes.

It felt like people were finally realizing the importance of women rappers' stories in 2021 when Lifetime aired the biopic *Salt-N-Pepa*, an eponymous film about the group. But its release faced controversy when group member Spinderella spoke up about being wrongfully excluded from its development and production. All in all, there just aren't enough biographical films out there that tell the full stories of the pioneering women in hip-hop who helped make the culture and the music what it is today.

I love a great music biopic. For one, it gives viewers another medium through which they can learn about certain figures. When we talk about hip-hop, especially those early days, there aren't as many recorded tracks, videos, or photos of some of the people who were there, which unfortunately means its participants run the risk of being left out of history if they aren't here to tell their stories themselves. Which brings me to my next point. While these people are still here with us, why not have them help tell their stories and cut them a check for an executive producer credit too? It's the least we could do for our hip-hop pioneers, considering its sheer existence has put a lot of money in the pockets of people who aren't of, from, and don't respect the culture. And lastly, they'll just be really damn interesting.

So I've decided to draft a few ideas for the biopics of women in rap that I would love to produce. To be honest, there are so many interesting and important women in hip-hop that I would want to produce a biopic on every last one. But, for the sake of time and limiting the amount of cramps I'm sure I'll get if I try to type up a biopic on every single woman, I'm going to keep the list short and give you ten. That's ten biopics, complete with a title, logline, synopsis, and an explanation of *why* we—yes, you and I—need it. Oh, and one more thing. This book is copyrighted, which means these ideas are too. So don't try to steal these—give me a producer credit and cut the check.

Aaaaand action!

Luminary: The MC Sha-Rock Story

Logline: From North Carolina to the Bronx and then to the stage at *Saturday Night Live*, this is the story of how a young lady by the name of MC Sha-Rock earned the title of "the first female rapper."

Synopsis: *Luminary: The MC Sha-Rock Story* follows the first female emcee from her beginnings as a B-girl in the Bronx to a rapper in the group Funky Four (later Funky Four Plus One and Funky Four Plus One More). A deal with Sugar Hill Records and a performance on *Saturday Night Live*—which is one of the first nationally televised rap performances ever—sends the group to the top. Along the way, bad contracts, tension within the group, and jealousy from other crews threaten to stop the story of Sha-Rock in its tracks, but her love for hip-hop and fight for credit, royalties, and respect cements her legacy as far more than a plus one.

Why we need it: I'm going to give you a bit of her story, because seeing it all play out on-screen is just a way to emphasize that what Sha-Rock has done, endured, and fought for is more important than anything I could write.

Known as the Luminary Icon, Sha-Rock has influenced everyone from MC Lyte—who posted on Facebook on October 15, 2021, that Sha Rock was the "first female I ever heard rock the mic"—to Run-DMC's DMC, who told detailed what it was like hearing her rhyme on "Rappin' and Rocking the House" for an episode of NPR Music's *Louder Than a Riot* podcast in 2023:

> *I heard her rhyming over the breakbeat "Seven Minutes of Funk" and it was just the craziest thing that I ever heard. And I heard a lot of people do it. But there was*

something about the way Sha-Rock delivered her rhymes that was just the prototype to be. She was already dominant. The echo chamber just made her invincible.

Sha-Rock told *Louder Than a Riot* that Sylvia Robinson called the group near the end of the tour to let them know that Debbie Harry of Blondie was going to host and perform on *Saturday Night Live* and she wanted to have a special guest.

From this podcast I learned that Sylvia chose Funky Four Plus One More for the history-making television spot because they "had a female and the fact that we were young and innocent-looking." The other acts on the label were pissed that they weren't selected to appear on the late-night comedy show, so much so that when the tour bus got back to the parking lot of Sugar Hill Records the groups started fighting. Yes, y'all, *fighting*, with Keef Cowboy of the Furious Five punching Lil Rodney Cee of Funky Four Plus One More.

As mad as their label mates may have been, that wasn't going to stop the show. On Valentine's Day in 1981 the group still took the *Saturday Night Live* stage and sent hip-hop into the homes of anyone who watched the performance. Unbeknownst to her group members at the time, Sha-Rock was pregnant, with the shirt she wore during the performance concealing her bump. When she told the guys she was pregnant the next day they were not happy. To them, Sha-Rock's pregnancy meant the group's continued success was at risk. And while it certainly didn't have to be that way, Sha-Rock revealed that "after the pregnancy, that's when things went downhill for the Funky Four Plus One."

When I think about this part of Sha-Rock's story I think about women rappers like Lauryn Hill and her seminal song, which we'll talk about later, "To Zion." I think about the people who bashed Cardi B after she revealed her pregnancy on *Saturday Night Live,* the same show where Sha-Rock made history decades before. And I remember the way people talked about Yung Miami of City Girls when she announced her pregnancy while her group mate JT was incarcerated. For each of the ladies it was the use of phrases like "bad timing" that set out to punish them for choosing motherhood and make it seem like you couldn't be a mom *and* have your career. It's crazy that in all the years that have passed we're still having the same conversations, because news flash: you can do it all and then some!

Sylvia Robinson would go on to be godmother to Sha-Rock's daughter, which makes the next part that I'm about to tell straight-up frustrating and sad. Seriously, there's no other way to put it. The group broke up and Sha-Rock had to take care of her kid. And despite Sylvia being godmother to her baby and assuring Sha-Rock that she would look out for her, the emcee wasn't making money off any of the music she made for Sugar Hill Records, and as Dan Charnas perfectly put it in a 2019 article about Robinson for *Billboard,* "her success with Sugar Hill did not satisfy a hunger for credit that ultimately metastasized into greed and tarnished her reputation."

This kind of greed and capitalization persists in all realms of music, but this is a book about women in hip-hop. And I know when you read that quote, someone's bad deal or royalties or social media rant against their label came to mind. How far we've come, how far we have to go.

Sha-Rock linked up with MC Debbie D and Lisa Lee and formed the trio Us Girls, with the ladies appearing in the 1984 movie *Beat Street.* Clover Hope's *The Motherlode* revealed that around that time, she also recorded an unreleased track with the Sequence's Angie B. But in the midst of her new chapter Sha-Rock was still bound by her contract with Sugar Hill Records. Dissatisfied by it all, she chose to get out of the game altogether.

In the 1990s Sha-Rock's interest in the industry was renewed when she saw a Sugar Hill Records compilation LP selling for a hundred dollars in a record store. Sha-Rock was determined to make sure that the artists who *made* said music could eat off it long after they stepped out of the booth. Sha-Rock got in touch with Artist Rights Enforcement in New York City, rounded up her old group and former label mates like the Furious Five and a member of the Crash Crew, and brought a lawsuit against Sugar Hill Records. On July 15, 2022, Sha-Rock announced on Instagram that they won their final judgment:

> *People use [sic] to think I was tripping, simply because I've always spoken on the lawsuit and was determined to see this through. Some said let it go. I can't discuss the amount; but it's finally over. Or we're [sic] be back in court if my money is short.*

Now tell me that wouldn't make a really good movie!

Ladies, My Mercedes

Logline: In the early days of hip-hop, a crew of girls by the name of Mercedes Ladies set out to shake up the boys' club and stake their claim in history.

Synopsis: A story of sisterhood and sodality, the girls in Mercedes Ladies are DJs, dancers, and emcees making it happen in hip-hop long before groups like J.J. Fad and Salt-N-Pepa hit the scene. As teenagers in the Bronx, the young ladies hustle hard to promote parties and put on shows in their community while fending off male detractors who attempt to sabotage them along the way.

Why we need it: They're widely regarded as the first girl group in hip-hop, and in my opinion there's just not enough content out there celebrating and highlighting the young women who formed Mercedes Ladies. As founding member Sheri Sher said in her book, *Mercedes Ladies*—which you should buy and read ASAP—they were "seven teenage girls from different areas of the Bronx whose paths came together during the late 1970s to create an everlasting bond." Hip-hop is rooted in community and that bond is important, especially when it comes to the ladies. Which brings me to the two reasons that come to mind when I think about the importance of this story.

For one, hip-hop was and remains a culture predominantly driven and influenced by men. It is men who are often given the space to dictate what's acceptable, who gets paid for what, who can perform where, and a host of other things. For the girls in Mercedes Ladies, creating the group was about getting the work done and demanding respect too.

Two, there's always a discussion (in other words, gossip and crap talk) about women and girls who rap not being able to get along. You could probably get on your Twitter right now and see some stans inciting friction between two women rappers as we speak. Now, don't get me wrong, I think beef between rappers—as long as all parties keep the battles over the beats—can produce some amazing records and encourage healthy competition. Moreover, women who rap should be given the space to beef and be angry and disagree with things just like the men are. My issue is with the notion that women who rap can't get along at all. It's an idea rooted in sexism and misogyny that's just flat-out not true. And what better way to show that than with *Ladies, My Mercedes*?

~~~~~~~~~~

Funked Up

Logline: A backstage audition for one of hip-hop's biggest executives changes the lives of three ladies from the South, and hip-hop, forever.

Synopsis: An audition by Gwendolyn "Blondy" Chisolm, Cheryl "The Pearl" Cook, and Angela "Angie B" Stone for Sylvia Robinson of Sugar Hill Records takes them from cheerleading teammates in South Carolina to the first all-woman rap group to release a record. As the Sequence, the trio make history as pioneers in the early days of recorded rap while battling shady business practices.

Why we need it: I know I talked about the Sequence a couple of chapters back, but there are a lot of reasons why people *need* to watch a biopic on the group. *A lot.*

First, their pen game. In *The Anthology of Rap*, editors Adam Bradley and Andrew DuBois noted that "[u]nlike some of the Sugar Hill performers, the women from the Sequence wrote their own rhymes; in fact they often wrote rhymes for their label mates." An amazing fact, made even more amazing when I learned earlier this year that the Sequence ladies wrote Sugarhill Gang classics "Apache" and "8th Wonder." Practically everyone knows "Apache," either from watching Will and Carlton dance to it on *The Fresh Prince of Bel-Air* or because they had an OG around to hip them to classic rap records. However *you* know the record doesn't really matter here. What you should know is that the ladies were behind it, one of the biggest songs in hip-hop history. That fact alone rejects the still far-too-commonplace idea that women can't write songs without the assistance of a man. The girls' pens have been penning from the jump.

Second, their influence on other women in rap. "A lot of female rappers say they've been there since Day One. I've been there since the night before. And they were there before *that*," Roxanne Shanté told *Rolling Stone* in a 2017 piece about the Sequence. She added, "When it came to hearing them on the radio, they automatically let me know, OK, that's what I'm supposed to be doing. If it wasn't for them, there wouldn't be no me. And if it wasn't for me, there wouldn't be *none of them*." Yet another example of pioneers influencing the pioneers who would come after that. And I mean, wouldn't it be cool to see a young Shanté turning on the radio in her living room in Queensbridge and rapping along to "Funk You Up"?

Third, they're from the South. Blondy, the Pearl, and Angie B were putting on for their region long before André 3000's proclamation at the 1995 *Source* Awards that "[t]he South got something to say." We know hip-hop started in the Boogie Down Bronx, but that doesn't mean that other places in the country, as well as the world, didn't contribute to the elevation and innovation of its music. Most of our hip-hop discussions on the South don't go all the way back to the 1970s, so it'd be nice for viewers to know that the Sequence had something to say too.

Fourth, the music itself. I know this one seems more expansive than the others, and it is. But for a reason. A lot of the Sequence's music includes them rapping and singing on hip-hop tracks long before artists like Lauryn Hill and Nicki

Minaj were doing it on their songs—check out "Funk You Up" and "Cold Sweat" to hear them in action. It'd be cool to draw a direct line between the musical stylings of the ladies we listen to today and the Sequence. Their music has been sampled by artists like Trina, Erykah Badu, En Vogue, and most notably on the Dr. Dre cut "Keep Their Heads Ringin'," for which they each got 6.5 percent of the royalties. Which brings me to the last reason.

Reason number five, and it's something I've mentioned far too many times in this chapter, is the Sequence's dealings with their label and lack of compensation for their artwork. Blondy told *Rolling Stone* that she first heard the Dr. Dre hit that sampled "Funk You Up" on the radio while she was cleaning her new apartment. "If I'm not wrong, I believe Sylvia gave us $10,000 for that song. They cut our percentage down to six percent each on the song. And then, you go into [Sugar Hill heir and former executive Joey Robinson Jr., who died in 2015]'s house, and Joey got a five-times platinum of 'Keep Their Heads Ringing' in his house with our song 'Funk You Up' on it," she told the publication. "How come we don't have one of those, and it's our music? So, you know, it hurts to know that, here you is, busting your ass, can barely feed yourself, can barely pay your bills, and everybody's just going on, and people making millions of dollars off something you created."

Angie B, who would go on to become a successful R&B singer under the name Angie Stone, also shared how a bad deal impacted her career as a solo artist. She told *Rolling Stone* in 2017 that she has never received royalties from the sales of her debut album, *Black Diamond*, or her sophomore output, *Mahogany Soul*. The music industry has a history of exploiting its artists, and I can only hope that seeing some of this stuff play out on-screen will inspire all kinds of artists to advocate for themselves and learn as much as they can about the business they're getting into, as well as rally viewers to make sure our current artists and our OGs are paid. We're stronger when we stick together. Don't get it funked up.

~~~~~~~~

B-Girl Baby Love

Logline: Back when breaking reigned supreme and all of hip-hop's elements were at the forefront, B-girl Baby Love of the Rock Steady Crew put on for the ladies.

Synopsis: Born Daisy Castro, Baby Love joins the legendary Rock Steady Crew at the age of fifteen. Baby Love performs the hook on the Rock Steady Crew single "(Hey You) The Rock Steady Crew," dances alongside a crew of only dudes, and appears in the classic movie *Beat Street*. In just about two years she will leave the crew altogether, but the impact of her breaking stands the test of time.

Why we need it: We've already established that you would be hard-pressed to find any movies that center any of the first ladies on the mic. That means it's even more difficult to find anything that looks at the ladies who DJ'd, designed, danced, graffitied, etc. Outside of a six-minute-long documentary on Dutch Public Television's *Top 2000 a gogo* that interviews Baby Love at her crib, there isn't much out there on Baby Love and her career. And to be fair, there might not be anything beyond those six minutes that she wants to tell us. But if she does, I'd love to hear more about what it was like for her as a B-girl in a crew full of guys, why she decided to leave the group and focus solely on college, and the impact that breaking has had on her life as a whole.

I came up watching dancing movies like *You Got Served* and *Save the Last Dance.* Let's run the concept back with Baby Love's story. Maybe if this movie gets made I'll finally learn how to helicopter, that movie breakdancers do when they spin their legs around under them really fast.

~~~~~~~~~~~~~~~~~~

Naturally, these aren't the only biopics I would want to see get made. I want one on J.J. Fad, who had a hit with their song "Supersonic" and were among the nominees for the first-ever Grammy Award for rap music. I also want one on Sweet Tee and DJ Jazzy Joyce, who linked up for "It's My Beat," to highlight the paths that women emcees and DJs have to take to find success. Hollywood should also take a look at pioneering rapper Lisa Lee, who was a member of the Universal Zulu Nation and appeared in two of the earliest hip-hop films: *Wild Style* and *Beat Street.* There should be films on Pebblee Poo and MC Debbie D too. Both of them made their case for being the "first female hip-hop soloist," and while I'm not sure we'll ever get a definitive answer on who was and who wasn't, Pebblee Poo's time as Kool Herc's first woman emcee and Debbie D's decision to break away from a group and record solo tracks are two story lines worth exploring on the big screen.

Outside of the emcees and DJs, I'd love to see a biopic on women in other spaces in hip-hop. Like fashion. Give me the documentary on April Walker. Or Angie Martinez. Or Cindy Campbell. There *has* to be a biopic on Cindy Campbell . . .

DEE BARNES, THE FIRST WOMAN TO HOST A HIP-HOP PROGRAM ON BROADCAST TELEVISION WITH *PUMP IT UP!*

Not to toot my own horn here, but I'm somewhat of a line dance aficionado. My mom and I went to line dance classes when I was a kid, and I intensely watched my aunts who line-danced at the cookouts and block parties held while I was growing up, hoping to have the steps mastered before my parents shouted "my crew, let's roll." If you've ever been to one of *The Gumbo*'s Sample Sunday parties then you probably saw me teaching someone or a crew of people the NJ Strut. So yeah, I take line dancing pretty seriously.

Which is why I hate that I haven't learned the moves to the line dance done to "Dance to the Drummer's Beat" by Herman Kelly & Life. One day a few years back I decided to look up the tutorial video again and practice my moves, thinking the tutorial would come up instantly in search. As I scrolled through the results, though, I came across a video for a song with the same name by Body & Soul and Trouble Funk. The only thing I hate just as much as not knowing a dance is not knowing a song, so I had to click it. When I watched it, I soon realized that

Dee Barnes was one half of Body & Soul. Yes, Dee Barnes, who made history when she became the first woman to host a hip-hop program on a broadcast television network with Fox's *Pump It Up!*

There's a lot about Dee that I want you to know, but I have to start somewhere, so let's take it back to her time as a member of the West Coast hip-hop duo Body & Soul. Dee had her sights set on music, television, and film at a young age, and was so empowered to make her career happen that she packed up all of her stuff and moved to Los Angeles from New York when she was just a teenager. Dee's cousin took her to all the spots in LA when she arrived, like the historic Avalon nightclub in Hollywood and the popular skating rink World on Wheels. It was at that second spot that she would meet her now best friend and the other half of Body & Soul, Rose Hutchinson. Dee spotted Rose performing at the rink, and as she told *HuffPost* in 2015, "I was like I got to meet this sister. You know, I want to work with this sister. As opposed to the mentality of 'I'm going to take her out, I'm going to take her spot.'"

As Body & Soul, Dee and Rose would release their debut single, "Dance to the Drummer's Beat," on the label Delicious Vinyl in 1989. The song's B-side was an upbeat, thumping cut titled "Hi-Powered" that sampled Stevie Wonder's "Sir Duke" and Uncle Louie's "I Like Funky Music," the latter of which was also sampled by Beyoncé, Missy Elliott, MC Lyte, and Free on "Fighting Temptations." That same year the label dropped an album showcasing its roster, with a new track by Body & Soul appearing on it titled "We Can Do This." The song is an affirmation that the ladies "get busy" on the track and a reminder that they're not to be messed with, rapping, "if you came in peace cool / But if you came to diss, miss, we can do this."

Put the girls on notice!

When the people behind *Pump It Up!* were looking for someone to host the show, Dee's label, Delicious Vinyl, presented both of the Body & Soul ladies for the audition. When it was time to try out for the role, Dee took inspiration from Carlos DeJesus, who hosted the syndicated music television show *New York Hot Tracks*; Ralph McDaniels, who created and hosted the pioneering hip-hop music video show *Video Music Box*; and Downtown Julie Brown, who hosted MTV's *Club MTV*, a half-hour music program described by the network as "a video age dance show." She got the deal. At the age of nineteen, Dee Barnes would be the host of *Pump It Up!*

The show wasn't national at first, airing only in LA. Dee recalled having to meet with executives at Fox before they decided to make it national. For Dee, being national wasn't her primary focus. Nah. Being positive and celebrating the music and the artists were her main concerns. Nonetheless, Dee made history hosting a show on a broadcast television network. While music shows on MTV and BET appeared on the TV screens of anyone who had paid for cable channels, broadcast networks like CBS, NBC, ABC, and FOX were free for anyone who had a television within the range of a transmitter. Basically, if you had a TV, you could watch Dee.

"They put me on after *The Simpsons* to keep up the momentum," she told Rock the Bells in 2022. "At the time, it was just *Cops, America's Most Wanted, The Simpsons, Married with Children*, and *Pump It Up!* and I believe Joan Rivers and Tracey Ullman's shows. That was it."

Barnes hosted the show for three seasons, from 1989 to 1991. She went to Ice-T's house and checked out what he had in his fridge long before MTV's *Cribs* was even an idea. She hung out in Times Square with Eric B and Rakim. She chopped it up with legendary women in hip-hop like MC Lyte, Salt-N-Pepa, and Queen Latifah. Dee was getting interviews with the GOATs long before their GOAT status would be solidified and showing what women in hip-hop could do on TV, setting the stage for hosts like *Rap City*'s Big Lez, *106 & Park*'s Free, and *Total Request Live*'s La La Anthony.

And in the midst of it all, she was still putting in work as an artist. In 1990 Body & Soul appeared on a posse cut by the West Coast

Rap All-Stars titled "We're All in the Same Gang." The song, pro-duced by Dr. Dre, featured King Tee, Body & Soul, Def Jef, Michel'le, Tone-Lōc, Above the Law, Ice-T, Dr. Dre, MC Ren, J.J. Fad, Young MC, Digital Underground, Oaktown's 3.5.7, MC Hammer, and Eazy-E. The track was nominated for a Grammy at the thirty-third annual ceremony, losing to "Back on the Block" by Melle Mel, Ice-T, Big Daddy Kane, Kool Moe Dee, Quincy Jones, and Quincy D. III.

The next part of this story isn't easy to write, but it's an important part of Dee's story and has to be told. What happened was detailed by Mankaprr Conteh in a 2023 article for *Rolling Stone*:

> *Ahead of an album release party where Barnes said that Dr. Dre assaulted her, a segment on her show aired that captured the tension between Dre's then-group N.W.A and former member Ice Cube. In a 2015 op-ed for Gawker, where Barnes recounted the incident, she said N.W.A later claimed Dre was angry about the clip she included in the show and beat her mercilessly because of it. The police were called and in the early hours of January 28, 1991, a warrant for Dre's arrest was issued. At the time, he was charged with assault and battery. He pleaded no contest, resulting in a $2,500 fine and a two-year probation sentence with community service. In the op-ed, Barnes wrote that she's suffered horrific migraines in the years since the incident, pulsing in the exact spot where she said Dre slammed her head into a wall.*

In the aftermath of the life-changing incident Dee Barnes said she was blacklisted from the industry, taking retail gigs and other jobs to pay the bills because she couldn't get work as a journalist. In 2019 Dee tweeted a GoFundMe link and revealed that she was facing homeless-ness and looking to raise $5,000. The community showed up and showed out for her, and as I write this the fundraiser has $33,805 in donations. A few years later, when she risked losing the *Pump It Up!* archives she held in storage to an auction, the community came through again.

And that kind of support makes me so happy!

Pump It Up! was fire. The handful of songs by Body & Soul that exist out here in the world are bops, and Dee was in the mix during hip-hop's golden age! Dee Barnes is a pioneer who deserves to have both her story told and her contributions to hip-hop celebrated, and I'll be first in line for the documentary and whatever else she does.

More Music TV Hostesses with the Mostesses

A Shout-out to ANANDA LEWIS

Ananda Lewis's skills as a VJ and television host resulted in her interviewing big names like Destiny's Child, Snoop Dogg, and Brandy, and heading up some of TV's most popular shows, including *TRL* and *Hot Zone* on MTV and *Teen Summit* on BET in the late 1990s and early 2000s, and on the TLC home decorating show *While You Were Out* in 2019. She has two NAACP Image Awards, one for an interview she did with Hillary Clinton and another for her hosting of the MTV special *True Life: I Am Driving While Black*. In 2001 she became the host of her own talk show, *The Ananda Lewis Show*, which ran for one season. After the show Lewis made the decision to take a break from the industry altogether. She decided to go back to school to become a contractor, which eventually led to her hosting some episodes on *While You Were Out*. When *Shondaland* asked her what advice she would give to someone who is trying to follow their passion, Ananda said, "Look for that feeling. If your heart fills up with goodness and you're smiling and you feel full, then that's probably the thing you want to do every day." That's how I felt when I started *The Gumbo*, so I can confirm that this is great advice.

A Shout-out to LA LA ANTHONY

Long before La La Anthony was playing the roles of Lakeisha Grant on *Power* and Flo DeVoe on *The New Edition Story* she was cohosting a radio show called *Future Flavas* alongside her friend Ludacris. In 2001 Anthony joined *TRL* and *Direct Effect* at MTV, where she interviewed a long list of rappers that included Lil Wayne, Redman, and OutKast.

Today it's damn near impossible to watch TV or a movie and not see La La's face, but that's just one section of her resume. She's been a *New York Times* bestselling author twice, inked a production partnership with ITV America, and even released a hair care line, Inala. Yet with all of those amazing accomplishments, whenever I see La La I'll always think of *MTV Spring Break*, the network's annual spring break coverage that featured performances from some of the biggest names in music in some of the most tropical places on the planet. La La talking to Missy Elliott after she performed "Gossip Folks" and "Work Out" while models walked the runway in their hottest swimwear is one of my favorite moments. La La was just so damn cool, calm, and collected in the midst of a bunch of screaming spring breakers. How could you not love her?

A Shout-out to FREE

BET's video countdown show *106 & Park* is one of the most important music programs to ever air on television. Free cohosted the show from 2000 to 2005 and interviewed some of the biggest names in hip-hop, R&B, and Hollywood, including Halle Berry, Denzel Washington, Jay-Z, Mariah Carey, Michael Jackson, and Aaliyah, just days before she passed away. Whether I was rushing to get in front of a TV to see if my favorite artist kept their spot in the countdown or intensely watching battle rappers duke it out on Freestyle Friday, *106* was an important part of my life for years because it placed me inside the world of the guests and the music on the show. To see a Black woman at the helm of it all made it that much sweeter.

Today she hosts *Rap Rotation Rewind* on Amazon Music, is the CEO of Pudding Stone Bath Company, and is the founder of Team Cancer Free, an organization whose mission on their Instagram reads: "Team Cancer Free is committed to providing education and resources surrounding Breast Cancer Awareness for women of color!" A true inspiration for getting it done and giving back too.

A Shout-out to DOWNTOWN JULIE BROWN

I'm a nineties baby, so I did not grow up watching MTV OG Downtown Julie Brown. She hosted *Club MTV*, which premiered on the network in 1987 and was influenced by *American Bandstand*. Here's what Brown said about the show for the 2001 book *MTV Uncensored*: "They were putting out music you could dance to, so MTV wasn't saying, 'This is dance music,' they were saying, 'This is music you can dance to—have fun with it.' It was basically club stuff. You know, when you go out. It wasn't just one particular song or one particular flavor that was out there. And so I became the little dance diva, and *Club MTV* was born."

As a host she was witty, charismatic, knew her music, and had the dance moves to match. So, yeah, shout-out to Downtown Julie Brown.

A Shout-out to RACHEL STUART-BAKER

Before she was hosting shows on BET, Rachel was competing in pageants like Miss Universe as Jamaica's ambassador. When she left the pageant game she got the job hosting *Caribbean Rhythms*, one of the earliest programs on American cable television dedicated to highlighting music by Caribbean artists. "Because we featured the culture, people, food, topography, and diverse islands that make up the Caribbean, it also was pivotal with increasing tourism in the region," Stuart-Baker told the *Jamaica Observer* in 2023. "I went on to host other shows for BET, but *Caribbean Rhythms* will always be the most special and meaningful. . . ."

She would later go on to host the BET shows *Planet Groove* and *Live from LA*.

A Shout-out to SHERRY CARTER

There's a scene in *The New Edition Story* where all of the guys from the group, who were pursuing careers as solo artists and in new musical groups, sit down for an interview on BET's music program *Video Soul* to talk about reuniting. It's a near-perfect reenactment of the real interview that was conducted by Sherry Carter, who also served as a host on more BET shows like *Video LP*. Over the course of her career she's interviewed Tina Turner, Tupac Shakur, Oaktown's 357, and more.

LESLIE "BIG LEZ" SEGAR, THE FIRST AND ONLY WOMAN TO OFFICIALLY HOST *RAP CITY*

The *Living Single* theme song is my favorite. Written and performed by Queen Latifah, it played at the top of the show to introduce the cast and took viewers on a journey through New York City, where the show was based. But there's another thing about those credits that I really love, and it's the dancing silhouette of a woman by the name of Leslie "Big Lez" Segar. If she were to send you her resume, I'm willing to bet money that it'd be the most robust resume you will have seen in your life thus far. And that's because Big Lez has done it all and then some (and then some more after that). Here's a quick rundown: Big Lez is a dancer and choreographer who has worked with Mary J. Blige, Bobby Brown, LL Cool J, Salt-N-Pepa, and Michael Jackson, a radio and TV personality, producer, fitness specialist, actress, and the first (and only) woman to officially host the influential BET music show *Rap City*.* Leslie literally puts the "multi" in multifaceted, but it's that very last thing that I mentioned that I'm going to talk about here.

---

* Other women appeared on *Rap City* as guest hosts, like Eve and Lil' Snoop.

The start of Big Lez's career is nothing less than inspiring. A "Jane of all trades" from the very beginning, she attended Springfield College in Massachusetts on a full scholarship for gymnastics, and as she told *2 Hype* magazine, got her hip-hop dance moves from "battling the guys at clubs Kilimanjaro, The Choice, Paradise Garage, The World, and The Red Zone." All of her skills came together when she performed a stellar gymnastics solo at a Kiss-FM basketball game, after which she received a bunch of business cards from different record and video companies. When she hit them up, one of the companies hired her to dance and act in a musical. Then when they needed a dancer for their artist Jay Williams, she got the job.

After graduating from college, she danced on her first tour—the Triple Threat Tour with Keith Sweat, BBD, and Johnny Gill. When she came across an ad searching for a dancer for a Paris Barclay–directed music video, she decided to audition. Not only was Paris familiar with her work when she showed up to the audition, but she got the gig: a spot dancing in the video for LL Cool J's classic track, "Around the Way Girl." It was her first mainstream video, and it was just the beginning.

The exposure from "Around the Way Girl" opened up more doors, and Lez started to dance and choreograph tours and videos for artists like Guy, Michael Jackson, Bobby Brown, and Whitney Houston. She was especially loved by Uptown Records, where she worked with a host of artists on their roster, like Heavy D and Mary J. Blige. In fact, she choreographed the moves for the "You Remind Me" and "Real Love" videos, the latter getting her an MTV Video Music Award nomination.

One day her dancing took her to the set of BET's half-hour, live viewer call-in music show *Video LP*, where she was invited to be a guest. She performed and sat down with the show's host at the time, Madelyne Woods, and talked about her experiences and relationships with the artists she had worked with. BET's producers thought she would be the perfect host on *Rap City*, but landing the role did not come without its challenges.

The producers from *Rap City* had two fights: for her voice to be taken seriously as a woman in hip-hop and with a BET executive who told Big Lez to her face that she was not what men wanted to see on television.[*] "That was around the time where . . . the light-skinned, long-haired girls were obviously getting more of the work than the rest of us," she said in a 2021 interview with *B High ATL*. "Whether it was in music videos or stuff like that, colorism is a real thing especially amongst our people." Big Lez said she had to prove herself at every stop, while also acknowledging she didn't get certain opportunities because she didn't fit certain beauty standards. It's a reminder of how far we *haven't* come, and how much work we still have to do when it comes to discrimination against people with darker skin.

In spite of the attempts to hold Big Lez back, she got the job and became *Rap City*'s first and only woman to officially host the show. But you already knew that, hence the title of this chapter. During Lez's seven-year-long tenure at the show she interviewed some of the biggest names in hip-hop. Whether she was riding on the back of a jet ski with Xzibit or hanging out with Lil' Kim on the set of the "Crush on You" video, it goes without saying that Big Lez had an exciting gig. But in addition to that excitement, she provided viewers with interviews that, in the words of *Adweek*, "brought the realness of hip-hop to the masses on *Rap City*." There's no way I can get into all of her interviews here, but what I *can* do is share some memorable moments from the ones that I like.

---

* Big Lez has spoken about this experience a bunch of times, including during the *B High ATL* interview I mentioned and a 2019 interview with *Rolling Out*.

~~~~~~~~~~~~~~~~~~~~~

Lil' Kim

The location: "Crush on You" video set

Year: 1997

The moment: Everybody was on the set for this video, and I mean everybody. The video had a bunch of cameos from some of the biggest names in hip-hop and R&B, including Aaliyah, Sheek Louch, and Big Lez herself, while other artists like Spinderella and Jay-Z showed up to show their support. Big Lez actually interviews those last two for this particular episode of *Rap City* as well and Jay-Z hilariously tells Lez that she has "like eighty jobs," but my favorite moment happens when she talks to Lil' Kim, who is seated alongside Biggie and Lance "Un" Rivera. Rocking the yellow wig, retro oval sunglasses, yellow crop top, and elbow-length mesh gloves for the yellow scenes of the music video, Kim answers Lez's question about a movie role she would love to play. Her answer? Sharon Stone's Ginger McKenna in *Casino*.

I'm not sure if you've ever watched *Casino*, but if you have, take everything you know about Ginger McKenna's character, table it, and keep reading. If you haven't, well, keep reading too. Ginger McKenna is easily one of the most stylish characters we've ever seen in a film. Easily. In a 2020 *Vogue* article titled "Sharon Stone on the Unforgettable Fashion of *Casino*, 25 Years Later," writer Liam Hess says the "movie's breathtakingly opulent fashions played an important part in Stone's journey to inhabiting the character of Ginger with such commitment." The same could be said of Lil' Kim, whose innovative fashions played an important part in her overall image.

Ginger was a hustler too. And while Kim's hustle wasn't in the casino, her enterprising, go-getter nature is evidenced by the endless campaigns and brand deals she did over the years. It was so prophetic for Lil' Kim to name that character in that moment. And it was pretty cool for Big Lez to ask that question in the first place.

~~~~~~~~~~~~~~~~~~~

MC Lyte

The location: The street (no, literally, they're walking down the street)

Year: 1995

The moment: Imagine MC Lyte and Big Lez just walking through traffic in their flyest fits, because that's exactly what's happening here. You could look it up too, but with the way the internet goes nowadays you know that something can be here today and gone tomorrow.

Big Lez asks MC Lyte about her verse on the remix to Brandy's debut single, "I Wanna Be Down." Lyte opens the joint rapping, "Yeah I get exotic with the melodic tune / I get hypnotic with the moon." Her tone, delivery, and lyrics come together to make one of my favorite verses on one of my favorite tracks ever recorded.

MC Lyte got a call from record executive Merlin Bobb, who asked her to be on the remix. But when Lyte got the track there was nobody else on it, so she told Lez, "I said damn what am I gonna do here? I can't feel the vibe of what everybody else is gonna do." Nonetheless, Lyte got it done. She drew inspiration from the original version of the song and thought about the things that would make her want to be down with somebody or vice versa. But the part of the story about how the track came to be that really shocked me was that all of the ladies did their verses in different studios and at different times.

Trust me, I know that people get sent tracks to lay verses on that they record from the comfort of their own studios all the same. That's not what got me. Before I came across Big Lez's interview on *Rap City*, I imagined Brandy, Lyte, Queen Latifah, and Yo-Yo all in the studio together vibing and yelling "ooooohhhh" after each of the emcees laid down their verse. The song is just so tight and seamless that I just assumed they were all together. So, to learn that they weren't actually together, but all contributed verses that fit so perfectly, made me love the song that much more.

~~~~~~~~~

Lost Boyz fans

The location: Outside of live music venue Tramps in New York City

Year: 1997

The moment: In this particular episode Big Lez is outside of Tramps talking to fans waiting in line for the Lost Boyz to perform in celebration of their sophomore album, *Love, Peace & Nappiness*. The first people she talks to are a Black girl by the name of Cherrelle and a Black woman who goes by Queen of Spades of the Chosen Few. I have no idea what that name means or how she got it, but rest assured that I would not want to mess around and find out.

Anyway, what I love about this Big Lez moment is less about the conversation being had, and more about the fact that it's happening between Black ladies and a girl who are fans of hip-hop. Like I said at the beginning of this book, we have been here from the very start. That means we can talk about the girls just as much as we can talk about the boys. Our knowledge of the hip-hop landscape doesn't, and shouldn't, have to be relegated to one specific gender.

~~~~~~~~~~~~~~~~

Remember when I said that Big Lez's job as a host of *Rap City* was what I was going to talk about in this chapter? I kind of lied. I mean, I *did* talk about that, but it's not *all* I'm going to talk about. I can't talk about Big Lez and not go into detail about a lot of the other stuff that she did. Impossible. But you've been reading a lot and I've been writing a lot, so how about we switch things up for the second half of this joint?

~~~~~~~~~~~~~~~~

Instead of giving you more paragraphs to read filled with facts about Big Lez, we're going to play a game. I don't know about you, but I like games. They're a great way to break up the monotony of reading for a long period of time, and they're also a really effective way for people to learn new information. So, we're going to do a crossword puzzle. Well, you are. I obviously know the answers so doing it would be no fun for me.

The answers to the clues in the puzzle are random facts and things from Lez's career. Some of them you should know already after reading this chapter; some of them you'll be able to figure out as you go. The game is on the next page, and the answers are at the bottom. Oh, and please don't cheat!

The Learn About Leslie "Big Lez" Segar Crossword Puzzle

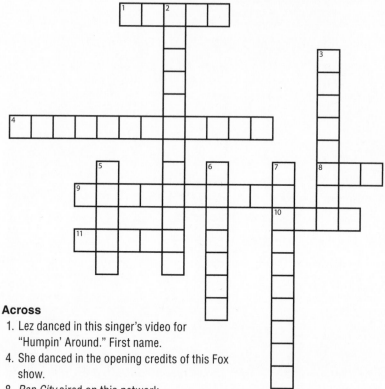

Across

1. Lez danced in this singer's video for "Humpin' Around." First name.
4. She danced in the opening credits of this Fox show.
8. *Rap City* aired on this network.
9. She danced in the sequel to this comedy film starring Kid 'N Play.
10. First name of the "Queen of Hip-Hop Soul," whom Leslie has choreographed videos for and interviewed.
11. In addition to television, she has also hosted shows on this audio broadcasting medium.

Down

2. She choreographed the music video "She's Dope!" for this group of former New Edition members.
3. She danced in this Egyptian-themed Michael Jackson video "_____ the Time."
5. She danced in the video for the classic Whitney Houston track "I'm Every _____."
6. She was the only woman to officially host this music television show
7. Her mother signed her up for this sport as a kid.

You Know All About Big Lez, but You Need to Know About These Dancers/Choreographers Too

FATIMA ROBINSON

The *New York Times* called Fatima Robinson "one of the most sought-after hip-hop and popular music choreographers in the world," and I'm about to tell you exactly why that's true. At twenty years old Fatima got her first big gig: to choreograph Michael Jackson's video for "Remember the Time." She killed it, and since then she's worked with what feels like everyone in the music world. Aaliyah. Beyoncé. Bobby Brown. Doja Cat. Mary J. Blige. Pharrell. Rihanna. The list is endless.

Her film resume is no joke either. She worked on the movies *Dreamgirls*, *Charlie Wilson's War*, *American Gangster*, *Public Enemy*, *Ali*, and *Confessions of a Shopaholic*, as well as with A-listers like Will Smith, Halle Berry, Eddie Murphy, John Travolta, the Rock, Sandra Bullock, Thandiwe Newton, and more. The Emmy-nominated and MTV Video Music Award–winning dancer, director, and choreographer is a legend.

TISH OLIVER

As a teenager Tish Oliver used to travel from South Central LA to Hollywood to battle the dudes at the club. She wasn't quite sure what career she was going to pursue after high school, but she knew she loved to dance and learn new moves.

The path was laid out for her when she entered and won a dance competition right before graduation. The prize was a spot in a major music video, and as I'm sure you can guess, Tish's career took off. She worked with Queen Latifah, Whitney Houston, Bobby Brown, and LL Cool J, killed it alongside Janet Jackson on the Janet World Tour, and was brought in by the legendary choreographer Tina Landon to freestyle to help her come up with some moves for Michael and Janet's "Scream." *So cool.*

From listening to an interview that Tish did on *The Kelly Alexander Show* in 2022 I learned that she made the decision to go to medical school and still teaches dance. She told the host it's the hardest thing she's ever done. If I had to guess what she'd say was the second-hardest thing, I'd go with the back bend she did in Michael Jackson's "Remember the Time" video. But maybe that's me projecting since I know I could never do that move. I'm sure it was very easy for her.

LAURIEANN GIBSON

You might recognize her from Diddy's iterations of *Making the Band*, where she helped the girl and guy group hopefuls with their choreography and stage presence. But long before that the Emmy-nominated choreographer, creative director, dancer, and actress was a member of *In Living Color*'s all-lady dance troupe the Fly Girls.

She's worked with Lil' Kim, Beyoncé, Megan Thee Stallion, Lady Gaga, Michael Jackson, Nicki Minaj, and Missy Elliott—she did the choreography for Missy Elliott's "The Rain (Supa Dupa Fly)." Her choreo work on Gaga's "Bad Romance" video won her an MTV Video Music Award and she played the role of Jessica Alba's rival Katrina in the film *Honey* (she choreographed the film too). Her signature "boomkack" catchphrase is not only used to emphasize the moves in an eight-count, but also as a reminder to "fight back against negative thoughts."

JOSSIE HARRIS THACKER

Jossie was working on Wall Street when she got her first big opportunity as a dancer. She was literally dancing in the club, having fun and doing her thing, when two men spotted her and asked her if she would be a part of a music video for the group Color Me Badd.

She danced with artists like Michael Jackson, Mary J. Blige, and Janet Jackson and became a Fly Girl on *In Living Color* before making the transition into acting. A few of her credits include *Sabrina the Teenage Witch*, *That's So Raven*, *Desperate Housewives*, *Chicago*, and the movie *Mississippi Damned*. Today Jossie teaches acting classes, with her students landing roles on networks like ABC, NBC, CBS, BET, Netflix, Showtime, and HBO.

ROSIE PEREZ

Long before being nominated for multiple Emmys and an Oscar, Rosie Perez had been scouted to become a dancer on *Soul Train* in the 1980s. With a performance style that was hip-hop through and through, she would go on to choreograph the Fly Girls, the all-lady dance collective on the popular sketch comedy show *In Living Color*, for four seasons. Perez worked with the Boys, Janet Jackson, and LL Cool J. She also choreographed Diana Ross's video for "Workin' Overtime."

Rosie's breakout film role came in 1989, when she played Tina in Spike Lee's *Do the Right Thing*. After that she was cast in *White Men Can't Jump* and the Peter Weir film *Fearless*, which earned her a Best Supporting Actress nomination at the Oscars.

She's published an autobiography, appeared in countless other movies and TV shows, and been an activist for a bunch of causes. If you have some free time later, type in "rosie perez soul train" on YouTube. You're in for a treat.

THIS IS THE TRUE STORY...
OF SEVEN STRANGERS...
PICKED TO LIVE IN A LOFT...
AND HAVE THEIR LIVES TAPED...

TO FIND OUT WHAT HAPPENS...
WHEN PEOPLE STOP BEING POLITE...
AND START GETTING **REAL**

HEATHER B. WAS THE FIRST BLACK WOMAN ON A REALITY TV SHOW

MTV's biography for Heather B. when the first season of *The Real World* aired read, "She has a lot of drive and dedication to whatever she is doing. She makes friends quickly and always speaks her mind regardless of the consequences." All facts. Heather B.'s personality and openness made her the perfect cast member for the new series, traits that arguably made the show more compelling and entertaining than it would have been without her. Reality television has gone through many changes since Heather B. appeared on TV screens in 1992, but none of those changes can undo the fact that she is widely regarded as the first Black woman on a reality TV show, appearing on the very first season of one of the most influential reality TV programs of all time. I cannot stress how important this is. But to understand this importance, you really have to understand the impact of reality television.

As a nineties baby, I can't really imagine what life would be like without it. As a kid, I made sure to have Cartoon Network, Nickelodeon, or any other age-appropriate channel queued up on the last channel button on my remote when I was watching *Flavor of Love* after my parents told me I wasn't allowed to. *Jersey Shore* was a constant talking point at the lunchroom table during my high school years. In the present day, I clock in to watch pretty much whatever *Real Housewives* franchise is currently on-air every week! I think NeNe Leakes and Tiffany Pollard are the queens, and moreover the first ladies, of this particular TV genre. Like seriously, could you imagine what reality television would look like *without* them? Exactly.

Reality television gives us a lens through which we can see and understand the world. And while many shows today are often accused of fabricating story lines and scripting scenes, I'd argue that those early seasons of *The Real World* were as real as TV could get. And that's what drew people in. That *realness*. Which brings us to Heather.

Heather B. Gardner, rap name Heather B., was raised in Jersey. And I was raised in Jersey. I highlight this not simply because some really cool people come from there, but because there's this special kind of hunger that exists for New Jerseyans who want to make it in the entertainment industry. I've felt it, and Heather B. felt it too. A personal message on her website reads:

> I have always wanted to do television, but growing up my parents knew NOTHING about taking me to New York City, getting me an agent, or auditions. Finally in 1992, the opportunity came to audition for a documentary MTV was doing called "The Real World." I was so frustrated with the music industry after only 2 years in the business, I thought "Why not TRY?" "What do I have to lose?"

Hailing from Jersey City, Heather had her sights set on becoming a rapper in the early 1990s. She went to the same college as KRS-One's little brother Kenny Parker, and after a meeting with the rapper and calling him a couple hundred times, KRS signed her to

Boogie Down Productions. See the hunger and drive? That "Why not *try*?" attitude led her to audition for MTV. It was that hunger that landed her a spot on the very first season of MTV's *The Real World: New York*, a new kind of reality television series that sought "to find out what happens...when people stop being polite...and start getting real."

And get real they did.

The entire first season took viewers on a journey through real-life issues and debates around topics like race, class, gender, and more— it was filmed during the 1992 Los Angeles uprising that occurred after four police officers were acquitted in the beating of Rodney King. Some conversations have aged well. A lot of them . . . not so much, lol. But it was truly unlike anything that had ever been seen on television before. Couple that reality with the fact that MTV was at its peak at the time, and the show was a hit! I wasn't alive when the first season of *The Real World* aired, so I went back and rewatched the entire first season and then the *Homecoming* reunion series that brought the crew back together in 2021.

Here's what I learned: Heather B. is a pioneer in the realm of reality television, and should be treated as such. So here are some of my favorite moments from the first season of *The Real World*, featuring the first Black woman on a reality television show.

"A lot of people tell me, you know, when I rap I sound so angry and so mad and so frustrated. But that's how I feel inside and that's what comes out, you know, when I get a chance to express myself."
—Heather B. ("Julie and Eric . . . Could It Be Love?", Season 1, Episode 2)

Heather B. is in the studio recording a song that touches on the topic of sexual assault, and two of the men in the studio tell her she should re-record one of her verses because it sounded like she had some water bunched up in her throat. You can see the frustration in her face, and when they cut to b-roll of her she recites the quote that kicks off this paragraph. I felt this moment because I've been there. You think you're doing something perfect, or at the very least to the best of your ability and in a way that is most authentically you, and then someone comes in to tell you that they "don't get it." I know we've all been there, women especially. Heather B. had a right to sound angry and frustrated while she recorded a verse about women being assaulted. That grittiness that the men in the studio said was coming from her throat only helped bring the pain associated with the story she was telling hit home harder. I love this moment because she basically said, "I hear you and I'm doing me. Thanks."

"But of course, you don't know nothing about hip-hop."
—Heather B. ("Julie and Eric . . . Could It Be Love?", Season 1, Episode 2)

I love this quote because this is really something I want to be said more. For context, Julie Gentry is one of the castmates who live in the house with the rest of the crew. She's from Birmingham, Alabama, her dad doesn't like Black people, and when Heather B.'s beeper goes off in the first episode, Julie foolishly asks her if she's a drug dealer. I'll pause so you can roll your eyes. Also, fun fact, Meredith Black, a writer for the *Los Angeles Times*, revealed in 2021 that Heather B. was being paged by KRS-One's brother, who was trying to get her to go to a Tribe Called Quest and De La Soul concert. I really hope she went.

Anywho, Heather B. brings Julie to the studio with her while she's recording her album. One of the producers gives her feedback, telling her that she's rhyming to the beat but just going through the motions. Julie chimes in to tell Heather that it sounded good to her, to which Heather replies, "But of course, you don't know nothing about hip-hop." And it's true. She literally doesn't. And I guess that kind of misunderstanding is a metaphor for all of this. If you think back to what I mentioned in chapter 1 when we discussed the party Cindy threw, Cindy talks about how much hip-hop was and remains a space for community. People who don't get that or the community shouldn't really comment on it. So I think it's pretty lit that Heather B. let her know she didn't know what she thought she knew. And she'll take her advice from the people who do.

"If I didn't have my father I would be lost, for real."
—Heather B. (Previously unaired, shown in *The Real World Homecoming*)

As a true daddy's girl, I loved this line. Now, this was filmed in 1992 for the first season, but it didn't air until 2021, during the finale of *The Real World Homecoming.* During this episode, cast member Norman Korpi asks one of the show's co-creators if there is anything that they wish they could have aired. He tells him that they would shoot sixty hours of footage a week that they would then have to cut down to twenty-four minutes for TV. It's at this moment that Heather B. reveals she wishes her scene with her dad—who has since passed on—would have made it into the final edit. She says, "Especially being a Black female, just to see her with her dad, I always had a very strong relationship with my father, and I think that always goes missing in every show, written or reality. It's just never there. People don't see Black women and their fathers together, and what that means, and it helps us to develop our relationships later on in life." As a daddy's girl, I feel her. And I'm glad we got to see this moment.

"The people at the record company, they don't care."
—Heather B. ("WWF Is in the House!", Season 1, Episode 12)

This quote is a pretty self-explanatory one. We know how the record labels do artists. We know all about the 360 deals and the bad contracts and shystie managers and everything in between. This was an important moment to show on-air, because this would not be the last time a Black woman in hip-hop or music as a whole expressed frustration with her career and how she was being handled. Even if people didn't know it at the time, she was speaking up about the practices that still plague so many artists today. It was important that she did.

After her time on the show, Heather B. would go on to sign with Pendulum Records in 1995, and in 1996 she released her first album, *Takin' Mine*. The album hit No. 36 on the Top R&B/Hip-Hop Albums chart and had three charting singles: "All Glocks Down," "If Headz Only Knew," and "My Kinda Nigga."

Women in Rap Reality TV Moments

Cardi B's "Foreva" moment on *Love & Hip Hop: New York*

If you haven't watched clips from Cardi B's time on *Love & Hip Hop: New York* then you're missing out on top-tier reality TV. Cardi was a cast member on the show's sixth and seventh seasons, touting herself as a "regular, degular, shmegular" girl from the Bronx with dreams of making it in the music industry. She gave viewers a whole lot of laughs, from using a hilarious tone of voice in an etiquette class to twerking in a Zumba class, but nothing tops the discussion she had with DJ Self in the studio. Here's what happened.

One of Cardi B's story lines on the sixth season of the show was about her hustle to make it in music, more specifically with her desire to get DJ Self—with whom she had some romantic history—to play her music on the radio and help her succeed in the industry. He gave Cardi B the runaround, much to her dismay, and it all came to a head when she got into an altercation with a woman Self brought to a party they were all at.

When the two met up to talk about what happened, Cardi B uttered a sentence that resulted in one of my favorite GIFs of all time: "If a girl have beef with me, she gon' have beef with me foreva." It was hilarious, poignant, and real, and practically impossible to escape on the internet for months. Type "Cardi B Foreva GIF" into your browser; you're in for a treat.

Babs, Da Band, and That Infamous Cheesecake Walk for Diddy on *Making the Band 2*

This right here is one of the most memorable moments in reality television. On the MTV series *Making the Band 2*, Diddy launched a talent search to create a new hip-hop group of singers and rappers, with the finalists being named Da Band. Yet in between the weeks of eliminations and auditions and the release of the debut album, *Too Hot for TV*, came a straight-up unbelievable request from the head honcho himself. Diddy instructed Da Band to walk from the Bad Boy office to Junior's in Brooklyn to bring him some cheesecake. Yes, y'all. Diddy had them walk from Midtown Manhattan—at night, in the cold, and over a bridge—all the way to Brooklyn to cop him some dessert.

The group argued and complained, rightfully so, throughout the entire trek, but the moment I love is when Babs remarks that despite being from New York even *she* had never made that walk. And she's right, because that trip can easily be made via a cab or the subway.

Getting there and back took five and a half hours, but when they returned the security guard informed them that Diddy had left for the night. The look on Babs's face is priceless, and the best way I can describe it as one that says "I'm *never* doing no shit like that again."

Lil' Kim's Farewell Dinner on
Lil' Kim: Countdown to Lockdown

Back in 2005, Lil' Kim was sentenced to 366 days in prison for perjury, and cameras were there to capture the last days before she started serving her sentence at Philadelphia Federal Detention Center. In 2006 the footage they captured aired on BET for the series *Lil' Kim: Countdown to Lockdown*, which showed everything from Kim shooting videos to prepping for a performance at a Marc Jacobs event.

In the midst of all of the glitz and glamour, the show gave fans an up-close and personal look at Kim and her loved ones mentally preparing for her to go to prison. In a moment that made me emotional when I watched it for the first time, Kim and her friends, family, and team have dinner at her favorite restaurant, Mr. Chow, the night before she is set to turn herself in. Everyone goes around the table and shares some touching words about the artist, but it was Mary J. Blige's speech that brought tears to my eyes. Mary laments about the way her and her friend have drifted apart, saying that her insecurities and thoughts resulted in her not being there for Kim as much as she should have. She wraps it up by saying that she loves Kim and would fight for her anywhere. Mary and Kim are two of my favorite artists who have each had their fair share of trials and tribulations. To see them be so vulnerable and honest about their friendship was so touching, and a reminder that no matter how big you get and how much history you make, you always need a good friend in your corner.

SOPHIE BRAMLY, THE WOMAN WHO BROUGHT "YO!" TO MTV FIRST

D an Charnas's book *The Big Payback: The History of the Business of Hip-Hop* is essential reading for hip-hop fans, music fans, entrepreneurs, and anyone who cares about pop culture. It was in *The Big Payback* that I first learned about Sophie Bramly, whom Charnas described as "the woman who first made MTV say 'Yo!'"

Bramly, a Franco-Tunisian photographer, producer, and writer, originally wanted to become a lawyer before deciding to study graphic arts at Penninghen, an art school in Paris. After graduating, Bramly started freelancing as a photographer, getting her work in publications like *Paris Match*, *Metal Hurlant*, and *Le Jardin des Modes*.

A move to New York City in 1981 would prove to be life changing, with Bramly becoming immersed in the still relatively young culture of hip-hop. After meeting the b-boy group New York City Breakers at a party, Sophie started to link up with various people and photograph them. "Although I did photograph numerous breakdancers during the four years I lived in New York, I rapidly shifted to DJs, rappers, and graffiti artists," she told *Lodown* magazine. Her contact sheets became filled with photos of people from all realms of hip-hop, including DJs like Kool Herc, GrandMixer DXT (who earlier in his career went by GrandMixer D.ST), and Jazzy Jay; rappers like Lisa Lee, Kurtis Blow, Run-DMC, and the Beastie Boys; graffiti artists like Zephyr, Dondi, Futura 2000, and Lady Pink; and breakdancers from crews like Dynamic Breakers, Magnificent Force, and the Rock Steady Crew. "I dropped everything else I was doing and I followed them everywhere they went for four years," she told *Dazed* in 2014.

When Sophie returned to Paris after those years in New York, she became the artistic director for *H.I.P. H.O.P.*,[*] a television show created in 1984 by Sidney Duteil, a DJ, rapper, and television and radio host often referred to as the "Father of French Hip-Hop." When Senior Vice President of International Programming Liz Nealon was tasked with launching the MTV brand in Europe a couple of years later, Bramly got the call to join the team. Before she knew it, she was in London helping to prepare for the channel's debut.

Here's the thing about MTV that you may or may not know. The channel premiered in the United States in 1981 and rarely ever featured Black musicians. The premiere of Michael Jackson's video "Billie Jean" on MTV in 1983 helped kick down the doors for Black artists on the network, and the following year Run-DMC's video for their song "Rock Box"—a guitar-based track that blends rock and roll with hip-hop—became the first all-rap video to air on the network.[**] But as Charnas wrote in *The Big Payback*, "Four years after MTV first aired Run-DMC's 'Rock Box,' the channel had programmed less than ten rap videos total." Which brings me back to Bramly and MTV Europe.

While preparing for the launch of the network in Europe, Bramly found herself constantly listening to *Yo! Bum Rush the Show*, the debut studio album by Public Enemy. Nealon saw Bramly's background in hip-hop through her time

---

[*] Fun fact, *H.I.P. H.O.P.* was one of the earliest television shows dedicated solely to hip-hop.

[**] Blondie's video for her song "Rapture," which featured a rap verse, aired on MTV when it launched on August 1, 1981.

photographing its early days in New York City and her work on *H.I.P. H.O.P.* and thought she would be the perfect person to host a show on the network. "She knew my background and thought it should be part of the MTV Europe she wanted to do, groundbreaking, innovative," Sophie said of Nealon's request in that interview with *Lodown*. "I was very surprised, as MTV back then was known for airing white music only, but I was thrilled too."

The show got its name from the album Bramly couldn't stop listening to, and in October of 1987, *Yo!* premiered on MTV Europe. The show featured rappers from Europe and the States. At the time that I'm writing this you can find Public Enemy and Eric B. & Rakim's performances and Sophie's interviews with MC Lyte, Salt-N-Pepa, and KRS-One on the show on Vimeo.

A year later *Yo! MTV Raps* would premiere in the states, co-created by Peter Dougherty and Ted Demme, with Bramly's friend and hip-hop legend Fab 5 Freddy as the show's first host.* As *Vulture* noted, not only was the American version of *Yo!* the network's first show "dedicated entirely to rap music," but it also "finally flung the doors to the genre wide open, expanding upon the mainstream success that hip-hop had already started to achieve elsewhere."

The American *Yo!* was responsible for so many big moments in hip-hop that are still talked about today, but as a nineties baby the ones that stick out to me might be different from someone who was able to watch the show when it aired. There's Tupac's interview with Fab 5 Freddy where he talks about his upbringing as the child of a Black Panther Party member, Mary J. Blige and Grand Puba's performance of "What the 411?," and the legendary

---

* Doctor Dré and Ed Lover would host the show when it expanded to weekdays. Dré's Original Concept group member T-Money often joined the show as a guest host.

freestyle session with a bunch of rappers that went down on the series finale! The show was also revived for Paramount+ in 2022 with new hosts Conceited and DJ Diamond Kuts.

Whether you're watching old clips or the reboot on Paramount+, remember that it was a woman by the name of Sophie Bramly who first brought *Yo!* to MTV.

Two More MTV Shows That I Love That Were Brought to You by Women

The Cut (created by Dr. Edna Sims)

A few years before Simon Fuller's singing competition television series *American Idol* made its television debut[*] came another show that was looking for the next big musical star: MTV's *The Cut*. Premiering on September 28, 1998, and hosted by Lisa "Left Eye" Lopes, *The Cut*'s concept came from Dr. Edna Sims, who wanted to create a show unlike anything ever seen before. When she discussed the program's format with the *Honolulu Star-Bulletin* in 1998, she noted that the contestants' "backstories give you a sense of who you're seeing and what they're like outside of the music. Having the judges tell them why they scored something can give the kids and the audience tips on things that can really make a difference in advancing their career." This structure would be replicated many times over in a host of singing competition programs, including *The Voice*, *America's Got Talent*, *Making the Band*, and of course, *American Idol*.

That wasn't the only thing that made the show so great. In a piece Charné Graham wrote on *The Cut* for *The Gumbo*, she added that it was also Left Eye's "charisma and quirky supernova

---

[*] *American Idol* debuted in 2002. The show was the American version of Fuller's British music competition television series *Pop Idol*, which aired from 2001 to 2003.

style that gave *The Cut* a unique edge. Not only did she style herself in some of the most innovative fashion, makeup, and hairstyles each episode, but she also brought with her a level of honesty and support that could only come from an artist themselves—and a Black woman more specifically."

A rapper and a singer by the name of Silk-E would go on to be the winner of the show's first and only season, taking home a prize that included a record deal, wardrobe, and funding from MTV to produce a music video that would then go into heavy rotation. Silk-E released her debut album, *Urban Therapy*, in 1999—"My Sista" is a great track from the LP.

If you watch some of the episodes of *The Cut* that are available on YouTube you'll see that Dr. Edna Sims is credited (as Edna Sims-Bruce) as the talent executive and the person responsible for the show's concept, with Adam Tyler listed as the creator. She sought out Left Eye to host the show and came up with the concept. There would be no *The Cut*, or at least not the version people watched, without Sims.

Sims made an Instagram post back in 2021 where she reminisced about Left Eye's charisma as a host and the impact of *The Cut*. Part of it read:

"I knew that I had a hit show, when I got a call from hit-maker producer #JimmyJam saying, in his Minneapolis studio he has a bay of TV screens on his wall with one big screen in the middle and whichever show attracted his attention, was moved to the big screen. He went on to say that every day, he couldn't take his eyes off 'The Cut' and asked if he could be a guest judge. Of course the answer was, 'Yes'! Now, my show was pre–*American Idol*, in fact Randy Jackson was a judge on the pilot, so you may not remember."

Dr. Edna Sims was at the forefront of creating the modern musical competition television show. So even if you didn't remember it, you certainly know now.

Cribs (created by Nina Diaz)

When MTV *Cribs* premiered on September 12, 2000, it was the seminal television show that took viewers inside the homes of their favorite celebrities. This wasn't like your average interview sit-down where we may have caught a glimpse of a celebrity's kitchen in the background of a shot. Nope. Stars were giving us full-on tours of their living rooms, bedrooms, guest bedrooms, in-house studios, garages, backyards, pools, and everything in between.

Cribs is the brainchild of Nina L. Diaz, who started at MTV in 1997 as a freelancer and today is the president of content and chief creative officer at MTV Entertainment Group. Diaz, a fan of the popular television series *Lifestyles of the Rich and Famous*, wanted to create a show that allowed people to go into a celebrity's house—or big-ass mansion—to see how they lived.

"You weren't supposed to have the peek behind the gates. You did not have access, as a fan, to that level of information about your favorite artist," Diaz told the *Washington Post* in 2020. "Celebrities had a high level of privacy. Outside of those promotional venues, they didn't need to let you that deep inside their world, and they had an image that they needed to maintain."

They *did* let us in, though, and we got to see everything from Missy Elliott's car bed to Mariah Carey using the Stair-Master in heels. Years later we learned that some people were capping on the show, renting mansions and cars for their episodes because they didn't have it or didn't want to show it.

The show was revived and new episodes started airing in 2021. And while times and views on celebrity status have changed, *Cribs* is an iconic piece of television history that influenced other shows, digital programs, and even the way we share our space on social media. None of that would exist without Nina.

QUEEN LATIFAH WAS THE FIRST RAPPER TO GET A STAR ON THE HOLLYWOOD WALK OF FAME

A lot comes to my mind when I think about Queen Latifah. The music lover in me thinks about the 1989 release of her debut album, *All Hail the Queen*, which featured the powerful single "Ladies First" and set the tone for a rap career that would champion women and reject objectification. There's also the bop she made with Faith Evans titled "It's Alright," where Queen shows off some serious vocals, and the way she opened up her verse on the remix to Brandy's hit "I Wanna Be Down," rapping, "About yay short, about yay tall / About so big, about so small." In 2023 she became the first woman rapper to have her music inducted into the Library of Congress. Nearly three decades before that announcement was made, Queen Latifah and Salt-N-Pepa became the first women rappers to win Grammys—Salt-N-Pepa won Best Performance by a Duo or Group with "None of Your Business," and Queen won Best Rap Solo Performance with "U.N.I.T.Y."

QUEEN LATIFAH

The telephile* in me thinks about Latifah's role as Khadijah James on the Fox sitcom *Living Single,*** where she plays the editor of a Black magazine called *Flavor.* The show follows the life of James and her friends, her childhood friend, roommate and boutique buyer, Regine Hunter, her cousin, executive assistant and office manager at *Flavor* and other roommate Synclaire James, and their neighbor Maxine Shaw, attorney at law. If you've never watched this show, please promise me that you'll do so after you finish this chapter or whenever you decide to take a reading break. It's a classic created by the incomparable Yvette Lee Bowser that would impact a bunch of shows long after it went off the air in 1998. And I really would love to know your reaction to Season 4, Episode 15. It's a flashback episode that shows us how Khadijah came up with the name for *Flavor* and also features a really funny fight between Maxine and Regine.

There's also the cinephile in me that gets transported to the hair salon and the movie *Beauty Shop,* where she played the role of hairstylist Gina Norris, a widow who quits her salon job because of a shitty boss and decides to open up her own shop. Oh! There's also *The Secret Life of Bees,* a personal favorite movie of mine where Latifah plays August Boatwright, the family matriarch who runs a honey-making business. And how could I forget the TV movie *Bessie*? It's one of my all-time favorite movies, and there's something extra special about watching Queen Latifah play the role of the iconic blues singer Bessie Smith, who used her music and lyrics to defy norms around gender and sex and speak openly about love, respect, independence, community, and more. She helped break down barriers for all Black women in music thereafter, and Queen Latifah did as well.

---

* I hate that this word hasn't really caught on. Cinephile is so smooth but if someone loves TV they'll just call themselves a "TV lover." This is my attempt to make the word *telephile* stick.

** Latifah also wrote and performed the *Living Single* theme song. Like come on. What CAN'T she do?!

Queen Latifah is a rapper, actress, talk show host, singer, songwriter, model, film and television producer, voice actor, businesswoman,* author, and a bunch of other things that would take up a bunch of space to write out. But if it helps, just think of a profession or job title or role and Queen Latifah has probably already done it ten times over. She helped stretch the limits of not only what was possible for women in rap, but everyone in rap as a whole, and helped take rap to new heights. With everything she's done, it should come as no surprise that Queen Latifah was the first rapper to get a star on the Hollywood Walk of Fame in 2006. Yes. The. First. Period.

The relationship between hip-hop and film is a tight one. When *Wild Style* was released in 1983 it was the first hip-hop movie, with a loose narrative around a graffiti artist that made it almost feel like a documentary. Next came *Breakin'* and *Breakin' 2: Electric Boogaloo* in 1984, musical films that centered the experiences of breakdancers. Then came the movies *Beat Street* and *Krush Groove*, which used narrative storytelling to show a young DJ and his friend on a mission to make it big with hip-hop and the early days of a fictional rap label, respectively. All of these films had people from hip-hop on the cast, and as the culture grew so did its presence and representation in movies.

When the 1990s came around, rappers were notching roles in films that weren't necessarily centered around the music. Kid 'N Play starred in the comedy *House Party* at the top of the decade. Ice-T had roles in *Breakin'* and *Breakin' 2: Electric Boogaloo*, and in 1991 played New York City police detective Scotty Appleton in the crime film *New Jack City*. In 1991, Ice Cube played the role of Doughboy in John Singleton's crime drama *Boyz n the Hood*, and a few years later wrote

---

* In 1991 Queen Latifah took MTV News on a tour of the video rental store that she owned in Jersey City, New Jersey. A few years later she started her own production company, called Flavor Unit Entertainment.

and starred in the comedy *Friday* (2005). Tupac notched starring roles in 1992's *Juice* and 1993's *Poetic Justice*. In 1995, five years after *The Fresh Prince of Bel-Air* premiered, Will Smith starred in the buddy cop film *Bad Boys*. He would go on to become one of the biggest movie stars in the world. Men who rapped were getting the space to do it all. Enter Queen Latifah.

With a few small movie roles under her belt and her own television show in production on Fox, Latifah starred in the 1996 movie *Set It Off*, a heist film that follows four women on their quest to rob a bank. *Variety* described Latifah's performance as "career-making," and though I first watched the movie about fifteen years after it debuted, I understand exactly what they meant. *Living Single* and her role in the romantic comedy *Brown Sugar* showed me the funny side of Queen Latifah, while *Set It Off*, and then *The Secret Life of Bees* and *Bessie*, showed me her abilities as a dramatic actress. Her ability to talk about diverse topics in her music manifested on the screen. Any role you want her to play—an HIV-positive woman in *Life Support*, a hilarious and determined hair salon owner in *Beauty Shop*, or a prison escapee determined to prove her innocence in *Bringing Down the House*—she can do it all, convincingly too. When Latifah played the role of Matron "Mama" Morton in the 2002 musical film *Chicago* she was so damn good she received a Best Supporting Actress Oscar nomination. If you haven't watched it, do yourself a favor today! She is a talented rapper who mastered the ability to tell stories in her music and on-screen. Why *wouldn't* you give her the star?

The process to get a star on the Walk of Fame is pretty straightforward, but let me break it down for you. First, somebody nominates a celebrity who has been active for at least five years in one of the six categories—motion pictures, television, radio, recording, live theater/performance, and sports entertainment (first awarded to Michael Strahan in 2023)—and sends in a form that includes the nominee's photo, bio and qualifications, a list of their contributions to the community and examples of civic orientation, and then a letter of agreement from the nominee or their management. The fee to apply is $250. The committee then looks at all of these applications, usually around two hundred each year, and selects twenty-four to thirty names to go on the Walk.

After the Walk of Fame Selection Committee makes its picks, the Hollywood Chamber of Commerce board of directors does a vote on whether to approve the star and then the names are submitted to the city of Los Angeles' Board of Public Works for final approval. Once all of *this* is done the celebrity must agree to attend a star-unveiling ceremony and a hefty sponsorship fee must be paid by the celebrity or whoever nominated them. That number today? Seventy-five thousand dollars.

"When I started in 1987, I think it was about $3,500," Walk of Fame ceremonies producer Ana Martinez told *Billboard* in 2023. "Then it went up to $5,000. It would go up every few years. The last time we had a big increase, was probably almost 10 years ago—it went from $40,000 to $50,000. Then it was $55,000. Everything is astronomical right now. Everything has gone up since we've been back from COVID."

That dollar amount covers a bunch of things, including the star's creation, installation, and maintenance, and the costs related to the unveiling ceremony.

So getting a star on the Walk of Fame is a *process* and far from a simple feat.

Queen Latifah is so damn good at everything she touches. In fact, she could get a star in every other category on the Walk of Fame too. Here is my case for that.

The Reasons Queen Latifah Should Get A Star In The Other Five Categories On The Walk Of Fame

THE RECORDING STAR

I don't understand how Queen Latifah *does not* have a star in the recording category, but she's a legend, so explaining this won't take long.

The New Jersey–bred Latifah started off as a beatboxer and rapper in a group called Ladies Fresh, also pulling double duty as a singer at her local church. She became a member of the Flavor Unit—a crew of rappers and DJs from North Jersey—and when her demo track landed in the lap of hip-hop legend Fab 5 Freddy, her rap career was set in stone.

Latifah signed with Tommy Records and dropped *All Hail the Queen* in 1989. Album cuts like the first single, "Wrath of My Madness," and the feminist anthem "Ladies First" combined with her Afrocentric outfits and hard-hitting delivery highlight what Rock the Bells described as a "remarkable fearlessness for a debut album, both in the embrace of guest appearances at a time when that was still novel in Hip-Hop, and Latifah and the 45 King's willingness to dabble in a wide array of genres." In addition to the inclusion of R&B, house, jazz, and reggae sounds, Latifah paired her commanding tone and lyricism. It was a stellar project that catapulted her to the front lines of the rap game, and also into the Library of Congress thirty-four years later.

Latifah's third album *Black Reign* became the first by a solo woman rapper to go gold, and featured one of my favorite songs of hers: "U.N.I.T.Y." Rooted in women empowerment,

Latifah used the track to address street harassment, domestic violence, and the disrespect of women. It was an important message, and in 1995 it won Latifah the Grammy Award for Best Rap Solo Performance. At that ceremony Queen and Salt-N-Pepa won the first Grammys for women in rap, period.

To date Queen Latifah has released a total of seven studio albums, two of which are jazz. Because naturally a pioneer like Latifah has a *bunch* of hits.

Somebody needs to give Queen Latifah her recording star on the Walk of Fame, like yesterday.

THE TELEVISION STAR

The fact that Latifah does not have a star in this category baffles my mind too, but I don't think I need to do much talking to convince you how she could get one here. Queen Latifah's been all over my TV screen for practically my entire life, from *Living Single* in the 1990s all the way up to the current CBS series *The Equalizer*. But there's one particular television gig she was excellent at that I don't think gets talked about enough, and that's her eponymous talk show that ran from 1999 to 2001 (and then again from 2013 to 2015). Billed as the "Dear Abby for the Hip-Hop Generation" when it debuted in 1999, Latifah's talk show had it all: performances, cooking segments, interviews with artists and everyday people, and more. Slick Rick, Fat Joe, Mary J. Blige, Ice Cube, DMX, Mike Epps, and Missy Elliott all guested on the show and were interviewed by Queen, who also moderated panels on difficult discussions around race and parenting. My personal favorite moment is when she is joined by Donna Summer around Thanksgiving and they candidly talk about what they are going to serve at dinner. Donna says she's going to serve turkey with two different stuffings to go in opposite ends of the turkey, one of which will be made with corn bread. Sounds delicious.

Please give her this star too.

THE LIVE THEATER/PERFORMANCE STAR

There are two specific stage performances that tell you everything you need to know about why she could get this star one day. Queen Latifah played the role of Ursula in *The Little Mermaid Live!*, a music television special created for ABC based on the classic Disney story, and she killed it. Seriously, you don't even need to watch the entire thing, because her performance of the character's signature song "Poor Unfortunate Souls" literally stole the show. Queen Latifah also played the Wiz in the *The Wiz Live!* on NBC a few years earlier and was stellar there. Fun fact: she starred in her high school's production of *The Wiz* too.

As an added bonus she starred in the film adaptations of the Broadway musicals *Hairspray!* and *Chicago*, so I feel like playing those roles on Broadway would be a lock as well. All somebody needs to do is cast her. If and when it happens she's certainly got a star coming her way.

THE RADIO STAR

If the talk show is any indication of how good Latifah is at hosting shows and having conversations, then it's not a stretch to say she could host a successful radio show too. All she has to do is host one and this star is a lock.

THE SPORTS ENTERTAINMENT STAR

I'm breaking the rules here, but I feel like since I've made such a great case for Queen Latifah to get a star in every other category, we can just let the whole "you have to do this for five years" thing slide. Queen Latifah has a bunch of sports notches on her belt. In high school she played varsity basketball, and her former coach Vinny Smith told Andscape that he was certain she would be a good player: "She had two sides: She had a desire . . . a vision, and she was fun." The team won the championship two years in a row—1985 and 1986—and Latifah's skills on the court helped them win the ship.

If that's not enough for you, have you seen the way she stole the ball from professional basketball player Shawn Kemp at the 1994 MTV *Rock N' Jock B-Ball Jam*? It was a TV series where famous people in Hollywood played famous people in sports, and in this particular episode she gets the ball from Kemp, takes it to the hoop, and makes the shot. If you watch the video on YouTube a lot of people in the comments are saying it's staged, but let me tell you something: I'm really bad at basketball. So bad I wouldn't even be able to fake a steal if the ball was placed right in the palm of my hands.

On top of all of that, in 1998 she was the first rapper to perform at the Super Bowl! The halftime show for this particular Super Bowl was "A Tribute to Motown's 40th Anniversary" and featured performances from the Temptations, Smokey Robinson, Martha Reeves and the Vandellas, Queen Latifah, Boyz II Men, and two new, young Motown signees D.J. Jus and Nique, who were seven and eight years old at the time, respectively. Latifah comes out a little under halfway through the halftime show to roaring applause as she sings her song

"Paper," which is basically a cover of the Motown classic "I Heard It Through the Grapevine." That's quite literally "sports entertainment." If they won't let it slide I'm recommending that Latifah pick up a super-low-risk sport like badminton, table tennis, or bowling. That should be enough to do the trick.

If they give her the star she'd be the only person to have one in all six categories. The committee knows it'd be cool, and they should just do it!

~~~~~~~~~~~~~~~~~~~~

In the years that followed Latifah getting her star, her professional career only continued to grow: her company Flavor Unit signed a multi-project first-look development deal, she became a CoverGirl for the second time, starred in the box office hit *Girls Trip*, played the role of Carlotta Brown on *Star*, and did so much more. She also let the world in on a part of her personal life, shouting out her longtime partner Eboni Nichols and their son when she accepted the Lifetime Achievement Award at the 2021 BET Awards, closing the speech by exclaiming "Happy Pride!" Fans immediately took to social media to express their happiness for Latifah and their feelings of being seen and affirmed by her words. I watched it all happen live, and it was beautiful to see.

I could go on and on about the Queen, but for the sake of time I'll just leave you with this. When you see a woman in rap stepping into film and TV and then other lanes after that, living honestly in their truth and standing up for women, you have to think of Queen Latifah. She made it clear that you could have it all, and then some. The star is just the terrazzo and brass representation of that. (But seriously, someone needs to give her the other five.)

MEGAN THEE STALLION, THE FIRST WOMAN TO PERFORM A RAP AT THE OSCARS

Megan Thee Stallion's ascent to stardom can be followed through a series of events that go back to 2013, when the rapper who hails from Houston started uploading videos of herself freestyling on social media while attending Prairie View A&M University. In 2018 she signed with 1501 Certified Entertainment and 300 Entertainment and released her EP *Tina Snow.* The following year she received her first entry on the Billboard Hot 100 with her song "Big Ole Freak" and released her second mixtape, *Fever.* In 2020 Meg released her debut album, *Good News,* and received her first and second No. 1 singles on the Billboard Hot 100 with the Beyoncé-assisted remix of her song "Savage" and her feature on Cardi B's "WAP." At the 63rd Annual Grammy Awards ceremony in 2021, Thee Stallion took home three awards: one for Best New Artist, one for Best Rap Performance, and one for Best Rap Song, the last of which she won with Beyoncé. That same year she signed a first-look deal with Netflix to create and produce content. And if that's not enough for you . . .

In 2020 she became the first woman to have three songs reach No. 1 on *Billboard*'s Streaming Songs chart, in 2021 she was the first rapper to cover the *Sports Illustrated* swimsuit issue, in 2022 she was the first Black woman to be on the cover of *Forbes* 30 Under 30 magazine, and a few months before that she was the first woman to perform a rap at the Oscars. She joined Becky, Luis G, and the cast of the animated Disney film *Encanto* for a performance of "We Don't Talk About Bruno," which featured a new verse from Meg.

If you do a quick Google search for "hip-hop oscars," you'll get results that tell you the rappers who have won Oscars at the Academy Awards—Eminem for Best Original Song with "Lose Yourself" in 2003, Three 6 Mafia for Best Original Song with "It's Hard Out Here for a Pimp" in 2006, and Common with John Legend in 2015 with *Selma*'s "Glory" for Best Original Song. If you dive deeper and look up "hip-hop oscar performances," you'll learn that Three 6 Mafia's performance of "It's Hard Out Here for a Pimp" in 2006 was the first time a rap song was performed at the ceremony, Pharrell performed "Happy" in 2014, Common performed "Glory" with John Legend in 2015, and that Queen Latifah sang "I Move On" from *Chicago* alongside Catherine Zeta-Jones in 2003. (This was also the first time a woman rapper performed at the ceremony, which I'm sure you were wondering about!)

There's also Pharrell's role as a music consultant alongside legendary composer Hans Zimmer for the eighty-fourth annual ceremony and Jamie Foxx's—who I consider a part of hip-hop—2005 win for Best Actor for his role as Ray Charles in *Ray*.

Considering hip-hop's tremendous impact on film, it's interesting how few hip-hop moments there have been at the Academy Awards. Be clear, I'm not shocked by any means. I know that a culture created by Black and Latino kids in the Bronx is not going to be easily accepted or even acknowledged by an institution that sat the first Black person to win an Oscar, Hattie McDaniel, in the back of the awards show and denied her entry to the "whites only" after-party and is still trying to grapple with the decades of exclusion highlighted by April Reign's

#OscarsSoWhite movement. But I also know there are movies starring rappers, rappers on movie soundtracks, movies centered around hip-hop, hip-hop lyrics shouting out movies, and story lines lifted from and "inspired" by rappers' lives and communities.

In Megan Thee Stallion's case, she's had music in films like *Birds of Prey*, *The Addams Family 2*, and *Queen & Slim*. She's been cast in the upcoming A24 comedy musical *F*cking Identical Twins*. She has a first-look deal with Netflix. She referenced *A Nightmare on Elm Street* in the "Thot S***" video. She's acted a few times in TV series. In 2020 she told *Marie Claire* magazine that she's writing a horror movie and hopes to collaborate with *Get Out* director Jordan Peele on it. And there's, of course, her historic rap performance. Thinking about all of this got my wheels spinning.

Meg's verse on "We Don't Talk About Bruno" was perfect for the Oscars stage, and there are so many songs of hers that could be perfectly turned into award-winning movies. I actually don't care if they win Oscars or not, because these films I'm about to describe would win awards in my house. And the same thing I said earlier applies here. This book is copyrighted, so don't try it!

Megan Thee Stallion Music into (Potentially Oscar-Winning) Movies

Hot Girl Summer

Genre: Romantic Comedy
Starring: Megan Thee Stallion, Halle Bailey, Raven Goodwin, and Ryan Destiny
Plot: When a young author (Megan Thee Stallion) breaks off her engagement with her high school sweetheart, each of her friends (Halle Bailey, Raven Goodwin, and Ryan Destiny) invites her to live in their respective cities—Savannah, Oakland, and London—to help her have a "hot girl summer."

Plan B

Genre: Comedy

Starring: Megan Thee Stallion, Regina Hall, Tyler James Williams, Ncuti Gatwa, and Mo'Nique

Plot: A group of graduate students (Megan Thee Stallion and Regina Hall) compete against their classmates (Tyler James Williams and Ncuti Gatwa) to get the highest grade in a class taught by the hardest professor at the university (Mo'Nique). Along the way they learn the importance of friendship and independence.

Opposite Day

Genre: Sci-Fi Comedy

Starring: Megan Thee Stallion, Maya Rudolph, Thuso Mbedu, J. Alphonse Nicholson, and Luke James

Plot: Bored with the monotony of her day-to-day life, a young woman (Megan Thee Stallion) pays a scientist (Maya Rudolph) for the ability to trade lives with whomever she wants. She meets some funny characters along the way (Thuso Mbedu, J. Alphonse Nicholson, and Luke James).

Cognac Queen

Genre: Drama

Starring: Megan Thee Stallion, Angela Bassett, Gina Torres, Kimberly Elise, Lovie Simone, and Joe Morton

Plot: When the family patriarch (Joe Morton) can no longer make the trips to France to run the cognac business, his eldest daughter (Megan Thee Stallion) returns home to help her younger sister (Lovie Simone), her mother (Angela Bassett), and her aunt (Gina Torres) with the business.

Do It on the Tip

Genre: Horror Comedy

Starring: Megan Thee Stallion, Queen Latifah, Zack Fox, and Method Man

Plot: When an anonymous letter detailing the location of $5 million ends up in a high school teacher's (Megan Thee Stallion) mailbox, she recruits her brother (Zack Fox) and cousins (Queen Latifah and Method Man) to help her get to the cash. The only problem? They have to go to "The Tip," a haunted island off the coast of her state, to get to it.

(This next one is a bonus for my little sister because she requested it!)

Freaky Girls

Genre: Romantic Comedy

Starring: Megan Thee Stallion, Taraji P. Henson, Keke Palmer

Plot: Two best friends (Megan Thee Stallion and Keke Palmer) sign up for an app that allows them to get advice from their older selves on dates. But when they break one of the rules and alter their futures for the worse, they have to track down the app's elusive creator (Taraji P. Henson) for help.

Someone tell the Academy that Meg and I got one (or six)!

Interlude

EVE, MY PERSONAL STYLE ICON

Writing about Cindy Campbell made me think about the first party I threw for *The Gumbo*. Writing about Dee Barnes reminded me of the hip-hop news videos I used to host for an internship I held in college. Writing about Queen Latifah took me back to my mom doing my hair on Sundays while we watched old episodes of *Living Single*. And writing about Big Lez and other women who hosted music television shows brought me back to the *106 & Park*–themed birthday party I threw in 2019. I asked all of my friends to dress up in their best early 2000s outfits or reference a moment from the show. I didn't really care too much about what people wore, though, because the party was really a ploy for me to get the chance to dress up as Eve. I wore a white tank top and leather pants, drew two pawprints on my chest with black eyeliner, and bleached my hair platinum and buzzed it short.

Eve means a lot to me and to hip-hop. She's the First Lady of Ruff Ryders. She won the first Grammy Award for Best Rap/Sung Collaboration when it was introduced in 2002 for her hit "Let Me Blow Ya Mind," featuring Gwen Stefani. She played the role of fashion designer

Shelly Williams on her eponymous UPN sitcom *Eve*. And she had a clothing line by the name of Fetish. In addition to all of that, Eve is really the first woman in rap that I 100 percent saw myself in as a kid.

That doesn't mean I didn't relate to the other women rappers I was listening to growing up, because I did. The thing about Eve, though, is that she's from Philly. And as a kid growing up in a part of New Jersey that's largely influenced by the Pennsylvania city, I recognized immediately that we had a lot in common. Eve ate the food I ate. Went to the places I went to. Wore the clothes that I wore.

In the video for "Satisfaction," the neighborhood Eve is hanging in looks just like my aunt's in Philly, where I spent plenty of days on her stoop eating pickles she bought me from the corner store. When Eve performed at the 2002 NFL Kickoff Concert in Times Square rocking an Eagles jersey I was hype to see a star repping a team I had worn on my back on more than one occasion. And when she did an interview with *Bon Appétit* in 2013, she told them the chicken cheesesteaks from Ishkabibble's are her favorite. They're mine too, and if you ever stop by the food spot make sure you get a "Gremlin" to drink.[*]

Eve wasn't just a part of my childhood. She's also been the inspiration behind a lot of my fashion choices. When I saw her in a jersey dress I asked my parents for one. When I cut all of my hair off and bleached it blond I brought a picture of Eve to the salon. (I would reference more pictures of her when I dyed my hair red and lavender.) And when I started working full-time I would stop by the beauty supply store to buy scarves to tie around my head like she did.

---

[*] A "Gremlin" is the half lemonade and half grape juice drink they sell at Ishkabibble's. It's delicious, and take it from me, no matter how many times you try to re-create it on your own it won't taste like the one at Ishkabibble's. Oh, they also have a chopped turkey cheeseburger that's my second favorite thing behind the chicken cheesesteak. So if you're ever in Philly stop by and try these items. There are two Ishkabibble's locations now: the OG one that you can walk up to with a few barlike seats and Ishkabibble's II, which has a lot of tables inside. Both are on South Street. Tell me if you go!

With countless hits under her belt and a career that's touched television, film, and fashion, Eve is undoubtedly "that girl." She's also my personal style icon, and that's the reason why I wanted to dress up like her for that birthday party I threw back in 2019.

I wonder if all of this talk about dressing up like a rapper reminded you of a moment you did the same, or when someone's look inspired you to try something new. There are so many women in hip-hop who have shaped the looks of our favorite emcees, created brands of their own, experimented with different hair colors and makeup, and influenced a lot of the trends we see today. They're style icons too, and the next few chapters are all about them.

Interlude

APRIL WALKER IS THE FIRST WOMAN TO HAVE A DOMINANT HIP-HOP FASHION BRAND

April Walker is the GOAT. Seriously. If I could copy and paste those five words six hundred times I would. But you purchased this book for a reason, to learn about the women in hip-hop who paved the way for any and everyone who came after them, so teach I will. But first:

April Walker is the GOAT. April Walker is the GOAT. April Walker is the GOAT. April Walker is the GOAT.

Now onto April's story.

Raised in Brooklyn, April was a hustler from the beginning. When she was thirteen years old, she charged kids five dollars each to learn gymnastics from her. When she got to high school, she would cop wholesale clothing items to resell to people when they got paid.

In 1987 April Walker started her first business, a custom tailor shop by the name of Fashion in Effect, which she ran out of Clinton Hill, Brooklyn. At this time she was a college student. The idea to create her own space in her borough was sparked by two people: her father, who managed jazz greats and artists like D Train, Jaz-O, and Jay-Z (you read that right!), and Dapper Dan, whose shop she visited one night after attending Amateur Night at the Apollo in Harlem. That kicked off the journey that would lead to her being the first woman to have a dominant hip-hop fashion brand.

"Fashion was the most natural thing that came to me," April tells me. "It was the perfect marriage because by the time I was in the eighties I knew I didn't want to work for someone else."

With Fashion in Effect April hit the ground running. She set up her office in the space next to the bathroom, hired tailors, purchased sewing machines, set up a showcase in the front so people could buy beeper covers, and purchased denim, velour, terry cloth, and corduroy so she could create whatever her customers desired.

"We made a lot of custom things. We made sequined tuxedos, we made gowns. We would do whatever, we could do whatever. I did a lot of shirt dresses, basketball dresses. There were different things we did that were ahead of their time, so to speak," April tells me. "We did goose down coats, leather, all kinds of stuff. It literally was like you come in the store and from the sales point, we can either create it for you, we can work with you and design it with the customer. Or you had a certain amount of ready-to-wear pieces that people could buy."

The people *were* buying it, with everybody from emcees like MC Lyte to the neighborhood hustlers and their wives pulling up to Fashion in Effect to get their fits. Even a young Biggie came to the shop one day to ask about an airbrush shirt he saw in the store's window. He became a customer, and by the time he got his deal the two already had a working relationship.

April started a styling division at Fashion in Effect too, landing her first styling job alongside the iconic brand Shirt Kings to outfit Audio Two for the cover of their album *I Don't Care*. From there it was on, with April going on to style Queen Latifah, Nikki D, Gang

Starr for their *Daily Operation* album cover, Jeru the Damaja, the rap duo No Face, Bytches With Problems (BWP), and Run-DMC, to name just a few.

In addition to all of this, April was laying the foundation for Walker Wear, her own official line of original clothing, by creating sweatsuits, beanies, crew neck sweaters, and her wildly popular "rough and rugged suit," which came together after her customers kept asking for clothing with deeper pockets, more legroom, a lower crotch, and jeans that were straight at the bottom. The "rough and rugged" suit was a hit, and customers flocked to Fashion in Effect to grab their version of the outfit they saw everyone rocking. April was onto something big, and she knew it. The people around her took notice too, and encouraged her to make the line official and show it at the Namsby.

The Namsby, founded by the National Association of Menswear Sportswear Buyers, was a fashion trade show where designers and brand owners could showcase their fashions to potential clients and retailers, and it was slated to happen at the Jacob K. Javits Convention Center in Manhattan soon. It was the perfect place for April to show her line, and she did. But not without some nervousness.

"I was terrified because I didn't want in from that side. I was totally on some like, being an underdog, the other side. But I did a show out of a suite at the Flat Hotel, where Motown would take their artists. It was a corporate hotel where artists would be," she remembers. "We took a clothesline and put it around the suite. We had hors d'oeuvres, we had champagne. And then Jam Master Jay and a few of my other teammates went over to the Namsby and stood outside so when buyers were coming in they would tell them they needed to go to the Flat Hotel."

A bunch of big fashion retailers pulled up to the suite to buy some of April's clothes, including Dr. Jays, Merry-Go-Round, and Simons. It was the beginning of Walker Wear, which would go on to become one of the first brands in hip-hop fashion to open distribution doors and command millions of dollars in sales. And to be clear, some people use the terms *streetwear* and *urban wear* to describe the clothing brands coming out of our communities. Whatever term you see, just know that April Walker was the first woman to dominate in the space.

"When I started there wasn't streetwear, there wasn't urban fashion. There was nothing, it was like going into the wild wild west, like, it wasn't there. So we were literally creating it, right, by trusting our instincts. . . . I didn't have a blueprint," Walker said on a 2021 episode of *Drink Champs*. "I was literally feeling hip-hop and listening to how we felt and expressing that and that's how my team was expressing it. And that's what translated into the clothing."

April was intentionally ambiguous when it came to her brand too—so much so that people thought it was owned by Run-DMC or Naughty by Nature at one point. Hip-hop and fashion were and remain two spaces dominated by men, so sexism affects women being taken seriously and respected in these spaces. In a conversation with her father, April told him, "I don't know if they'll accept a woman making men's clothes." He told her if she had to chance it, don't do it. So she let the products speak for themselves. The products did more than speak, though. They took the industry by storm.

Walker Wear received celebrity endorsements from Biggie, the fictional characters Beavis and Butt-Head, and Tupac, who recruited Walker to create some clothes for the movie *Above the Rim*.* Naughty by Nature, LL Cool J, Wu-Tang Clan, EPMD, Shaquille O'Neal, and Method Man all wore the brand, with Meth's denim "rough and

---

* A really cool story that April Walker told on *Drink Champs* is that Tupac called her personally and told her he wanted her to do all of the clothes for *Above the Rim*. The costume designer told them she couldn't do them all, so he made it a point to let them know he wanted all Black designers for the movie. April made a camouflage outfit and vest that he wore in the film, and recommended another brand, 5001 Flavors.

rugged suit" on full display in the "I'll Be There for You/You're All I Need to Get By" video. Walker Wear was also one of the first hip-hop fashion brands to get distribution from Federated and FootLocker and introduce product placement to MTV and BET.

She was in business before FUBU, Sean John, Rocawear, Baby Phat, and Enyce, and when artists and hip-hop executives were thinking about starting clothing brands of their own, April Walker was there to lend an ear and give advice. In her *Drink Champs* interview she recounted the time Roc-A-Fella Records cofounder Damon "Dame" Dash was trying to get Rocawear off the ground and initially wanted to sew the clothes himself before deciding not to. Left with a bunch of sewing machines he wasn't going to use, he called none other than April Walker to give them to her.

April Walker laid the groundwork and helped create the multibillion-dollar industry known as streetwear/urban wear. But when she peeped the exploitation and appropriation that was affecting Black artists on the music side she knew the writing was on the wall for hip-hop fashion. She made the decision to shelve her brand.

People who weren't rooted in hip-hop culture set out to capitalize on what designers like April Walker did, while actively removing people who looked like her from the process. "Fashion has made billions from black culture for decades, from zoot suits to stolen streetwear," Lela London wrote for *Forbes*. April relaunched her brand in the 2010s, and in June 2020 she penned an open letter to the fashion industry calling out the racism and discriminatory practices:

> Our enduring cultural currency is not reflected in equity, own-ership, or legacy stories. Today, despite the foundations we laid, many brown and Black designers still face the same "invisible" challenges I did as a young, Blexican woman start-ing out three decades ago. The gatekeepers in fashion still deny access, resources are still limited, and obtaining capital and

financial backing is still "a dance" for Black designers. Big fashion houses constantly loot our creativity without repercussions, knowing we'd be outgunned if we challenged them in legal proceedings.

I don't know what fashion would look like today had April not opened Fashion in Effect and launched Walker Wear, and I honestly don't want to. She is a hip-hop pioneer whose impact is undeniable, and when we talked she told me she's pushing hard to make fashion the sixth element of hip-hop: "It's a part of the DNA, let's start acting like it." April herself is a part of hip-hop's DNA too. Don't ever forget.

Some Gems from My Chat with April Walker

The only thing cooler than getting to write about the women in hip-hop that I admire is getting to talk to them and share it with you. Here are some more great moments from my chat with Ms. April.

NS: We have a bunch of different phrases for these clothes, streetwear, urban wear, hip-hop fashion. I want to get your opinion on the use of these words.

AW: Best analogy I could have is we've gone from Afro-American and even before that, Negro to African American, Black. All the people that get all of those different names, right? It's the same thing with urban wear, streetwear, with hip-hop [fashion]. I think that I embrace it all because I don't run from the things that we created. But I also am much more than just that. People rarely bring up Fashion in Effect. And the fact that we started with a custom shop that did couture. Like all those hustlers back in the day, that's all they were wearing. And we were making stuff for the wives. That was the base of our business starting out.

NS: Yes.

AW: In terms of the coined terms, it's a code word to say who's wearing it. Just like you have multicultural dollars and advertising dollars. I think that's where those lines need to go away, for that purpose. Because we need to get away from the codes and one budget for one genre of people and another budget for another genre of people. When we get to the point where we're all people and all respected in the same way and have the same equity space that's different.

NS: I want to touch on something you said about the early styling, so many interviews touch on Fashion in Effect and then immediately go into Walker Wear. And they should, it's a gigantic brand. But when I think about what you told me about having the hustlers come in and you're styling them—those were the hood celebrities.

AW: That's how I started! Like, you know, it's funny. My father's like, if you ever do your story, you have got to give them credit first. And I always would. Because I wouldn't be here without them. At one point the 88th Precinct had on us their watch list for selling drugs out of Fashion in Effect!

NS: Wait, what?

AW: That was because so many Mercedes and Bentleys would pull up in front of our shop. And you're talking about the eighties when the crack era was starting and stuff.

NS: That is crazy! Did anyone ever come in there to question y'all?

AW: I only knew because I was cool with a few of the police and one of them told me and I was like wow, that's crazy . . . If I had that ledger from Fashion in Effect? We made eighty-something thousand that first year. And you can imagine in 1987, 1988, that was like, a lot.

NS: Yes, that's a lot! This is why we need the biopic! Now, when we talk about all of the work [you did], what did you do when you weren't doing fashion? Was there something you did as a hobby or to decompress—

AW: [*Laughs*]

NS: I love that you laughed!

AW: That's where I learned about self-care, after [I stepped away from the industry].

NS: What was it like for you to make the decision to leave?

AW: It just became heavy and it wasn't fun anymore. It was really like falling in love with something. And then you start falling out of love with it because the thing you fell in love with doing, the creating, and the relationships and the building—all the things that really draw you in . . . it became about numbers more . . . I watched it become this megabillion-dollar industry and very few of us were participating or had a seat at a revenue table.

NS: What reignited it for you? Where you're like, all right, now is the time for me to come back in.

AW: I think it was the digital era, because two things happened. I took a lot of time off and it gave me a lot of time to get my mind, my body, and my spirit together and my second wind. And then realizing I don't have to play by anyone's rules. I can come in this real lightweight and just be creative if I want.

NS: Mhmm.

AW: But I knew when I came in, part of my objective coming back in was to bridge the gap, because I saw the tools of technology and how impactful they could be, but also how there could be a disconnect. And so I said I wanted to storytell through our brand without being preachy. And I knew I would be able to do that and talk to young people and grow with them and learn also . . . I believe in reverse mentorship.

NS: I love that.

AW: I think the biggest part for more seasoned people is not to become rigid as we age, because that's how you stay open to growth and creativity. And I think if you're lucky, the more seasoned we become, the more we realize how much we don't know. We *can* grow.

NS: When we talk about your legacy, what is the most important thing you want people to think of when they think of April Walker?

AW: I would like them to think that I lived in my truth. And that I was a giver and a game changer and I was here for my community. I believe that when we empower each other, we're helping to bring a healthier—we're empowering our communities. So I believe when we empower individuals we're empowering our communities, and I believe when we empower our communities collectively, we are helping to create a healthy global ecosystem. And I want to be remembered as one of those game changers that did that.

NS: Absolutely, absolutely. Well, you are to me!

AW: Thank you.

~~~~~~~~~~~~~~~~~

had the honor of attending the New York Liberty WNBA team's annual UNITY Game in 2022, where the theme was "See Black Women." As a part of the initiative designed to "amplify Black women who are transforming mainstream spaces and creating pathways to racial, gender, social and financial equity,"[*] April Walker curated a

---

[*] Via a July 2022 press release.

pregame panel discussion and a Black Women-Owned Business Expo on the concourse. It was beautiful to see. What I've decided to do is share the stories of some more ladies in the world of hip-hop fashion who you should know, love, celebrate, and learn from. After all, that's what April Walker would do.

SHARA McHAYLE

I interviewed Shara for *The Gumbo* back in 2021 and hearing her stories of her time in the industry was so fun, and a part of the reason why we ended up video chatting way longer than the time I slotted in the calendar. Shara worked for PNB Nation, one of the first hip-hop fashion brands to exist, period. The brand abbreviated the phrase "Post No Bills," three words that are often seen on New York City buildings and construction sites forbidding the posting of advertisements or any type of signs. The brand's politically conscious messaging is what drew Shara in,[*] and it was there she began her career in the marketing department, rising in the ranks to marketing and sales director and being offered a partnership by the five founders. She was the only woman, and in her second year took the company from $250,000 to $1.2 million in sales.

Today Shara runs Hoop88Dreams, a company that exclusively sells hoop earrings, with her daughter. The "hoop" in the name references the product, while the "88" is a reference to her favorite year, 1988, in which you have classic albums from artists like Biz Markie, Big Daddy Kane, and MC Lyte. In her years post-PNB, Shara managed the career of her husband and iconic hip-hop DJ, producer, and rapper Pete Rock, and focused on family. She told me that at her core she was an entrepreneur, and creating Hoop-88Dreams was a space through which she could reengage with the culture. A culture that she was a part of with one of the first hip-hop fashion brands, from the beginning.

---

[*] It was the messaging on a shirt specifically that drew Shara McHayle to PNB. The shirt was originally titled "Three Names," and then it became "Hello My Name Is," and on it were the names of three people killed by the New York City Police. She told me, "It just struck a chord, and that was 1991. It was then that I knew I wanted to be involved in the brand PNB Nation and that I knew fashion would be the gateway to the conversation [and social commentary]."

ELENA ROMERO

If anyone knows anything about hip-hop fashion, it's Elena Romero. She got her start as a journalist in 1993, working at New York radio stations WNYC-AM and WBAI-FM. Three years later she transitioned to the newspaper business, becoming a fashion journalist for the now-defunct *Daily News Record* and then *Women's Wear Daily* (*WWD*).

Today she's an assistant professor and assistant chair in the Marketing Communications Department at the Fashion Institute of Technology; an award-winning correspondent and producer for *LATiNAS*, which airs on CUNY TV; author of *Free Stylin': How Hip Hop Changed the Fashion Industry*; coauthor of *Fresh, Fly, and Fabulous: Fifty Years of Hip Hop Style*; and co-curator of the Museum at the Fashion Institute of Technology exhibit of the same name, which housed over one hundred garments and accessories to tell the story of hip-hop style from its beginnings.

TONI SCOTT GRANT

If you do a quick search of Toni Scott Grant on IMDb, you'll find credits for the Showtime series *Billions*, Hulu's *Wu-Tang: An American Saga*, the Super Bowl LIV halftime show, and more. Her very first styling job was for Timbaland, who paid her $5,000 for her work. The following week the girl from Texas was in Los Angeles styling Baby Stase, Mase's twin sister, for the "I Really Like It" video by Harlem World.

SYBIL PENNIX

The January 1995 cover of *The Source* magazine is so excellent. I was only a few months old when it hit newsstands, but a little over a decade later, armed with the internet and Tumblr, this cover is one of the earliest memories I have of finding something online and going "whoa!" Mary J. Blige is one of my favorite artists and in my opinion one of the greatest artists to ever do it—there's a reason she has her own chapter later in the book! Couple that fact with how fire her outfit looks—a white puffer coat, knee-length silver boots, a furry hat that the fashion girls would scramble to get their hands on today—as she sits on a literal chair made out of ice, and it's one of the coldest—no pun intended—fashion moments in music, to me. The look was styled by none other than Sybil Pennix.

After she got her bachelor's degree in industrial engineering from the University of Pittsburgh, Sybil's dream of starting a modeling agency led her to the Big Apple. In New York she landed a job as Diddy's assistant at Uptown Records and when tasked with styling the one and only Mary J. Blige, Sybil more than rose to the occasion. Pennix became the first in-house stylist at the label, outfitting artists like Heavy D, Jodeci, Mary J. Blige, of course, and more. When Diddy started Bad Boy Records in 1993, Sybil styled the artists on his roster, and also discovered, developed, styled, and managed the Bad Boy–signed R&B group Total.

KIANGA "KIKI KITTY" MILELE

Kianga's resume is long. And I mean looooonnnnggggggg. Over the years she's designed for multiple fashion brands, including Jay-Z's Rocawear, Diddy's Sean John, Eve's line Festish, Kimora Lee Simmons's Baby Phat, and Beyoncé's Deréon and also served as the creative director for Nicki Minaj's Kmart line. She's damn near worked with every artist who's ever made their foray into the business of fashion. It's no surprise, considering she got her start as one of the first designers for the iconic brand FUBU and as an assistant to Sybil Pennix. Over the course of her career she rose in the ranks, becoming the creative director at FUBU Ladies and then launching her own lines: K.A. Kitties and a resort brand, K. Milele.

BEVY SMITH

The 2012 *BET Remembers Whitney* television special with Bevy Smith as the host was so touching. As a then-aspiring music journalist, I especially loved the care Bevy took when it came to asking questions and getting heartfelt stories from the people she was interviewing.* She's a great interviewer and host, which is why

* There's a moment in the special where Bevy talks to some of the women who danced in Whitney Houston's "I'm Every Woman" music video when they were children. One of the women, Mercedes, was diagnosed with colon cancer as a kid, and told Bevy that Whitney paid for all of her surgeries. It's such a touching story, and one that I think everyone should know. Because when you get to a certain point, helping others is so important.

she cohosted the Bravo fashion talk show *Fashion Queens* and *Page Six*'s syndicated entertainment show *Page Six TV*, as well as currently hosts her own Sirius XM radio show, *Bevelations*. In 2021 she released her memoir, *Bevelations: Lessons from a Mutha, Auntie, Bestie.*

Before all of this, though, Bevy was making history as a fashion advertising executive at *Vibe* magazine. It was there that she landed *Vibe*'s first luxury fashion client, pitching fashion houses for *Vibe* in 1998. As she told *InStyle*, "I remember the white guy I replaced said, 'Oh, they'll never talk to you. They don't even take my calls, so they'll never talk to you.'" Surprise, they did. She remembers seeing a quote in *WWD*, where Tom Ford—then the creative director at Gucci—described making a collection for Whitney Houston "if she married a hip-hop star and they were vacationing on a yacht." She sent Gucci a laminated copy of the quote and put it in a box along with some pictures of some iconic looks that *Vibe*'s fashion director (and later editor in chief) Emil Wilbekin had styled using Gucci clothes, and the next summer they got two pages of ads in the magazine. After that, Prada had ten pages in the magazine. This helped open doors for advertising opportunities and luxury fashion collaborations within hip-hop.

SHARENE WOOD

In 2012 Sharene Wood and her husband, Guy Wood Sr., created Harlem Haberdashery, a fashion boutique that's designed for big names like Beyoncé and Jay-Z. Twenty years before this the Woods established 5001 Flavors, which originally started as a personal styling service before growing into a custom clothing company. 5001 Flavors had outfitted everyone from Biggie and Missy Elliott to Alicia Keys and Diddy. They also did that No Limit *Vibe* magazine cover where the entire crew is outfitted in leather camouflage fits. Hip-hop history.

JUNE AMBROSE

A 2022 interview with June Ambrose by *Fashionista* calls her a "creative multi-hyphenate, for whom 'stylist' hardly begins to convey her role." And it's true. She's a designer, author, host, award-winning creative director, and entrepreneur with a career that spans four decades, working with some of the biggest names in hip-hop in the 1990s, 2000s, 2010s, and now the 2020s. She started off with a career in investment banking before shifting gears and taking a role at Uptown/MCA Records. It was there that she booked her first styling job.

Ambrose would go on to mastermind some of the most memorable looks in hip-hop history, like the shiny red suits Diddy and Mase wore in the video "Mo Money Mo Problems," DMX's sparkly jacket at the beginning of the movie *Belly*, and, of course, Missy Elliott's blowup vinyl suit that she wore in the video for "The Rain (Supa Dupa Fly)." And that's not even scratching the surface!

To be honest, it's impossible to talk about hip-hop fashion without talking about June Ambrose, not only because of the iconic moments she created, but also because she was one of the first stylists to bridge the gap between luxury fashion houses and hip-hop artists. As she told *NBCBLK* in 2016, "I wanted to be that style ambassador who was going to move the culture forward by introducing high fashion to urban music. I was determined to get black music played on pop radio, I was determined to turn hip hop into 'hip-pop.'"

With a resume that includes being creative director for Puma, hosting her own style rehabilitation show *Styled by June* on VH1, dressing her longtime client Jay-Z and more, June set the tone for what fashion and hip-hop could do and the heights that it could go.

MISA HYLTON

There's no way I couldn't mention Misa! She has a whole chapter later on in the book, so you'll learn about her when you get there!

LIL' KIM, THE FIRST "BLUEPRINT" FOR THE MODERN WOMAN IN RAP

There are a lot of ways to talk about Lil' Kim, and that's because she has done a lot and means a lot to a lot of people, myself included. You can start with Junior M.A.F.I.A., the hip-hop group from Bedford-Stuyvesant ("Bed-Stuy"), Brooklyn, who saw success with songs like "Player's Anthem" and "Get Money," of which Lil' Kim shone as the brightest star. Then you can visit her debut album, 1996's *Hard Core*, which received critical acclaim and set the stage for a new kind of sex-positivity for women in rap. There's also Lil' Kim the fashion muse. Take, for example, her appearance at the 1999 MTV Video Music Awards,* where she pulled up in a one-sleeved lavender jumpsuit made out of Indian bridal fabric and a seashell pasty that covered her left nipple. There's also her monochromatic outfits and matching hair in the "Crush on You" video, which were inspired by the "Emerald City

---

* Misa Hylton was the architect behind her 1999 VMAs look, which was inspired by Missy Elliott. She told *Essence*, "I was with Missy Elliott, and we were talking fashion and music, and she was like, 'If I was Kim, I would just have one boob out, like f—k it. I wouldn't care, because Kim can do that.' Missy got my imagination working. The next big event was the 1999 VMAs, and I brought that idea to life. It was risqué, so I made it really pretty with Indian bridal fabric to soften it."

Sequence" in the film *The Wiz* and would go on to be replicated a bunch of times, especially in costumes. There's also my personal favorite outfit of hers, the all-pink ensemble she wore on the Met Gala carpet in 1999, where she became the first woman rapper to attend the event.

Almost everything that Kim did was a moment, either as they were happening or through discovery years later. It would be ahistorical to deny the reality that we still see Lil' Kim's influence today, from her musical content to her overall style, Kim was an "it girl," a muse, and for the modern woman in rap, the first blueprint.

I'm going to be really transparent here. This chapter was the hardest one to write. Lil' Kim is not just an important figure in hip-hop, but she's also one of my favorite rappers. It's hard to write about someone you love and admire when their impact seems so obvious. I tried to use charts and graphs to make my point but none of it was clear, so I scrapped it. Then I tried to write a bunch of paragraphs, but none of

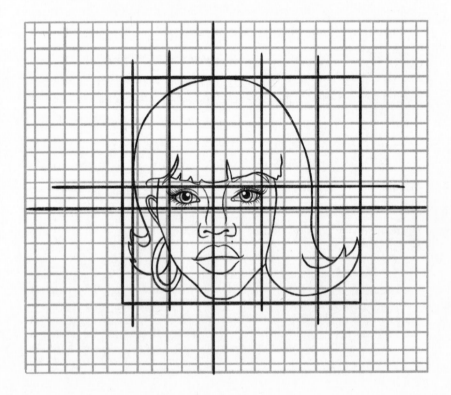

them were strong. So I deleted those. And when I realized my idea for a graphic representation of Lil' Kim's influence would look more like a spider than a proper diagram, I erased that whole thing too.

What I did next is what I always do when I can't figure something out: call someone I love and tell them I can't figure it out. On that night in particular it was my best friend, listening on the other end of the phone while I vented about not being able to articulate the theme of this chapter well.

"I've explained Lil' Kim's influence and impact to so many people. Calls, text, in person, and I just don't know how to write it down," I told her. That's when she gave me the best idea I've ever heard: "Why don't you have a conversation and make it look like the #TextCheck series you do for *The Gumbo*?"

#TextCheck is a digital interview series that we do on *The Gumbo*'s social platforms, where we talk to artists, DJs, and other women in hip-hop solely through texting. It's one of our most popular content series and it's one of my favorite ways to talk to people. It's relaxed, loose, and creates the space necessary for authentic conversations just like the ones you have with the homies. It's also the *perfect* way to explain what I couldn't with those charts and paragraphs and diagrams.

The next few pages are a conversation between myself and someone who's listening to me explain Lil' Kim's standing as the first blueprint for the modern woman in rap. My messages will be on the left, and the other person's messages will be on the right.

NADIRAH

Thank you so much for doing this!

> **FRIEND**
>
> Of course! I'm excited to talk to you and learn some things lol!

NADIRAH

I'm excited for you. So let's get right to it, how much do you know about Lil' Kim?

FRIEND

A little bit I guess. I'm sure not as much as you though.

NADIRAH

If I tell you she's the first blueprint for the modern woman in rap, do you feel like that's accurate?

FRIEND

What do you mean by blueprint?

NADIRAH

The Cambridge Dictionary defines the word blueprint as "an early plan or design that explains how something might be achieved."

FRIEND

Okay. But I feel like there are other women in rap who are blueprints too . . .

Yeah there definitely are lmao.

NADIRAH

Oh absolutely! Women rappers who came out before Kim are the blueprint for a lot of things, and you knowwwww there are women who came out after Kim who are as well.

FRIEND

Hmm. So why is she the first?

NADIRAH

Two reasons. She's the first for the modern woman in rap, as in the women who are rapping now and in recent years. She's also the first blueprint because she came out before women like Trina and Nicki Minaj, who are also blueprints for women in rap today.

FRIEND

Oooohhhhhhh I get it.

NADIRAH

Do you or are you lying?

FRIEND

Lmao! I kinda get it, but I think I will even more after you keep explaining.

NADIRAH

Typing . . .

FRIEND

What are the things that make her this blueprint?

NADIRAH

Glad you asked lol! So there are two things that are crucial to Kim's blueprint, and that's sex positivity and style.

FRIEND

Oh yes! Kim had no problem telling you what she enjoyed on her songs!

NADIRAH

For sureeee. But here's the thing. Kim wasn't the first woman to rap about sex. Salt-N-Pepa's "Shoop," "Whatta Man," and "Let's Talk About Sex" all dropped before Kim's *Hard Core* hit the shelves. There was also Rap-A-Lot Records signee MC Choice, whose 1990 debut album The Big Payback was bold, braggadocious, and very, very explicit—her song "Cat Got Your Tongue" is probably one of the most sexually straightforward tracks I've ever heard. Left Eye was rapping about having both sets of lips kissed on TLC's 1991 debut single "Ain't 2 Proud 2 Beg." And the rap duo Bytches With Problems (BWP) had absolutely no problem calling out a "Two Minute Brother" when they released the song in 1990.

FRIEND

Oh wow. I have to look up MC Choice and BWP, I've never heard of them!

NADIRAH

Definitely do that, I'll send you some songs after this too.

FRIEND

Bet! Okay. So she's not the first woman to rap about sex . . .

NADIRAH

Not at all. But the thing about Kim is that she took it to another level. She was honest and explicit about sex and her right to pleasure. She made it an important part of her music and it empowered so many women who listened to it.

If you listen to Junior M.A.F.I.A.'s 1995 single "Get Money," Lil' Kim raps "rather count a million while you eat my pussy." On *Hard Core* the intro is literally the audio of a man masturbating; she proclaims that she "used to be "scared of the dick" before shouting out porn legends Heather Hunter and Janet Jacme on "Big Momma Thang" and on "Not Tonight" the chorus explicitly states that Kim is only in the mood for oral. It was bold, direct, and liberatory. She took a lot of heat for it. And she owned it.

FRIEND

What were people saying?

NADIRAH

A LOT. But there's one interview in particular that I always reference, and that's the one Lil' Kim did on Rolanda Watts's talk show *Rolanda* in an episode titled "Is Lil' Kim Sexualizing Our Children?"

The episode opens with Kim and Diddy performing "No Time," followed by a panel that included Lil' Kim, her mother, Ruby Mae Jones-Mitchell, president of Morality in the Media Robert Peters, Love Yourself, Stop the Violence founder and New York City police officer James Davis, and Hot 97 radio personality and former *Yo! MTV Raps* cohost Ed Lover.

FRIEND

Oh wow, all of them people?

NADIRAH

Right? Damn near the entire episode is Kim going toe-to-toe with the panel and the people in the audience who thought she was a bad representation of women, a bad influence on children and that her music should be banned.

James Davis asked her, "Why open up your legs and show us in a negative light?"

Robert Peters said if it were up to him during certain times of the day, lyrics from *Hard Core* "would be against the law to air . . ."

Some random man in the audience said that there were people who could tell him Lil' Kim's lyrics but didn't know their multiplication tables lmao.

It went on and on and on and on.

An important moment happens when a twelve-year-old girl by the name of Chanel who's a big fan of Kim tells Rolanda she listens to Lil' Kim's music on the Walkman because she knows her mom wouldn't approve. When Rolanda asks Lil' Kim to respond to the concerns, she gives the best answer:

"I think that she listens to it for the sound and for me being a young, positive Black young woman . . . doing my thing and getting over a hump . . . If you're going to listen to my music make sure you do the right thing. Don't go out and have sex for the wrong reasons. And if you do decide one day that you want to have sex, use a condom because I'm pretty sure you're old enough to get pregnant and catch a disease."

Despite all of the people at the show trying to shame her, she still took the time to talk to that girl and empathize and be honest with her.

FRIEND

That's powerful. But also, damn. I mean I'm not surprised people were being mean to her, but that's a lot to handle, especially when you're just one person! Talking about multiplication tables while I know the men rapping about sex were just walking around unbothered lol.

NADIRAH

Double standards at play for sure. She talked about this exact thing with bell hooks for the May 1997 cover of *Paper* magazine. She told her straight up, "[We] have people like Too Short, Luke Skyywalker [of 2 Live Crew], Biggie [Smalls], Elvis Presley, Prince, who are very, very, very sexual, and they don't get trashed because they like to do it. But all of a sudden, we have a female who happens to be a rapper, like me, and my doin' it is wrong. And 'cause I like doin' it, it's even more wrong because we've fought for years as women to do the same things that men are doing."

She was taking up space and stood firm in her right to do so.

FRIEND

That's fire. Wait, so what about the second thing, the style stuff?

NADIRAH

Lol the style stuff! So that's the other part of the blueprint. She married her music with her image.

FRIEND

Typing . . .

NADIRAH

Typing . . .

FRIEND

What do you mean?

NADIRAH

Salt-N-Pepa wore eight-ball jackets and leggings to match the cool, upbeat vibe of "Push It." Queen Latifah rocked Kufi hats and Afrocentric garments to go with the messages of Black feminism and empowerment on songs like "U-N-I-T-Y" and "Ladies First." For Kim, whose lyrics were charismatic, unashamedly sexual, feminine, and confident, her fashion had to be all of those things too. For a woman in rap it was new, exciting, and unprecedented, and with the legendary Misa Hylton as her stylist there was no way she couldn't make it happen.

FRIEND

Oooohhhh. Okay that makes a lot of sense!

I know a little bit about Misa but I want to learn more!

NADIRAH

She's one of the GOATs! I'll give you a little bit here and we can talk about it after we wrap this, but there's a whole chapter in the book dedicated to her that I don't want to spoil here.

FRIEND

Word word, makes sense.

NADIRAH

Misa is a stylist, designer, and pioneer in the fashion industry. She had a rep for killing it on the fashion front, so when her label needed someone to style Kim, Misa was the perfect person.

FRIEND

Can you send me the next chapter? Lol.

NADIRAH

Ha, yes. I got you.

When Clover Hope talked to Misa for her book *The Motherlode: 100+ Women Who Made Hip-Hop*, she said this about Lil' Kim: "Kim created another lane, allowing women to shape their own images and express themselves in any way they want through style. We don't have to be just one way as women. We get to choose what we wear and how we wear it."

FRIEND

Period!

NADIRAH

From the monochromatic fashions* and matching wigs** in the video for "Crush on You" to the mink she rocked in the video for Junior M.A.F.I.A.'s "Player's Anthem," the self-proclaimed "Black Barbie dressed in Bulgari" was unapologetic about her love for luxury and looking good. The fashion world took notice, and it wasn't long before the four-foot-eleven rapper from Brooklyn was working with the likes of Giorgio Armani, Donatella Versace, and Marc Jacobs.

FRIEND

Oh shit! I didn't know they worked with her!

NADIRAH

They didn't just work with her. They WORSHIPED her too!

In 1999 Lil' Kim got invited to present fashion designer Alexander McQueen with the Avant-Garde Designer of the Year award at the VH1/Vogue Fashion Awards. In 1999 McQueen was a GOAT, a big dog, whatever other word you can think of that describes someone at the top of this field. He had put on a fashion show that featured a model being spray-painted by robots, won two British Designer of the Year awards (he would win

---

* Ballroom icon and HIV/AIDS activist Hector Xtravaganza did the colorful furs Kim rocked in the "Crush on You" video, as well as a few more furs the rapper had in her closet. Xtravaganza was featured in Jennie Livingston's 1990 documentary on LGBTQ+ ballroom culture in New York City, *Paris Is Burning*, and served as a consultant on the FX television show *Pose*. Rest in peace to a legend.

** Just wanted to use this moment to big up Eugene Davis, the man behind the wigs in "Crush on You." In 2013 he told a really cool story to *Vice* about how the wigs in that video came to be. He got to the set and saw the stages "turned from blue to green to yellow to red." When he saw that her outfits were the same colors he left the shoot in Long Island City, Queens, bought some wigs, came back, and then styled them on her accordingly. The rest is history.

two more in 2001 and 2003), launched his own label, and was the chief designer at Givenchy.

FRIEND

Hold on, I gotta go look that spray paint thing up!

NADIRAH

Do it! It's cool as hell.

Five minutes pass . . .

FRIEND

Okay I'm back. Yeah that was cool as hell.

NADIRAH

See what I mean? Fashion GOAT. Anywho, when he got onstage to accept his award, guess what he did? He literally *bowed* to Lil' Kim and called her his idol. That's it. He didn't give an acceptance speech or anything. Bowed, said "thank you," and walked off the stage holding her hand.

FRIEND

Omg lmao. He wasn't playing!

NADIRAH

The designers loved Kim! That same year she was the first woman rapper to go to the Met Gala and she was Donatella Versace's guest!

FRIEND

Oh shoot go Kim!

NADIRAH

She rocked a studded pink bra top and hot pants, a full-length pink mink Versace coat, and pink python boots, and the whole fit was custom made.

FRIEND

I just looked it up. It's fire! And her hair matched too. I love how colorful her hair was.

NADIRAH

In the rap world Kim really changed the game with her hair. Some of my favorite Lil' Kim hair looks were done by Dionne Alexander. This one joint had the Chanel logo on the bangs! Beyoncé had it re-created for her Lil' Kim halloween costume.

FRIEND

I remember seeing that on Instagram a few years ago! And wow, a lot of the rap girls rock really colorful hairstyles today.

NADIRAH

Oh yeah. Flo Milli, Saweetie, Cardi B, and Nicki Minaj, just to name a few, have all been seen rocking colorful tresses on more than one occasion. The last two women have also sported monogrammed locks too.

FRIEND

Mhmm.

NADIRAH

The other thing I want to tell you is that Kim's style kept her booked and busy too. In 1998 she signed with Wilhelmina Models, landed ad campaigns with Candie's, Iceberg Jeans, MAC Cosmetics, and Old Navy. The commercial for that last one gave us the hilarious meme where Lil' Kim says "you're in the hood now baby."

FRIEND

Lmfao I know that meme!

NADIRAH

Yup! Kim took her love for fashion and parlayed it into endorsement deals and a long-standing position as a muse to the biggest designers. She paved the way for the relationship we see between fashion and women in rap today. When it came to her looks, Kim's team set new standards and trends for the ensembles rocked by women in rap.

FRIEND

Mhmm. Okay I see the blueprint!

NADIRAH

It's everywhere! So let's talk about some modern women in rap. Cardi's wigs in the "WAP" and "Shake It" video are reminiscent of Kim's colorful wigs in the "Crush on You" video and the monogrammed ones she used to rock. There is Meg's flower-printed wig she wore in the "Cry Baby" video. And Nicki's hair! The two definitely have had beef over the years, but Nicki hasn't let that stop her from acknowledging Kim's impact in the space. And Nicki's wigs are always LAID.

FRIEND

Okay period lol!

NADIRAH

And alllllll of them have had really big fashion and beauty brand deals because of their impact and style. Kim had a big makeup deal with MAC, and Meg, Cardi, Doja Cat, Saweetie, and Nicki have all collabed with big makeup brands.

They've all been to the Met Gala as muses too! And specifically when it comes to Nicki and Doja, they've really pushed the boundaries with their look like Kim did. Doja's red crystal fit at Schiaparelli's spring 2023 couture show was crazy. Her whole body was covered in CRYSTALS YO! And Nicki switched things up when she started rocking hair down to her feet. Literally sweeping the floor. Just different.

And then their lyrics? We don't get songs like Cardi B and Megan Thee Stallion's "WAP," Nicki Minaj's "Anaconda," or Meg's "Big Ole Freak" without Lil' Kim. *Hard Core* really shook the table and made the space.

FRIEND

Forreal. Wow, she really is a GOAT! And the blueprint, I get it. Now I have a question.

NADIRAH

Hit me!

FRIEND

Can we go see her the next time she has a show?

NADIRAH

Lmao, yes!

I don't know what rap would look like had it not been for Lil' Kim, but thankfully that's not something I have to ever worry about. With her lyrics and fashion she didn't just influence, she also built a new road for the modern generation of rap women to travel—oftentimes with much more ease than she did. That needs to be acknowledged and celebrated at every stop.

(Some of) the Ladies Behind
Lil' Kim's Looks

DIONNE ALEXANDER

Raised in Washington, DC, Dionne Alexander spent a lot of time at the salons owned by her cosmetologist mother. "I would go into my mom's salon and observe the hairdressers, who were all so glamorous," Alexander told *Vogue* in 2023. "Being around so many creative women, I was drawn to the lifestyle."

Alexander got hired to be a hairstylist on the set of the 1992 hip-hop film *Fly by Night*, where she met MC Lyte. Lyte became Dionne's first celebrity client, and she styled her hair for the "Ruffneck" and "Keep On, Keepin' On" videos. In the years that followed, Alexander racked up a clientele that included Mary J. Blige, Faith Evans, Ms. Lauryn Hill, Missy Elliott, Yo-Yo, SWV, Rosie Perez, and Lil' Kim.

She did Kim's wig for her MAC makeup campaign with Mary J., the zipper wig Kim wore in the "In the Air Tonite" video, the lavender locks she rocked at the 1999 MTV VMAs, and, of course, those monogrammed and logo wigs Kim rocked over the years. For the blue wig with the Chanel logo on the bangs, Alexander purchased a blond wig, dyed it turquoise, and drew the logo on with a Magic Marker. For the blond wig covered in the Versace logo that Kim wore to the design house's spring/summer 2001 show in Milan, Dionne used a gold marker to create the look.

After being diagnosed with endometriosis, Alexander decided to step away from the industry to focus on her health. In 2017 she launched hair care system LaTure Hair. In 2023, Lil' Kim wig replicas that she created went on display at *The Culture: Hip Hop and Contemporary Art in the 21st Century* exhibit at the Baltimore Museum of Art, and today more and more people are learning about her work. Getting my hair blessed by Ms. Dionne is on my bucket list, for sure.

NZINGHA

When she was interviewed for *Complex* about her work in 2022, makeup artist Nzingha said, "I wanted everybody to look like themselves. I didn't want anyone to look at the makeup and say, 'That's Nzingha's makeup.' I wanted them to see the individual artist." Born in the Bronx and partly raised in the United Kingdom, Nzingha comes from a family that she describes as the "OG influencers." Her uncle Robert (Bob) Gumbs, an artist, designer, writer, and photographer; godfather, Elombe Brath, a prominent Pan-African activist; and godfather Kwame Brathwaite, a legendary photographer and activist, were three of the founders of the African Jazz-Arts Society & Studios (AJASS) and Grandassa Models. AJASS pioneered the Black Is Beautiful movement in the 1960s, producing concerts and hosting "Naturally" shows, fashion shows that celebrated natural hair and Afrocentric clothing. The Grandassa Models, of which her mother was a member, were ambassadors for the movement. OG influencers *for real*.

Their work also inspired Nzingha, whose upbringing and Caribbean background helped shape her makeup artistry. A gig assisting a makeup artist on a *Black Hair Care* magazine shoot helped catapult her career, with her going on to work with artists like Janet Jackson, Prince, Mariah Carey, Destiny's Child, Brandy, Mary J. Blige, Missy Elliott, and Lil' Kim.

She first worked with Kim for the "Crush on You" video, and would craft amazing looks for the rapper as her makeup artist for years. One of my favorite looks she did for Kim appeared on the cover of *Interview* magazine, initially intended to be the cover of her album. On it Kim is covered in the Louis Vuitton logo, which Nzingha and her team spent six hours spray-painting onto the rapper.

Nzingha's makeup skills can be seen in your favorite shows and movies too, including *Power*, its spin-offs *Power Book II: Ghost* and *Power Book III: Raising Kanan*, *Wu-Tang: An American Saga*, *The Sopranos*, *The Cookout*, *The Forty-Year-Old Version*, and *Sex and the City*. She even did makeup on Broadway's Wicked. Wherever you catch her, just know that nobody does makeup like Nzingha.

NIJA BATTLE

An article published in the *New York Times* on July 26, 2000, said Nija Battle "brought a swaggering sense of sophistication to the furs she designed for the music world's most tireless clothes-horses." Battle had just passed away while on a business trip in

Montreal, leaving behind a legacy as a furrier to the stars and some of the biggest names in hip-hop.

Battle officially started making furs in the 1990s, but her skills were put to work when she was just a child, using the skins given to her by her father, a hunter, to create blankets and clothes for her dolls. Raised in Brooklyn by a Black and Italian father and Tuskaroran Native American mother, Nija frequently visited her grandmother in North Carolina, who raised minks. She also worked under furriers on Orchard Street and Seventh Avenue in Manhattan to gain experience.

Battle launched her own business and started bringing in big-name clients like Mary J. Blige, Whitney Houston, Diddy, and of course, Lil' Kim. In addition to the furs, Battle helped bring a bunch of looks the rapper rocked to life, including the mink-embellished jeans that she rocked in 1999. You can find a picture of Misa and the furrier styling the fit online. When speaking about Nija during a chat about Lil' Kim's fashion impact with *Complex* in 2019, Misa and Kim sang their late friend's praises. "She would meet you at the club and take your order . . . she was like a ball of energy and she was so creative and I miss her so much," said Misa. Kim echoed the sentiment: "She did all kinds of stuff that a lot of people are doing now . . . she was amazing."

Of course, the way we look at fur today is different, with many designers abandoning it and a statewide ban on the sale and manufacturing of new fur products going into effect in California at the top of 2023. In a 2019 *New York Times* piece, Jasmine Sanders noted that when it comes to Black women "this broader, cultural disavowal of fur has coincided with our increased ability to purchase it." Being able to purchase a fur coat as a Black person was a big deal, because it represented progress, ascendence, and, to Sanders, "resilience and glamour." Nija, with all of her knowledge and training, recognized this. That's what made her work so impactful. And that's why the customs she made for artists, including Lil' Kim, were so fire. Rest in peace, Nija.

MISA HYLTON, THE FIRST GODMOTHER OF HIP-HOP STYLE

Misa Hylton is one of the coolest people ever, to me. She's the woman behind so many artists' iconic looks, like Lil' Kim's lavender pasty look at the 1999 MTV Video Music Awards, Mary J. Blige's outfits in the "Not Gon' Cry" video, and Beyoncé's custom MCM logo bustier-jacket-hat-and-earrings combo for her and Jay-Z's "Apeshit" video. She's really really good at what she does. In fact, when she was asked by the *Daily Front Row* in 2018 if she was concerned that the MCM look wouldn't make it into the video, she smoothly replied, "[M]y looks always make it in." I know that's right. But what else would you expect from the first godmother of hip-hop style?

I call her the first godmother because of the role she's played in so many artists' careers. In families godmothers nurture and help promote the well-being of the children they said they would look out for, often being a safe space for them to express thoughts and ideas they might not want to share with their parents or guardians. In the honorific sense of the word, she pioneered new ways of dressing within the hip-hop space that would change the music and fashion landscape forever.

Misa Hylton got her start as a teenager, still a student in high school, when she was given the opportunity to work with Diddy* and R&B group Jodeci. Diddy had just been promoted from intern to A&R, and he was tasked with putting together the quartet's first album, *Forever My Lady*. Strongly influenced by hip-hop, Misa wanted to create a look for Jodeci that was inspired by the culture. At the time, R&B singers dressed up when they sang, which for the men meant suits and hard-bottomed shoes. What Misa wanted to do would be the complete opposite: hoodies, combat boots, and baseball caps, to be specific. She talked to Uptown Records founder Andre Harrell, who gave her the go-ahead to style the guys how she imagined, and she did, with the looks being seen in the video for Jodeci's song "Gotta Love," Misa's very first big styling project. What she did would change not only her life, but also the way R&B artists dressed from there on out.

When Misa received her first woman client in Uptown Records signee Mary J. Blige, the two ladies clicked instantly. Mary was from Yonkers and Misa was from Mount Vernon, both in Westchester County, New York.

"Our high schools played each other in sports, so there was this whole perspective that we shared. I actually loved her tomboy style. I thought it was dope, and I just added a touch of femininity to it," Hylton told *Garage* magazine in 2020.

Her work with Blige was groundbreaking. Putting Mary in jerseys, tennis skirts, and baseball caps separated her from the other singers at the time who might have been sporting dresses or heels. Mary's style wasn't that of the stereotypical singer. It was representative of the woman she was, the music she listened to, the city she came from, and the hip-hop soul genre she would become the "queen" of. And Misa understood that.

---

* Misa and Diddy were dating at the time.

Then, of course, there's Lil' Kim. Misa told *Billboard* that working with Lil' Kim allowed her to get into her "creative bag." From the cover of Kim's *Hard Core* to the "Crush on You" video to the fur-covered tan jumpsuit she wore to the 1999 *Source* Awards, Misa and Kim weren't afraid to push the limits and try anything and everything—which is how you get iconic looks like Kim with her boob out and covered with a pasty on the VMA carpet. Her work with Kim also pushed her to add another skill to her creative arsenal. "When I started working with Lil' Kim, she was so little (4'11" and size 4-½ in shoes) and by that time even though I had access, nothing fit her," Misa told *Billboard*. "She wore like kids size 11 or 12, which is how I got into designing."

Misa is a pioneer who has done a lot. Like, *a lot* a lot. She's been interviewed countless times and talked about a lot of things. She's talked about damn near every look that she's styled and designed; she's talked about working with Lil' Kim, Mary J. Blige, Missy Elliott, Faith Evans, Foxy Brown, and more. She was one of the stars of the Netflix documentary *The Remix: Hip Hop x Fashion*, which visually showcased her and other fashion designers' impact in the hip-hop fashion space and beyond. She led her own fashion styling and image consulting company with Chyna Doll Enterprises. She's designed collections with INC and Teva. And she still has her foot on the gas, running her eponymous fashion academy, holding court as Global Creative Partner for luxury fashion brand MCM, and styling and designing fits for the biggest names in music. As you can see, herein lies a struggle. How do you talk about someone who has been talked about in what seems like every way possible? Then it hit me. Why not let Misa tell it herself?

As a godmother, she's taught us so much through her words and work over the years. Thus, I decided to pick some quotes from a bunch of those interviews and tell you what each of them taught me, and which outfits Misa has styled or designs directly reflect the message.

What she said: "Working with Mary and Kim were life-changing moments for me because with them I found kindred spirits. . . . We were also fearless with our ideas and willing to try new things that reflected the culture." (*Hypebae*, 2019)

What it taught me: Think outside the box.

Misa took the bold and daring approach to her styling for Jodeci and applied it to Mary J. Blige. When it was time to shoot the videos for Mary's first and second singles, "You Remind Me" and "Real Love," Misa didn't put her in a gown and heels like the other songstresses were wearing. Mary had what Misa described to Hot 97 as a "tomboy edge," and Misa leaned into dressing Mary in a way that reflected who she was as a person and where she came from. That meant combat boots, jerseys, bandanas, oversized jackets, baseball caps, gold jewelry, and more. With Misa's help, Mary's standing as the "Queen of Hip-Hop Soul" showed in her outfits just as much as it did in the music.

What she said: "We were always challenged to change our authentic Black fashion choices. I always knew how to stand my ground on what I thought was beautiful." (*Nylon*, 2021)

What it taught me: Never tone down who you are to make someone else comfortable.

The reason I love this quote so much is that it's directly tied to one of my favorite Misa moments. When Misa was on the set of Mary J. Blige's "Not Gon' Cry" video she put the singer in a Fendi Mongolian fur fresh off the runway and a pair of gold twist hoop earrings. Misa described the earrings as a "staple in hip-hop style and the Black community" to the Museum at FIT in 2022, and they were representative of what the people within the community, as well as Misa and Mary, were really wearing in their day-to-day lives. (I have a few pairs too!)

There was a management team at the shoot that wanted to work with Mary, and one of them proceeded to ask Misa if she could change the earrings to something softer and less "distracting." Misa told the dude no, Mary loves them, and they're not distracting. Should've been the end of it, right? Nah. Dude came back and said something *again*, y'all! Misa stuck to her guns. And you won't believe what I'm about to say next, but this guy came back *again* with another person to try to convince Misa to take the earrings out. They would not let up, then recruiting Mary's then-manager Steve Lucas in the hopes that he could convince Misa to take the earrings out. His response? Basically, what Misa says goes.

There are so many instances where Black women are asked to do less in order to make someone else feel comfortable, and Black women in hip-hop are not exempt. Despite being asked a bunch of times, Misa never wavered. She was not going to compromise her integrity or her culture for people who wanted to "tone it down," and that's something I take with me everywhere I go.

What she said: "Wherever there's an obstacle, there's an opportunity." (*MadameNoire*, 2019)
What it taught me: Don't let a hurdle throw you off your game; roll with it.

Almost everyone who knows about Lil' Kim knows about the look she rocked at the 1999 VMAs, but not everyone knows that a part of the ensemble was the product of an accident.

Misa got the idea to put Kim in an outfit with one of her boobs out from Missy Elliott, so she decided on Indian bridal fabric and had the look custom-made: a sheer lavender jumpsuit with sequined seashells, a single bell sleeve, and her left breast exposed with a seashell-shaped pasty covering her nipple. Misa collaborated with the glam squad on the rest of the look, which would be complete with her makeup, Steve Madden heels, and a blond wig.

If you've never dyed your hair blond, I'm here to let you know it's a complicated process. Bleaching the hair helps lighten it, but adding in a purple toner or purple hair dye and conditioner mix helps neutralize the yellow and brassy tones that are often left in the hair when you bleach it. It's the difference between your hair being an orange-yellow color or a lighter, more powerful blond. But you *have* to have a good radio and time it correctly or else your whole head will be purple—trust me, because I've done it before.

That's basically what happened to Kim's wig. Dionne Alexander got some more purple on the wig than she wanted to, leaving Kim with a lavender-tinted wig. When it was time to show Misa the wig, Dionne told her she had to redo it. But Misa thought it was perfect, and the rest was history. A testament to turning an obstacle into an opportunity.

> **What she said:** "Zerina calls me and she's like 'Misa, okay I'm ready for the trench, but guess what? I need a whole look and I need it in three days and I need it shipped to Paris on Memorial Day weekend.' We got it done. . . . " (Museum at FIT, 2022)
>
> **What it taught me:** Stay ready so you don't have to get ready.

Imagine you get a call from Beyoncé's personal stylist and wardrobe curator, Zerina Akers, asking you to make something for the Queen. Then imagine you have to make it in three days and ship it to another country on a holiday weekend. Misa Hylton doesn't have to imagine it, because that's exactly what happened when she made Beyoncé's outfit for the "Apeshit" video.

Zerina and Bey loved the MCM trench coat that Misa—now global creative partner for the luxury fashion brand—made for Big Daddy Kane, so much that Zerina hit up Misa to ask her to make the same thing for the singer. When asked when they needed the coat, Zerina told Misa she would follow up with her. A few weeks went by, and Misa decided to reach back out to Akers to check in about the coat. Zerina wasn't sure if she still needed it, and didn't want to waste

Misa's time by having her make something that wouldn't even get worn. Makes sense. But then . . .

A month later Misa got a call from Zerina, who told Misa she needed not just the coat, but now an entire outfit made and shipped within the timeline I detailed two paragraphs up. With assistance from fashion stylist and creative producer Naomi Jonas, she got it done. Akers told Misa that Bey wore it, but outside of that she had no idea when or where she would see it.

The moment came when she was scrolling Instagram one weekend and saw a clip from "Apeshit." Bey was wearing the full MCM fit in the Louvre Museum in Paris. That couldn't have happened without Misa and her team being ready to go. Stay ready so you don't have to get ready.

> **What she said:** "I've worked in television, in film, I did celebrity fashion styling, editorial, runway, every area of fashion styling I have done it. And so I said you know what, I want to give back in this way and I want to create a program that will support the next generation of creatives." (*Love from a Distance*, 2020)
>
> **What it taught me:** Make sure you give back.

This example isn't an outfit, but it's a part of Misa's legacy that's far too important to leave out. In 2012 she founded the Misa Hylton Fashion Academy with stylist Jai Hudson. With certificate programs in fashion styling, streetwear business and marketing, and fashion technology, and courses in personal shopping and sneakers, the academy is designed to help the next generation of designers, stylists, and fashion creatives succeed in the business.

Given all that Misa has done, her commitment to giving back is important for all to see. You're never too big to help the people following in your footsteps.

WHAT DO YOU KNOW ABOUT **ESG?**

naturally listened to a lot of music while writing this book. I
played music videos for hours on end, kept albums by various
emcees on loop, and went to the record store as often as I could. I read
liner notes. I watched studio sessions. I researched samples. I wanted
to be completely immersed in the songs from the culture I was writing about, and by doing so I discovered a group of women whose
music has had a tremendous impact on rap. Those women make up
ESG, the band formed by the Scroggins sisters in the same area that
birthed hip-hop and whose song "UFO" is one of the most sampled
cuts in rap music history.

"Playing music was more my mother's dream than mine initially," Renee Scroggins told the *Chicago Tribune* in 2018. "At first I
didn't appreciate what she did for us, but as years went on, I realized
the key sacrifices she made. She was a cook making a meager salary
but she scrimped and saved to get those instruments. She was trying
to make sure what happened to my older sister and brothers didn't
turn out that way for the rest of us kids."

Renee's mother wanted to keep the girls out of trouble, so she purchased a guitar for Renee and a drum set, bass, and tambourines for her younger sisters, Valerie, Deborah, and Marie, respectively. Hailing from the South Bronx, the ladies formed ESG in 1978, an acronym for emerald, sapphire, and gold, and set out to perform at different clubs and make some money. Their sound, as Matthew Trammell perfectly put it for the *New Yorker*, "hit upon an original style of live dance music that combined funk, hip-hop, punk, and Latin grooves."

In 1981 the band released their eponymous debut EP on 99 Records, a six-track offering that included the popular club record "Moody," one of the best tracks to dance to, titled "Earn It," and of course "UFO," one of the most sampled songs in rap. The funny thing about "UFO," though, is that it almost didn't get recorded. There were three minutes left on the master tape—the original copy of an audiotape that is sent off for copying and distribution—when producer Martin Hannett asked if they had a song that would fit into the empty space.

"I said, 'Yeah, we've got "UFO."' He said, 'Go ahead, knock yourself out,'" Renee told Canadian music outlet *Exclaim!* in 2006. "It's funny because if there wasn't three minutes on that tape, we may have never done 'UFO.'"

Good thing they did do it, because not only would the song not exist, but neither would the 567 songs (according to WhoSampled.com) that sampled it. The group acknowledged this fact when they titled their 1992 EP *Sample Credits Don't Pay Our Bills*, because like the name says, they literally don't.

"l would go to different clubs and hear 'UFO' in the background on different records and think someone was stealing from me," Renee told the *Chicago Tribune*.

As a result, Renee made it a point to learn all about the music business, copyright laws, and the importance of owning her masters.

She also hired lawyers to help with the legal side of the sampling process.* And while at this moment in time there's no way to retroactively get ESG all of the money they're owed for being sampled without payment, at the very, very least we can acknowledge that so many songs, specifically rap records, would not exist or sound the same had it not been for the sisters from the South Bronx.

Their music stays on repeat in my crib now, along with the music by the artists in these next few chapters.

Interlude

* From an interview Renee did with the *L.A. Record* in 2006.

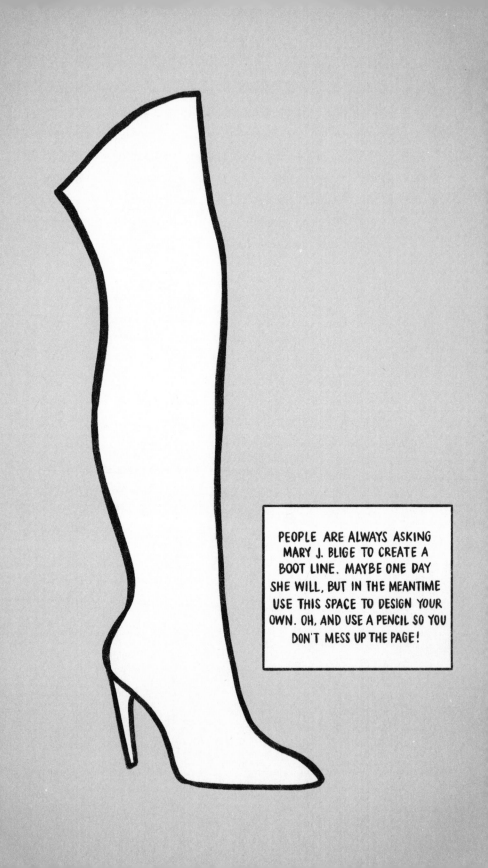

PEOPLE ARE ALWAYS ASKING MARY J. BLIGE TO CREATE A BOOT LINE. MAYBE ONE DAY SHE WILL, BUT IN THE MEANTIME USE THIS SPACE TO DESIGN YOUR OWN. OH, AND USE A PENCIL SO YOU DON'T MESS UP THE PAGE!

MARY J. BLIGE, THE FIRST (AND ONLY) "QUEEN OF HIP-HOP SOUL"

I don't think you can talk about women in hip-hop or hip-hop, period, without mentioning Mary J. Blige. That just feels wrong. And I don't like to do things that are wrong. So we're going to talk about some of the songs that I love by the woman who was the first of her kind with her sound, style, and approach. We'll call it the Mary Mixtape because I love alliteration and it's only right! But I need to preface this chapter . . .

There's one thing you need to know about me: there are a handful of artists I will fight for, hypothetically and literally. Mary J. Blige is one of them. Mary J. Blige, the first and only Queen of Hip-Hop Soul. Nobody was doing it like her, and to say her sound became the blueprint for music thereafter her debut would be an understatement.

If you don't know the story of Mary's path to stardom I got you covered. In the 2021 documentary *Mary J. Blige's My Life*, Mary talks about how she was living in Yonkers and went to the mall where she recorded a cover of Anita Baker's classic "Caught Up in the Rapture." She brought the tape home, and her stepfather was so impressed that he passed it along to Jeff Redd, a recording artist at the record label headed up by the late Andre Harrell. Harrell pulled up to where Mary lived in Yonkers, where she sang the entirety of Anita Baker's *Rapture* album for him inside of her family's apartment. I wasn't there, but I can guarantee you that she killed it. From there, Mary J. Blige became a part of Uptown Records. In 1992 she released her multi-platinum[*] debut album, *What's the 411?*, which peaked at No. 6 on the Billboard 200, landed at No. 1 on the Top R&B/Hip-Hop Albums chart, and produced Blige's first Top 10 hit single with "Real Love" peaking at No. 7 on the Billboard Hot 100. *Entertainment Weekly*'s senior writer Dave DiMartino visited Blige in Los Angeles ahead of a taping of *In Living Color* in 1992 and attributed the success of the album to "her powerful, soulful voice and hip-hop attitude," saying that both things solidly connected with an audience that had never seen a woman do what she was doing. And that's true. It was new. It was fresh. It was hip-hop soul.

As a nineties baby, it's hard for me to imagine music without the fusion of hip-hop beats and soul singing. It's pretty much embedded in my DNA, but I love it for two reasons. For one, it's because of the way Method Man describes it in the *My Life* documentary I mentioned earlier. He points out that Mary singing over hip-hop beats meant "we can groove to this, we can do our dances to this." And this is true. I hit all of the same dances to my favorite hip-hop songs and my favorite Mary J. songs.

Then there's what it did for women, Black women more specifically. The Queen of Hip-Hop Soul is a hefty title. Let's be real, we're not just handing that out to *anybody*. To put it in perspective, Aretha Franklin is the Queen of Soul, Michael Jackson is the King of Pop, and James Brown is the Godfather of Soul. Social media may have watered down honorific titles in the past few years, but there's no

---

[*] The album was certified triple platinum by the Recording Industry Association of America in 2000.

questioning that the names I mentioned and their music, talent, and skill have made them inimitable. They were able to sing about their experiences and feelings in a way that made you feel so connected to them. When Mary J. Blige came out the gate singing like that on beats usually reserved for rap songs, she was carving out the same space as her honored predecessors in music. To tell you what I mean I have to give you a quick history lesson.

The title of Mary J. Blige's debut album was a callback to her time working as a 411 information operator, and that in combination with the opening track "Leave a Message" are a clear signal that Mary is as real as it gets. Her music is as well. A lot of R&B and soul singers at the time were using their music to talk about happiness, pain, and relationship troubles while many of the rappers used their tracks to talk about the neighborhood conditions, oppression, decriminalization, economics, and more. Now, obviously this doesn't apply to everyone; music is not a monolith and there were plenty of artists who talked, sang, and rapped about everything. Because Mary was influenced by the genres I just mentioned she was able to amplify themes in hip-hop music in a way that wasn't really done before. She took themes that were hallmarks of blues women like Ma Rainey and Bessie Smith— abandonment, betrayal, romance, physical and emotional abuse— and fused them with hip-hop. Or as *Rolling Stone* described it, Blige's songs provided "a gritty undertone and a realism missing from much of the devotional love songs ruling the charts at that time." It's true. And it's the reason I felt every single word in "Your Child" at the age of five, when I had certainly never experienced a man cheating on me let alone a man having a baby with another woman.

One of my favorite scholars, Treva B. Lindsey, said something so profound about hip-hop soul artists in her 2013 article "If You Look in My Life: Love, Hip-Hop Soul, and Contemporary African American Womanhood" that I think perfectly describes why Mary is just so damn great. She writes, "Hip-Hop Soul artists challenge the invisibility of multidimensional African American womanhood within popular culture, and become conduits through which Black women of the Hip-Hop generation express personal aspirations, intimacy, and love." That's what Mary does and has done for over three decades. And that's why she is and will always be a pioneer, the first and only Queen of Hip-Hop Soul.

Now that I got all of that out, on to my Mary Mixtape!

"Everyday It Rains" (1995)

I sing this song out loud at least ten times a day. Not kidding. Just randomly, "everydayyyyyy" accompanied by a little bop. Usually out of nowhere. The crazy thing about this joint is that Mary is lamenting having to pretend she is happy when in reality she is not, because she lost the person who, as she sings in the song, brightens up her life. Hence why "everyday it rains." The reason I say it's crazy is that the beat is not what you would expect to hear someone singing about lost love over.[*]

P.S. If you want to know what dance I do to this song, look up "Mary J. Blige - Everyday It Rains (MSG)" on YouTube. That's me the entire time the song is on.

P.S.S. That's Faith Evans singing background on this track.

"You Remind Me" (the original and the remix) (1992)

It would be pretty insane to not have this on my list. Not only is it the first single from her debut album, but it's also one of my favorite Mary remixes. It's a straightforward love song, in which a man she meets reminds her of a love she once knew. The beat on both versions is hard. The remix has one of my favorite random rap lines too, on which Greg Nice (half of the New York rap duo Nice & Smooth) says, "N-n-n-now, M-M-Mary's infatuated, in love with you, Skiddly wah wah, Pepe Le Pew." It's a really funny line with a really funny rhyme, and I just love rapping it.

---

[*] The beat samples Lou Donaldson's "Who's Making Love," which was also sampled on rap tracks like "Hot Sex" by A Tribe Called Quest, "Pump It Up" by Nice & Smooth, and "Droppin' Science" by Marley Marl featuring Craig G, to name a few.

"Searching" (1997)

A Roy Ayers sample, a piano, the sound of turntables scratching, some boom-bap, and the repetition of the word *searching* over and over come together to create the *perfect hip-hop soul song*. The beat is so hard and so hip-hop, and on top of it Mary croons about her quest for peace of mind, love, unity, and happiness. Plus you can dance to it, cry to it, and smile to it. Mary opened up the door for listeners to experience any and every emotion. It's hip-hop soul at its finest.

"Enough Cryin" (featuring Brook Lynn) (2005)

A Darkchild beat.* This is a dance track and a diss track at the same time. Basically I'm not crying over this man anymore; he stinks and I'm gonna hit my dance on my way out of your life. She did that.

"Telling the Truth" (2017)

This one's not really a hip-hop track, but it's an excellent Mary track that I love so much and I wish people talked about more. It features production by Kaytranada and BadBadNotGood and it goes so crazy. Promise me you'll play it while you read this chapter?

"My Love" (1992)

Mary asks a very direct question in this song: "What you gonna do without my love?" In fact, she repeats it throughout the chorus so much that I imagine her looking at whoever she's talking to with her arms folded and eyes staring directly at them while really asking them, "You know you fucked up, right?" It's like an R&B ballad and rap diss rolled into one. It's perfect.

"Changes I've Been Going Through" (1992)

---

* Darkchild has won multiple Grammys. He was raised in New Jersey and made the beats for some classic tracks, including "What About Us?" by Brandy, "Enough Cryin" by Mary J. Blige, "It's Not Right but It's Okay" by Whitney Houston, "Say My Name" and "Cater 2 U" by Destiny's Child, "He Wasn't Man Enough" by Toni Braxton, "You Rock My World" by Michael Jackson, "One Wish" by Ray J, and "Déjà Vu" by Beyoncé.

It's the Queen of Hip-Hop Soul crooning over a sample of Biz Markie's "Make the Music with Your Mouth, Biz." Obviously it's going on my Mary Mixtape.

"All That I Can Say" (1999)

This song was written and produced by Ms. Lauryn Hill, who also sang the background vocals! Two music legends linking up on one track! Two ladies whose impact on hip-hop is undeniable! This song is just so good. I can't wait to talk about Lauryn later on in the book!

"Mary Jane (All Night Long)" (remix, featuring LL Cool J) (1995)

I went back and forth between trying to decide if I wanted to include the original, the remix, or both. They're both fire, but then I thought about the amount of times I played the remix over the course of my life and without a doubt the remix with LL Cool J has been played probably a couple thousand more times than the original—which, again, I really love. This version lands on the mixtape not only because of LL's verse, but because of the extra little trill that the late, great Chucky Thompson added to the beat. The only thing better is the live version where Mary adds a little "ohhhh" after singing the chorus.

"Mary's Joint" (1994)

Turn this on right now. I'm not even going to write about this one. Just listen to it. One of the best tracks in Mary's catalog.

"Testimony" (2001)

Something about Mary saying "it's alright, it's okay" is so comforting. And she's hitting all of what I highlighted from Treva earlier in the chapter. Easy pick.

"Share My World" (1997)

One thing I love about hip-hop is the way call-and-response techniques have been incorporated into the music. If I were to say "hip-hop hooray" I would expect you to reply with "ho, hey, ho." This technique is found in blues music too, like on Bessie Smith's "Empty Bed Blues," where trombonist Charlie Green musically responds to Smith's audible lyrics. In both genres the musicians are building upon a musical technique that drew inspiration from Black work songs and spirituals, it's a cool way to highlight the importance of conversation and community. Which brings me to this song.

On the chorus Mary sings "share my world," which is followed by the harmonies of the instruments that almost feel like they're saying "yes" in affirmation to Mary's statement. Masterful if you ask me.

"I Can Love You" (featuring Lil' Kim) (1997)

On June 5, 2020, I tweeted a picture of two ladies stepping into their bags along with the words "mary j blige and lil kim making 'i can love you.'" I feel like that tweet perfectly describes this song and why it's so great. Those two were in their bags, and as a result of stepping into said bags made one of the greatest hip-hop tracks ever. On the song both of the women use their verses to lament men who are with someone else. Kim makes it clear she'll go to extreme lengths for her dude,* rapping "Under pressure, I lie for you, die for you / Ruger by the thigh for you, right hand high for you." When it's Mary's turn she makes it clear that she's the woman he should be with, harmonizing "I can love you a little better than she can." The themes of love and heartbreak are directly in line with her musical foremothers in R&B and soul, and Lil' Kim's verse is hip-hop to the core. And the beat? A sample of Lil' Kim's *Hard Core* track "Queen Bitch." They did that!

"MJB Da MVP" (2005)

Mary got on this jawn and talked her shit. Well, sang her shit. "'91, I stepped in this game / After 'What's the 411?' things ain't been the same" is what she sings at the top of the song, and for three minutes and twenty-one seconds Mary takes you on a journey through her career to remind you why she's considered royalty. My favorite part is when she sings, "Go 'head, envy me, I'm the soul hip-hop queen" before reminding you she isn't going anywhere. I saw her perform this song *live* in concert in 2022 and it was everything. She is the Queen of Hip-Hop Soul. And you better not ever forget it.

---

* The dude in question here is Biggie, evidenced by the "In love with you since the days of 'Juicy'" line.

YEAR 3000

MISSY ELLIOTT, THE FIRST WOMAN IN RAP TO GO TO THE FUTURE

This chapter on Missy Elliott was one of the very first chapters I wrote when I started the book. She's one of my favorite artists and one of the greatest musicians of all time. So when it was time to get to work on the book back in 2022, I devoted weeks in the library to rewatching all of her videos, replaying her albums and features, watching old interviews, and marveling at her outfits.

Because I wrote this chapter when I did, it's not centered around the history-making announcement that was made on May 3, 2023: that Missy was a member of the Rock & Roll Hall of Fame's 2023 class, making her the first woman rapper to be inducted and one of only three women to be inducted in their first year of eligibility.

I don't need to break down the history of rap in the Rock & Roll Hall of Fame or analyze the 2023 class. This chapter on Missy shows you exactly *why* she's more than deserving of this honor and whatever other ones come her way long after this book is published. Enjoy!

T ruth be told, I've never been to outer space and I might not be the best candidate for NASA or SpaceX. I'm claustrophobic, for one, and the sight of a spacecraft's tiny interior terrifies me. Then there's microgravity, which makes you literally just float up there. I don't know about you, but I like my feet to touch the ground, okay? Oh, and of course there's the whole I-have-no-idea-who-lives-out-here-or-on-any-of-these-other-planets thing. I'm not naive to the fact that there are likely other life-forms out there in the universe, but I would personally like to meet them formally in the comfort of my home planet. Not out and about in an endless void and vacuum. So yeah, physically going up there might not be it for me. But the idea is still very cool. Missy Elliott not only made it cool, but cemented the idea as important when she used her music to become the first woman in rap to take us out of this world.

This chapter has a lot of info in it. Honestly, probably more information in it than any of the other chapters in this book. I read a lot, wrote a lot, rewrote a lot, and then repeated the cycle over a span of twelve months. Because there is so much information, I've decided to treat this chapter like a class and break it down into sections. That way it will be easy to follow and digest, and you won't feel like I'm throwing a bunch of facts and definitions at you for pages on end. Plus, I've always wanted to teach a class, so why not pretend I'm doing it in my first book? The syllabus is as follows:

First Things First University

MISSY ELLIOTT WAS THE FIRST WOMAN IN RAP TO GO TO THE FUTURE 101

Class Meeting Time and Location
Whenever and wherever you're reading this book

Semester
Spring, Summer, Winter, and Fall

Nadirah Simmons

nadirahsimmons@youknowthisisafakeemail.com

No office hours :)

Course Description

In the simplest of terms, Black people use Afrofuturism as a means through which they can imagine alternate worlds, spaces, and places for Black people. In our day-to-day lives we consume art that is a product of Afrofuturism, and music is no exception. With the use of the philosophy in her music and videos, Missy Elliott created a means through which Black people, and more specifically Black women, could see themselves beyond the scope of what is real and in front of them. This course will take a brief look at Black artists' Afrofuturism and then look at some examples of Afrofuturism throughout Missy's career.

Course Goals

Students who complete this course successfully will have an understanding of both Afrofuturism and how important it is to Missy Elliott's music. They will be able to articulate the importance of Missy's use of Afrofuturism to Black women and how the philosophy has impacted music and culture as a whole. They will also be able to spot Afrofuturism in film, television, books, music, and all other media.

Required Texts

This book.

Daily Work/Homework

Read this book.

Assignments

Again, simply read this book. That's it.

Lesson Plan

Intro

Intro to Afrofuturism

When you examine how many sci-fi and fantasy TV shows or films you've seen, how many can you name that had a woman as the protagonist, or more specifically a Black woman? Only a handful, I am sure, because historically when speculative fiction and imaginative and futuristic concepts are portrayed in media they are often delivered through a white lens. A 2016 Vox study pointed out that "only 8% of the top grossing sci-fi and fantasy films featured a protagonist of color, half of which were played by Will Smith (*Hancock, I Am Legend, Independence Day, Men in Black*)." They added that there were less than twelve Black characters in the entire *Star Trek* franchise—on the original television series that premiered in the 1960s, Nichelle Nichols played the role of Uhura, making history as one of the first Black women on television to play a role that was not a stereotype. Zero in *The Jetsons*. Only one episode of *The Twilight Zone*, which I will argue is one of the greatest shows of all time, featured an all-Black principal cast.

Enter Afrofuturism. The term was first coined by cultural critic Mark Dery in the 1990s in his essay "Black to the Future," describing it as "speculative fiction that treats African American themes and addresses African American concerns in the context of the twentieth century technoculture—and, more generally, African American signification that appropriates images of technology and a prosthetically enhanced future."

There's another definition I want you to know too, and it's that of filmmaker and author Ytasha Womack. For her, Afrofuturism is an "intersection between black culture, technology, liberation, and the imagination, with some mysticism thrown in, too." (In fact it was through reading her book *Afrofuturism: The World of Black Sci-Fi and Fantasy Culture* that I learned Dr. Mae Jemison's outer-space aspirations were inspired by watching Lieutenant Uhura on TV.* How cool is that?)

Then there's Ashley Clarke, curatorial director at the Criterion Collection, who describes Afrofuturism as "the centering of the international black experience in alternate and imagined realities, whether fiction or documentary; past or present; science fiction or straight drama."

All of these definitions are important pieces to the puzzle that is understanding what Afrofuturism is. But if they are a little hard to remember as you keep reading, just remember this one common theme: Black people use Afrofuturism to imagine alternate worlds, spaces, and places and then place themselves there. And for Black women it means that much more.

Afrofuturism in Music

One of the earliest Afrofuturistic approaches to music dates back to Sun Ra in the 1950s. Ra led "The Arkestra," with whom he recorded music that used hard bop and modal elements, and crafted space-themed titles to reflect his connection of ancient African culture to the Space Age. To put it simply, he was light-years ahead of his time. Ha. There's also George Clinton, who alongside his Parliament-Funkadelic collective has fashion, live performances, albums, and songs like "Mothership Connection" to quite literally

---

* Dr. Mae Jemison became the first Black woman to go to space, in 1992 aboard the space shuttle Endeavor.

take fans out of this world. (I mean, he's literally emerged from his space vehicle the P-Funk Mothership while onstage. Come on now.)

Black women who made music before Missy were Afrofuturists too. Grace Jones's 1985 single "Slave to the Rhythm" is one of my favorite examples. The cover art, which features Grace with a high-top fade and an elongated mouth, looks like it's something out of another dimension. The synths on the beat of the song itself are enough to make you feel like you're transcending as you listen to it. And the video . . . To have your own head emerge out of the ground and then have a car drive out of your mouth is the kind of thing that can only happen in an imagined alternate world. There's also the trio LaBelle's* incorporation of Afrofuturism in their music and dress, notably sporting space-age outfits that blew what Judy Jetson wore out of the water.

You can of course look to hip-hop prior to the release of Missy's first album for Afrofuturism as well. Here are the two things I will say. First, I think sampling is Afrofuturistic. We've already talked about how technology and imagined futures are important parts of Afrofuturism. And since sampling in hip-hop is a process in which classic cuts are reimagined for a new era, I am of the belief that when our Black artists participate in this process they are practicing Afrofuturism. Second, OutKast's *ATLiens* is another great example and also so important. The album's title nodded to them feeling excluded and therefore "alien" in hip-hop because they were from Atlanta, and the video for the album's lead single, "Elevators (Me & You)," opens with the rap duo trekking through a blue and red earthlike planet followed by a crowd of people. Afrofuturism again. Now let's get to Missy.

---

* LaBelle released their single "Lady Marmalade" in 1974 and it was a hit, topping the Billboard Hot 100 chart. In 2001 a cover of the track was recorded for the *Moulin Rouge!* soundtrack. Produced by Missy Elliott and Rockwilder, the track featured Lil' Kim, Christina Aguilera, P!nk, and Mya. The song won the award for Best Pop Collaboration with Vocals at the 44th Annual Grammy Awards in 2002. It was Lil' Kim's first Grammy win.

Before she was a solo artist, Missy Elliott was a member of the R&B quartet Sista. The group signed to DeVante Swing of Jodeci's Swing Mob imprint and recorded an album titled *4 All the Sistas Around Da World*, which was shelved. (Thankfully you can stream it!) It's one of my favorite albums, and songs like "I Wanna Be Wit U" give you an early look at the undeniable talent of Elliott, who wrote, sang, and rapped on the album.* DeVante's artist roster, often referred to as Da Bassment, included names like Ginuwine, Playa, Tweet, and Timbaland. Timbaland and Missy met in their home state of Virginia, and when she went to record Sista's debut, Timbaland went too, joining Swing Mob and producing the R&B group's debut album. When the work environment became increasingly volatile and unhealthy under DeVante's leadership, Missy left Da Bassment.** She spent some time at home in Virginia to regroup and then decided to move to New York City, ready to get to work.

By the time Elliott's debut album, *Supa Dupa Fly*, was released in 1997—five years after Jemison's trip to space and three years after I was born—her experience as an artist and behind the scenes working on projects for Aaliyah, 702, and SWV made her more poised to make her impact on music. Produced solely by her friend and frequent collaborator Timbaland, the futuristic beats, muffled ad-libs, and warped effects on her debut album created a sound that was quite literally out of this world. *Supa Dupa Fly*'s first single, "The Rain (Supa Dupa Fly)," is infectious and electric, using the sample of Ann Peebles's 1974 track "I Can't Stand the Rain," and breathy exhales and thunder and chirping audio components to set the stage for what a vast, new, virtually

---

* You didn't ask me, but here are my favorite songs on the album that you should listen to: "Hit U Up," "Good Thang," and "Feel of Your Lips," the last of which features vocals from my girl Mary J. Blige.

** Sourced from Missy's episode of *Behind the Music*.

uninhabited planet would sound like if you happened upon it during a space expedition somewhere in the future.

The video for the track found Missy sporting the iconic blowup vinyl suit conceived by her longtime stylist and fashion icon June Ambrose. The look, exaggerated by the fish-eye lens of the legendary Hype Williams, was more than a simple departure from the mainstream look of rap at the time. It was alien . . . worlds away from what anyone else was doing and an affirmation that Missy, and anyone who came after her, could create without the restrictions of what hip-hop and music at-large was supposed to be at that moment. Without restrictions on who *she* was supposed to be at that moment. In a behind-the-scenes interview for the video, Missy echoed this sentiment, saying, "You're not gonna hear nothing on the radio like that. So it's like the year 2000. It's futuristic. The music that we make is futuristic." Music that literally *sounds* like it came from an imagined reality.

The video for "Sock It 2 Me" upped the stakes by placing Missy, Lil' Kim, Da Brat, and Timbaland on a planet in outer space where they are fleeing their alien robot attackers. It was the video for the third single, "Beep Me 911," that reimagined Missy, Magoo, and 702 as robotic dolls, staggering across illuminated backgrounds reminiscent of the Milky Way. Each video literally centers Black people in the future. What I wouldn't give to have been a fly on the wall when they were being made.

The Future in Missy's Career

Now we're at my favorite part of the class. We're going to examine some of the ways Missy Elliott took us to the future with her lyrics, production, and music videos.

Her Verse on Gina Thompson's "The Things That You Do (Bad Boy Remix)"

In a 2011 episode of the VH1 documentary television series *Behind the Music*, Missy Elliott detailed how her verse on Gina Thompson's

1996 single set off a chain reaction of events on the path to stardom. Diddy,* whom Missy had previously met through DeVante, saw her in the studio and asked her if she still rapped. She said yes and Diddy played her Thompson's record. She remembered being nervous, but also knew that this was her chance. It was through that passion and drive that fans got "hee-hee-hee-hee-haw," a masterful ad-lib that made Diddy and listeners alike say "Oooh" when they first heard it. It was nothing like anything they had heard before. (See where I'm going with this?)

The ad-libs didn't stop there, with Missy creating a bunch of sound effects throughout the duration of her verse. There's the "BRR-RRRRR-CLICK!" noise that she makes to mimic picking up her car phone and an audible squeaking noise that sounds like the chirp my Boost Mobile phone** had in the 2000s. Mind you, the year was 1996.

When a video of Lil Wayne stating how Missy's use of sound effects and ad-libs influenced his rapping circulated online, Missy tweeted:

> When i 1st came in the game people laughed at me doing sound effects in my music 😩 I used to cry when they clowned me but then I kept doing wild sounds/crazy adlibs in my songs & people began to rock wit it 🙌 Years later those same sound effects are big in songs today 🙌 🔥

Missy Elliott's lyrics and sound effects were ahead of their time. Literally.

~~~~~~~~~~

* I'm a nineties baby so he's Diddy to me.

** Do you remember Boost Mobile phones? They had a walkie-talkie feature that allowed you to "chirp" someone with a compatible phone within a six-mile radius and talk to them. They also had some of my favorite rappers like Ludacris and Eve do campaigns with them at their peak.

Her Work on "Beats 4 Da Streets (Intro)" from Aaliyah's *One in a Million*

Shortly after the release of Gina Thompson's single came Aaliyah's sophomore album, *One in a Million*. Atlantic Records hired Missy Elliott and Timbaland to write and produce on the album, and the music that they created was . . . well, let me have the chairman and CEO of Atlantic Records, Craig Kallman, tell it. When speaking about the album in the VH1 documentary that I mentioned, he said "The sound of the beats, the sound of the production, the writing, everything had its own unique flavor and was a dramatic contrast to what was on the radio at the time."

The songs that Missy and Timbaland worked on were innovative and became bona fide classics. But that intro is what I'm going to talk about at the moment. An introduction is when you get to see or become acquainted with something for the first time, and in the context of an album it's an important component that sets the tone for the songs that will follow it. Timbaland's production on "Beats 4 Da Streets (Intro)" features ambient noise and beeping effects that make the track sound like it was pulled directly from one of the opening scenes of *Star Trek*. Atop the beat Missy calmly speaks: "Aaliyah, Aaliyah, wake up / You just now entered into the next level / The new world of funk, as we do it one time."

A new world of funk. A. New. World. Need I say more?

The Video for "She's a Bitch"

I mentioned him already, but it would pretty much be an injustice for me to not talk about Hype Williams some more. He's a GOAT, and a person I could listen to talk about his career all day. He directed the movie *Belly* and some of the best music videos ever, like TLC's "No Scrubs," Jay-Z's "Big Pimpin'," and Busta Rhymes's "What's It Gonna Be?" The thing about Hype Williams's videos that I love so much is that they all feel like mini movies. For those three, four, or five minutes that

I'm watching his videos I feel like I'm being introduced to a new space and a cast of characters, given a problem and by the end of the video a resolution. They're cinematic. They tell a story. And they're a testament to the sheer genius that is director, screenwriter, and producer Hype Williams. It's only right that his genius should work with Missy's genius.

Funny story here. Hype originally met Missy on the set of Jodeci's "Feenin'" video. Hype was directing the video and Missy was there doing craft services, y'all, which basically means she was responsible for providing the artists and crew with snacks and drinks. Missy was still in Sista at the time, and neither she nor Hype had a clue that a few years down the line they would work together and make some of the most impactful music videos in history.

The video for "She's a Bitch" is so insane. To start with, it shits on basically every other video ever made. I'm serious. If you want to take out your phone or laptop while you read this part so you can follow along, be my guest. I'm the kind of teacher that's cool with it. And if not, don't worry, I'm still going to explain the video.

The shiny black chrome letters that introduce the video's director, artist, and song title immediately transport viewers to another dimension. We then see Missy in a room full of lights that remind me of *The Matrix*. This part is extra cool because not only were these lights flown in from Germany to build the set, they were also integrated into Missy's costume, making her light up just as much as the room did. Next, Missy's on a black set rocking a bald head and jewels on her face and wearing a full-body latex outfit complete with a cape—shout-out to June Ambrose on the fit and Billy B on the makeup!

Just when you think the video couldn't get any better, a few scenes later Missy and her dancers come up out of the water on top of a giant letter *M* and start dancing. This scene is black as well, and the addition of the dark clouds behind the ladies as they dance on top of this hydraulic *M* in the middle of this body of water is simply not something that was a product of 1999. No.

Missy celebrated the video on her Instagram a few years back and made it very clear where her mind was during this time. "I was in the year 3000 in 1999 ," she wrote. "This video changed things visually in HipHop videos FOREVER "

It did. And with a budget that was reportedly $2 million, we might not see anything like this again until the year 3000 *actually* rolls around.

The Beat for "Lose Control"

I have to talk about the beat for "Lose Control," the lead single from Missy's sixth studio album, *The Cookbook*.

The track, which features Ciara and Fatman Scoop, samples "Clear" by Cybotron and "Body Work" by 1980s band Hot Streak. The beat is electric and infectious, so much so that whenever I hear it I just let my body relinquish control to the music. It's everything that I've talked about so far. Perfectly Afrofuturistic.

The video for the song, directed by Dave Meyers, won the award for Best Short Form Music Video at the 48th Annual Grammy Awards. We're going to talk about his work with Missy next.

The Video for "Pass That Dutch"

Dave Meyers directed, as the *Atlantic* put it in 2017, "some of the most iconic videos of the 2000s." And one of my favorites is "Pass That Dutch." In a 2003 interview with *MTV News* Dave talked about his creative process for the video. "Every time she calls, she demands to be totally different," he said. "In addition to trying to keep up with her growth, I have to reinvent my wheel every time. She loves having a dance element, so we always find new ways to do innovative things around dance."

Dave had already directed the videos for Missy's "Work It," "Get Ur Freak On," and "One Minute Man" by the time he got asked to do "Pass That Dutch." And if we're going off of his track record alone, then it was guaranteed to be fire before it was even shot.

Missy came to the call with a few things she was certain of: the album was militant and she wanted some black outfits and Riverdancing in the video. From there it was what Dave would describe as "very stream-of-consciousness," and when the finished product hit TV screens Missy was set in a postapocalyptic society recovering from the "unknown virus that's attacking all clubs" that Missy mentions at the top of the song. It was militant. There were black outfits. There was Riverdancing—in a crop circle under the light of an unidentified flying object, might I add. Plus, the video closes with Missy standing on top of a building like King Kong. But when asked about those final scenes Dave told *MTV News* he wasn't actually trying to reference the 1933 film. Nope: "It was more about Missy being on top of the world." On top of the world, and in a universe far out of it too.

One Last Thing

I know we're at the end of class, but I'm so hype that I'm just going to keep talking in the hope that you don't have anywhere to be and can stick around for a few more minutes.

There is no artist out there like Missy and I say this with 100 percent conviction because she can do it all: rap, sing, write, produce, direct, and so much more. If there were more time, I'd talk about more of the artists she's worked with like Janet Jackson, Whitney Houston, Beyoncé, Fantasia, Monica, Tweet, and Mary J. Blige, to name just a few. Or I'd talk about how when she signed her deal it also included her own label, the Goldmind Inc. Or I'd go into all of the accolades, including multiple Grammys, the MTV Video Vanguard Award, a Songwriters Hall of Fame induction, honorary doctorates, her own street, and a nomination to` the Rock & Roll Hall of Fame. Or I'd talk about how she has some of the most inspirational tweets of all time. Or I'd talk about how her sheer existence inspired a generation to think outside the box. But like I said, there's not enough time. So I'll leave you with this: thank you, Missy, for taking us to the future!

GANGSTA BOO, THE FIRST LADY OF CRUNK MUSIC

started working on this chapter a few days before Gangsta Boo, born Lola Mitchell, passed away on January 1, 2023. I told myself I wasn't going to write or work on or even think about the book for a few days during the holiday season, but "Wanna Go to War"* came on shuffle and I couldn't help myself. I *had* to put at least a few words on paper, even if the only words that came at the time were: "Chapter ?: Gotta talk about Gangsta Boo." After the song went off, I turned on Latto's "FTCU," a track featuring Gangsta Boo and her fellow Memphis rapper Glorilla that was released exactly one month before Boo passed. Both Latto and Glorilla, two rappers from the South, have spoken openly about their love for Boo. So when "Where Dem Dollas At" came on shuffle I couldn't ignore the voice in my head telling me there should be a chapter about Gangsta Boo. The woman who joined

---

* This song this song this SONG! The way it kicks off is crazy. It features a haunting beat produced by Juicy J and DJ Paul over which Gangsta Boo repeats the words "Wanna go to war wit me baby? This gangsta bitch can get crazy. Don't you deceive this lady. Don't fuckin' play wit me baby." It's HARD, exists in the collection of horrorcore rap that Boo and Three 6 helped shape, and really let listeners know that she was not the one to go to war with. One of my favorite songs by her.

Three 6 Mafia when she was just a teenager. The woman who influenced a generation of rappers and was a pioneer from the South. The woman who deemed herself the "First Lady of Crunk Music" in a 2012 interview with the blog *Passion of the Weiss*.

Before we go any further, though, it's important to say just what crunk music is. So here's a really simple explanation, courtesy of MasterClass: "Insistent, jarring synths, club beats generated by drum machines, and shouted call-and-response vocals anchor this Southern hip-hop subgenre."

Gangsta Boo rapped under the name Tinkerbell when her rhymes were, in her words, more positive and had no curse words. After her parents divorced, she told *Yahoo* in 2013 that "she moved to the hood" with her mom and changed her rap name to Suicide. She later became inspired by the Memphis rappers who had Gangsta in their name, so Mitchell combined that word with the nickname "Boo," which her aunt used to call her. Gangsta Boo was born. What a cool-ass name.

She used to call people's phones and rap on their answering machines as well as perform in talent shows. Her skills caught the ear of Three 6 Mafia's DJ Paul, with whom she went to junior high school, and he put her on his mixtape *Volume 16 "4 Da Summer of '94"* on a track called "Cheefa Da Reefa."* She would soon join the group. And when Three 6 dropped their debut album in 1995, Gangsta Boo was only fifteen years old. Fifteen and rapping *that well*? See why I love this part?

Her solo debut album, *Enquiring Minds*, came out three years later in 1998, and the songs on the album confirmed what was already clear: Gangsta Boo was in a league of her own. On her songs she rapped over really hard beats and called out to her listeners with a special kind of confidence and braggadocio that defined her music.

~~~~~~~~

* In an interview with *Billboard* in 2022 it was noted that "Cheefa Da Reefa" was the first solo song she recorded with Three 6 Mafia.

She easily infused her rap style on tracks with themes of all kinds, like songs about sex like "Suck a Little Dick," songs about relationships like "I'll Be the Other Woman," songs about straight-up fighting like "Wanna Go to War," and songs about getting to the cash like her hit "Where Dem Dollars At." Every single song was crunk, but when I think about the impact of that last one in particular, I can't sum it up better than Zandria F. Robinson did for NPR in 2020: the song "is the template for cash-as-women's-agency that reverberates throughout subsequent women rappers' work, from Trina to Megan Thee Stallion to Cardi B, as laborers in the music industry."

Her story doesn't end at "Where Dem Dollars At" either. She appeared on OutKast's classic album *Stankonia* on a track called "I'll Call B4 I Cum" and the Foxy Brown track "BWA," a track from *Chyna Doll* that also featured her sister in southern rap Mia X. Gangsta Boo released her second album, *Both Worlds *69*, in 2001, after which she left Three 6 Mafia and dropped her third album, *Enquiring Minds II: The Soap Opera*, in 2003. She was just twenty-one years old when she left the group, telling *Red Bull Music Academy* in 2013 that she was in a dark state and wanted to pull herself "closer to the light." She became more spiritual and even changed her name to Lady Boo for a period of time before reverting to Gangsta Boo and briefly reuniting with some of the original members of Three 6 Mafia to release an album as a new group name Da Mafia 6ix. In addition to all this she dropped a bunch of mixtapes and projects, including the 2014 EP *Witch* with fellow Memphis rapper and friend La Chat,* appeared on a Yelawolf track alongside Eminem, and collaborated with Run the Jewels.

But wait, there's more! Everything about Boo you can hear in music today, and not only in women rappers from Memphis like

* La Chat joined the Hypnotized Minds camp, a label started by Three 6 Mafia's DJ Paul and Juicy J. Her major-label debut, *Murder She Spoke*, sold over 100,000 copies and features the pulsing track "You Ain't Mad Iz Ya." Press play on that song later.

Glorilla and Gloss Up, but in rappers from the South as a whole and in men and women who rap, period. She didn't call herself "The Boo-Print,"* a play on the word blueprint, for no reason. "I would honestly say that I have to admit, respectfully and humbly, that I am the blueprint. I hear my cadence in a lot of men and female rappers," she told *Billboard* in 2022. "I used to run away from it. I used to didn't want to even give myself flowers because I've been so low-key and humble, but I'm on some f— that s—. It's time to claim what's mine. I'm one of the main b—." I'm sure you can fill in the blanks.

I rounded up some of Boo's crunkest lines for you to read and learn from. Maybe you'll learn the same thing I did the first time I heard them, or you'll think something *completely* different. That's what makes it fun.

When Gangsta Boo rapped, "What you do know won't hurt you in the long run" on "Don't Stand So Close," **I learned something very important**: that it's sometimes beneficial to know the truth instead of running from it. I also learned that it's good to deviate from the norm. People are always saying what you know won't hurt you, but, and follow me here, sometimes the stuff you don't know is hurting you more than you could ever know. So yeah. Don't be afraid to know the truth, it might make you feel better.

When Gangsta Boo rapped, "We be the roughest, my team be the buckest, my team be the quickest" on "Oh No," **I actually didn't interpret this line as** being ready to fight, as I'm sure many people did. No. Actually, I took this line by Boo to mean your crew should quite literally be rough, buck, and quick, on the off chance that you need to muscle your way to the front of a concert

---

* Gangsta Boo was also working on an album that she planned to title *The Boo-Print* at the time of her death.

venue if you see a space open up. I'm short. Like, really short. So having a group of friends who possess these qualities is important.

When Gangsta Boo rapped, "They say a gangsta ain't 'posed to cry, when I'm sheddin' tears and I'm a gangsta until I die" on "Love Don't Live (U Abandoned Me)," **I was reminded** that no matter how "hard" or "strong" you might be, it's okay to cry. A simple concept that's often hard to grasp. The reminder is good.

When Gangsta Boo rapped, "Why you up in the club wit no money, trying to see a little ass?" on "Can I Get Paid (Get Your Broke Ass Out)," **I actually laughed out loud** because an image immediately popped into my head of some lame at a strip club spending no bread. Boo might not have been talking about the strip club here, but that's where my mind went. And because that's where my mind went, I just want to say, if you go to the strip club, support the ladies and pay!

When Gangsta Boo rapped, "Badder than a school of kids, ages one through fuckin' six" on "This Is Personal," **she took me back** to my days at summer camp, where there were kids of all ages. The young ones often got into a bit of trouble for being "bad," but they actually weren't doing anything other than what kids do, and that's being kids! Having fun and making decisions without the arbitrary expectations or rigid boundaries we place upon ourselves as we get older simply because we think we have to. In fact some of the things we think are bad actually aren't, like staying in my pajamas all day, for example. Gangsta Boo reminded me of this.

When Gangsta Boo rapped, "Or is you copycattin' the Boo because you want it like that? You cannot get it like that" on Project Pat's "Ballers," **she affirmed something** I've always thought:

being as original as possible is always going to be more rewarding than being a copycat. I mean honestly, who likes being a copycat anyway? I can't imagine feeling good about biting an idea that didn't come from you. Like she said, you cannot get it like that.

When Gangsta Boo rapped, "Catch me off in Gucci sheets. Sleeping living luxury" on "M-Town Representatives," **she let me know** to treat myself every once in a while. The treat is not going to be some luxurious Gucci sheets, though. An acai bowl is a treat enough for my pockets and me.

When Gangsta Boo rapped, "Still gonna keep it real, still gonna get a deal. Still got my niggas looking trill with the gold grill" on "We Ain't Playin'," **she stressed the importance of community**. Basically, be yourself, get your bag, and take care of your people too. Read that last line again.

And when Gangsta Boo rapped, "Time to get real crunk, time to tear the club up" on Lil Jon & the East Side Boyz's "Move Bitch," **she shouted out the genre of which she proclaimed herself the first lady**. She also let me know it's cool to go out and party and have a really good time. Remember what I said about going to those parties where people stand on the wall? None of that was happening here. Not on the First Lady of Crunk Music's watch. Rest in peace, Gangsta Boo.

TRINA, DA (FIRST AND ONLY) BADDEST B****

I can't remember the first time I heard "Look Back at Me," but I do know it's a song that my best friend and I rapped and danced to together on more than a hundred occasions in undergrad. The Trina track, which features Killer Mike, is a raw and raunchy cut that is quite literally about looking back at your partner while you're having sex with them, and, as I'm sure you can imagine, encouraged a lot of twerking and grinding when it came on at the famous student center parties Rutgers was known for.* Those parties were the first time I really turned up the way I wanted to. I was in *college*. And college meant no curfew. No chaperones. No censored music. Just the freedom to dance and rap and dress how *I* wanted to. And Trina's song about her sexuality and pleasure was the perfect background music

---

* This is a shout-out to all of my Rutgers–New Brunswick homies. If you attended the school or visited the campus and hung out with the Black students you definitely went to a student center party on more than one occasion and you *know* they got crazy. Apparently they were more lit before I got there in 2012, and I can definitely say they dropped off sometime around the end of my junior year. But man, when they were lit they were *really* lit.

for those liberating moments. But what else would you expect from "Da (First and Only) Baddest B****"?

"Look Back at Me" appeared on Trina's fourth studio album, *Still Da Baddest*, released in 2008. The album was a reminder that she was indeed still "Da Baddest B****," a moniker that was also the title of her debut album and debut single. But don't get it twisted: being "Da Baddest B****" wasn't simply about having your hair and your makeup and looking good. Nah. For Trina, it meant being "confident, uplifting . . . eager to get out and work and make it happen and achieve your goal[s]," as she explained in a 2022 interview with Pandora. This confidence and eagerness inspired Trina to set out to get her real estate license, and she was literally about to sell a home when she got a request from her friend Trick Daddy. Trick, whom Trina had first met in the Liberty City neighborhood of Miami, wanted her to lay a verse on "Nann N****."

In a 2023 episode of NPR Music's *Louder Than a Riot* podcast, Trina told hosts Sidney Madden and Rodney Carmichael that she went to the studio with her girls, and after some convincing from Trick she agreed to do the verse. Trina asked Trick and all of the guys with him to leave the room and went to work on her rhymes—she was nervous. "They was like, yeah, you got to say that. I was like, no, I'm going to say this. No, say this," Trina said, recounting that night in the studio. "And I was like, should I say this? That's too nasty. They was like, no, that's perfect. I—my friends, I have the nine-to-fivers, and I have the all-nighters. So in a balance of both of them, there you go. That's how the verse came."

"Nann N****," released in 1998, was a hit, made all the more stellar by her verse. From there it was on. Trina signed with Miami-based label Slip-N-Slide Records, which was also home to Trick

Daddy, and got to work on *Da Baddest B*****. The album dropped in 2000, and on it Trina upped the ante on the raunchy rap lyrics of the women who came before her, using her bars to let the girls know how to get down in the bedroom and get to the money at the same time. In the NPR episode Sidney Madden said, "Trina was giving game because, to her, it wasn't just about promoting sexual freedom but financial freedom, too. Those two ideals were intertwined." It's that combination that epitomizes the confident and uplifting nature of Trina's persona as "Da Baddest B****," and also places her at the front of a very long line of women rappers who infused her style and lyrics into their music.

In 2012, *XXL* magazine named Trina the "most consistent female rapper of all-time," citing her output of albums as rare in the realm of women in rap. At the time that I'm writing this, she has released a total of six studio albums, the most recent being 2019's *The One*. For context, Missy Elliott has released a total of six studio albums and Queen Latifah has released a total of seven studio albums—two of which are jazz albums.[*] For Trina to have an output that matches some of the most important women emcees is not only a testament to the impact of her rhymes on multiple generations but also cements her status as an icon in rap. Yes, I said icon.

Trina was the recipient of the I Am Hip-Hop Icon award at the 2022 BET Hip-Hop Awards and was honored with her own day in Miami. That's right, every May 14 in

THE BIRTHPLACE OF THE BADDEST B****

[*] Again, Queen Latifah can really do it all!

Miami is "Trina Day." Her impact is large. And with *Da Baddest B***** being the starting point in Trina's solo career, there's no denying that the influence of the album, the single, and the nickname are all over the ladies in rap today.

I haven't done a Venn diagram yet in this book, so I've decided to do a few here. I feel like that's the easiest way to show the influence of Trina's "Da Baddest B****" persona. Remember, in order to be "Da Baddest B****," you have to be confident and eager, which Trina showed clearly when she intertwined lyrics about sex and getting to the bag. All right, let's look at some Venn diagrams!

Venn Diagram #1

TRINA

Make it quick, then slow head by the night stand

Like lightning, I wanna nigga with a wedding ring

—"Da Baddest B****" by Trina (1999)

BOTH

Getting head (and later on the song getting bread)

LATTO

First I make him eat it 'til he lockjaw

Give it to him good, knock a nigga socks off, uh

—"B**** from Da Souf" by Latto (2019)

The influence of Trina's track "Da Baddest B****" is all over Latto's single celebrating her region, "B**** from Da Souf." Latto is confident when she raps about the oral pleasure she wants to receive, much like Trina is about the pace of what she's getting by the nightstand. Right after that both ladies jump straight into the money. Trina will find a dude with some hefty bank accounts to cut them checks, rapping "Bank accounts in the Philippines / Blank note to take everything," while Latto's bag only gets larger in the midst of chitchat from detractors: "I run it up, they busy running they mouth." When Trina hopped on the "B**** from Da Souf" remix—which also features Saweetie—it only made sense.

Venn Diagram #2

TRINA

I'm da baddest bitch you got to admit that

69 ways? You know I went that!

And I'mma shake my money maker

—"Pull Over" by Trina (2000)

BOTH

Reclaiming terms that are often deemed derogatory toward women and making cash with their likenesses and assets. On *their* terms.

MEGAN THEE STALLION

Hands on my knees, shakin' ass, on my thot shit

Post me a pic, finna make me a profit

—"Thot Shit" by Megan Thee Stallion (2021)

"Pull Over" is one of my favorite Trina tracks. I remember hearing it on the radio growing up, and the image of Trina dancing on the beach in the music video always pops into my head when I think about videos from my childhood. The premise of the song is that Trina's butt is "too fat," so much so that it warrants being pulled over. Trick Daddy can be heard mimicking sirens on the chorus with his repetition of the words "whoop whoop." When we get to the third verse of the track, Trina affirms herself as "Da Baddest B****" and continues her reclamation of the word "b****," while also making it clear that her assets make money too. The same tone is reflected on Texas-bred rapper Megan Thee Stallion's "Thot Shit." When asked by a fan on Twitter why she made the track, Meg responded, "I'm really just talking shit and taking ownership of the words 'thot' and 'hoe' bc they're not the drag the men think it is when trying to come at women for doing them 🙍🏽‍♀️" Trina tells listeners she is "Da Baddest B****" and Meg embraces turning up on her "thot sh*t." Trina raps that she's going to shake her money maker, and Meg spits about making bread simply by posting a picture of herself online.

Venn Diagram #3

TRINA

Slob on a nigga

Take all his dough and then I dodge a nigga

—"Nasty B****" by Trina (2001)

BOTH

Without being too graphic here, just know the ladies are talented enough in the bedroom to get a man to come up off his money.

CITY GIRLS

Suck the soul out you

Rodeo show, get the bankrolls out you

—"Rodeo" by City Girls (2020)

One of my favorite hip-hop fun facts is that Trina is godmother to Yung Miami. Trina and Yung Miami's mom, Keenya, grew up together and hung out in the same spots in the city. In fact, Trina's mom used to do Keenya's hair. Their friendship manifested into a declaration that Katrina would be godmother to Yung Miami, and that's basically how it happened.

Now, obviously I can make all the connections in the world to Trina and women in rap today because the influence is clear, but one of the easiest lines to draw is between Trina and the City Girls. All of the ladies are from Miami, there's a familial connection between one of the City Girls and Trina, and much of their music has that Miami bass sound. "Nasty B****" is, well, nasty, as I'm sure you can glean from the lyrics I put in the Venn diagram. "Rodeo" by the City Girls is too, with the song standing firm in Trina's legacy of intertwining sexual pleasure with financial achievement. We might not hear Yung Miami rap that her rodeo show will "get the bankrolls out you" if it weren't for her godmother.

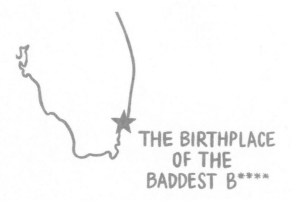

THE BIRTHPLACE
OF THE
BADDEST B****

NICKI MINAJ, THE FIRST WOMAN RAPPER TO COMPLETELY DEMOLISH TWO GOATED MEN ON A TRACK

I don't really remember when I first discovered Nicki Minaj because she's one of those artists I feel like has always been around. What I *do* know is that the first songs I heard by Minaj were "Itty Bitty Piggy" and "I Get Crazy." The latter I remember rapping in the mirror in the bathroom while I was supposed to be taking a shower—I used to let the mirrors fog up like crazy. Both songs appeared on her mixtape *Beam Me Up Scotty*, which dropped while I was a freshman in high school. She captivated what seemed to be everyone with her rhymes, from kids to adults to industry veterans alike because she was creative with her lyrics, animated onstage and in the booth, and last but certainly not least, talented beyond measure. So when she appeared on the Kanye West track "Monster" in 2010 alongside Jay-Z, Kanye West, and Rick Ross, it was a testament to her skills and the adoration of her fellow rappers, two of whom are widely considered to be among, if not *the*, greatest to ever do it. And let me be the one to say it: she outshined both of them. In fact, it was the first time a woman rapper completely demolished two goated men on a track.

Before we get to "Monster," though, I need you to be very clear about who Nicki Minaj is. Born in Trinidad and Tobago and raised in South Jamaica, Queens, Nicki was destined to be a star. As a teenager she auditioned for admission to Fiorello H. LaGuardia High School of Music & Art and Performing Arts, where students pursue their talents in art or music while completing the academic curriculum. "I sucked @ my singing audition for Performing Arts HS & I was crying & walking out the door," Minaj tweeted in 2022. "My mthr [sic] had to get rlly [sic] stern w|me so that I went back inside & did my drama audition & they ended up loving me. If she gave me a pity party that day I would've LEFT & never known. . . . " Nicki was accepted into the school, and after graduation pursued a career in acting, even being cast in the off-Broadway play *In Case You Forget* in 2001. But it wasn't long before music took its place at the forefront.

She joined the rap group the HoodStars—whose song "Don't Mess With" appeared on the 2004 WWE compilation album *ThemeAddict: WWE the Music, Vol. 6*—before setting out to chart a path of her own in the genre. Her debut mixtape, *Playtime Is Over*, dropped in 2007 and two years later she was signed to Lil Wayne's Young Money label. In an essay accompanying Minaj's appearance on *Time*'s 100 Most Influential People list in 2016, Wayne remembered watching Nicki rap on a DVD and being so impressed by her bars. He wrote that "it wasn't even about her rapping better than any female rapper," but instead that she was "rapping better than other rappers—period."

What Wayne said was right, and Nicki's talent showed in her sales, features, and influence. When Minaj released her debut album, *Pink Friday*, in 2010 she moved 375,000 copies the first week and took the No. 2 spot on the Billboard 200 chart.* It was the second-best album sales week for a woman in rap right after Ms. Lauryn Hill,

---

* Kanye West took the No.1 spot, selling 496,000 copies of his album *My Beautiful Dark Twisted Fantasy.*

whose album *The Miseducation of Lauryn Hill* debuted at No. 1 with 423,000 copies sold in its first week in 1998. The three albums that followed *Pink Friday*—*Pink Friday: Roman Reloaded, The Pinkprint,* and *Queen*—all went platinum. She also collaborated with some of the biggest artists in the game, like Beyoncé, Mariah Carey, Rihanna, Usher, and of course Drake and Lil Wayne (and left no crumbs, might I add). Nearly every young woman in rap who has come up after her has cited her as an influence, and in 2022, fifteen years after she released her first mixtape, she received her first solo No. 1 single when "Super Freaky Girl" rose to the top of the Billboard Hot 100 chart. An achievement that was long overdue.[*]

Despite the tardiness of the delivery of some of the many achievements Nicki should have, she has remained ahead of the pack with one crucial element: her performance. On tracks, Nicki shifts between speeds and incorporates alter egos. She raps with accents and delivers punch lines with precision and power. Her lyrics are creative, fun, and witty. Nicki is a *performer* on the mic, and without knowing that Nicki studied acting in high school or that she was a music lover since she was a kid, you might not fully grasp how destined she was to become an innovator and legend in the rap game. And if you don't fully grasp *that*, then you won't really understand why she smoked Hov and Ye on "Monster." But since you do know, we're ready to talk about the song.

Now, to be clear, I'm not saying that there has never been an instance before "Monster" where a woman rapper lyrically bested a man on a song. Music is subjective, of course, but there have been many, many, many instances, to me. Take "Knuck If You Buck," for example. Everyone killed their verses, but we'd be dishonest if we acted like Princess and Diamond's rhymes didn't outshine everyone

---

[*] "Super Bass" and "Anaconda" should have gone to the top of the charts. Both songs are so creative and innovative and you couldn't go anywhere without hearing them when they dropped. Still can't.

else's. Second, I'm also not saying there has never been a song on which a woman had a verse better than a GOAT of any gender expression. It has happened more times than I can count. Again, many, many, many instances. And last but certainly not least, I'm not saying it can't happen again. In fact, I would love for it to happen again. What I *am* saying is that out of all the songs that I have heard featuring two men who are considered rap GOATs and one woman, *this* is the first one where a woman absolutely demolished their verses. She didn't just rap better than them. She didn't just have a more entertaining verse. She didn't just have the most memorable lines. She took their verses, nicely packaged them, sprayed some perfume on the box, and returned them to the senders.

To try to make this point as clear as possible, I picked five moments from Nicki, Hov, and Kanye's verses and assigned each set to a round. I can't write them all in here, but you can follow along on your favorite lyric website. And as with any game, the person with the most points wins. Simple enough.

THE "MONSTER" MATCHUP

★ ★ ★ ★ ★ ROUND 1 ★ ★ ★ ★ ★

JAY-Z: Hov opens his verse rapping about mythical creatures and monsters like Sasquatch and the Loch Ness Monster.

──────── VS. ────────

KANYE WEST: Kanye starts off his verse by proclaiming he's the best to ever do it, dead or alive. Simple.

──────── VS. ────────

NICKI MINAJ: Nicki begins her verse by letting you know she's pulling up in a gangsta, monster-sized automobile accompanied by a bad chick from Sri Lanka.

Results: As much as people have made jokes about the way **JAY-Z** opens this song, I actually like it. It's pretty funny to me and is very much on theme. **KANYE**'s opening line is different from Hov's in that he starts off real braggadocious, and to be honest I would have if I was him at that moment in time too. The way **NICKI** kicks off her verse always puts an image in my head of her in a pink wig pulling up in a big-ass monster truck. If she's pulling up in a monster automobile then it has to be big, right? *Genius* says that the second line is about her friend Sri Lankan rapper M.I.A. But the reason I love it is that somehow she rhymed "gangsta" with "Sri Lanka." **ONE POINT FOR NICKI.**

★ ★ ★ ★ ★ ROUND 2 ★ ★ ★ ★ ★

JAY-Z: We're five lines into his verse, and at this point Jay's calling out other rappers' "silly nonsense," as well as asserting that they don't know where the swamp is. Here, the swamp likely serves as a metaphor for the neighborhoods he grew up in.

——————————— VS. ———————————

KANYE WEST: Kanye keeps up the braggadocio in his bars, this time proclaiming that his talent is unmatched: he can produce the track and rap on it. He compares his skills to that of a basketball player getting a triple-double with no assists.

——————————— VS. ———————————

NICKI MINAJ: Nicki continues her car talk, now asserting that she's in a Tonka truck the color of Willy Wonka. After that she makes it clear that she's the queen and she's here to conquer it all.

RESULTS: A good bar from **JAY-Z**, letting other rappers know they are in fact not monsters like they may have thought they were.

For **KANYE**, I had to ask one of my friends what a triple-double was because my basketball knowledge doesn't extend that far. I learned that it's when a player puts up double-digit numbers (at least 10) in three of the five major statistical categories. He told me it's very good. Then he started talking about how badly he wants the 76ers to make it to a championship. Kanye is reminding you who he is again, using a basketball metaphor to make it clear that no one can do what he can do let alone as much as he can do. It's cool.

NICKI confirms that she was indeed in a truck, and while I'm not quite sure what she meant by the color of Willy Wonka, I'm more captivated by her staking her claim as a queen right out of the gate. This round is a bit tougher than the first one, because Kanye's triple-double bars put up a good fight against Nicki's lyrics. However, Nicki's prophetic assertion of her queendom as a new artist on a track with two veteran rap kings has the edge. **ANOTHER POINT FOR NICKI.**

★ ★ ★ ★ ROUND 3 ★ ★ ★ ★ ★

JAY-Z: He raps about seeing dudes he's made millionaires milling around and sharing their feelings in the atmosphere—he specifically says "in the air." More on that below.

——————— VS. ———————

KANYE WEST: He raps that he's a dude from the Chi—short for Chicago—who still gets love for his accent.

——————— VS. ———————

NICKI MINAJ: Nicki raps some of the things she's heard from her haters, including lines about her character and her being on a diet. That second part she follows up with a proclamation her pockets are eating cheesecake.

RESULTS: JAY-Z's wordplay here is pretty impeccable. Many of us have assumed Hov was talking to Beanie Sigel, who was signed to the label the Brooklyn rapper cofounded with Dame Dash and Kareem "Biggs" Burke, Roc-A-Fella Records. Beans is one of my favorite rappers ever, and he has a song titled "Feel It in the Air" that also happens to be one of my favorite rap songs ever. The two were not on good terms at this point, though they appeared to have made up when

Beanie Sigel joined Jay-Z onstage for a surprise appearance at Jay-Z's "B-Sides" show in 2015. There are a bunch of other people Hov could have been talking about too, but those last few lines always make me think of Beans.

Ye's wordplay here is amazing as well. "Chi" sounds like "shy," and **KANYE** is basically saying that even though he's shy he still gets play and the ladies love his midwestern accent. It's a great use of homophones: words that sound the same but differ in their meaning or spelling.

Then there's **NICKI**, who starts rattling off the comments of her detractors in a high-pitched tone before seamlessly jumping in to set them straight. To hear her say her pockets were *eating*, and that they were eating *cheesecake* at that? Whew. She wanted you to know that they were really full and she was really paid. That was really historic.

This might have been the hardest one to pick because each of these lines is the perfect representation of the artist who rapped it. Everyone gets a point if you want me to be honest. And if everyone gets a point, then that just means **ANOTHER POINT FOR NICKI MINAJ.**

★ ★ ★ ★ ★ **ROUND 4** ★ ★ ★ ★ ★

JAY-Z: Hov basically calls out all of the fake people out there and raps that they have no fangs.

———————— **VS.** ————————

KANYE WEST: Ye lets listeners know about a woman who gave him her number and told him to use it if he wants to demote his current chick to number two and make her his new number one.

———————— **VS.** ————————

NICKI MINAJ: Minaj invokes the film *Bride of Chucky* here, proclaiming that it's "child's play" the way she kills careers.

RESULTS: My favorite **JAY-Z**, as I'm sure you've figured out by now, is the subtle-shot-sending Jay-Z. It makes me laugh! So him getting on a song called "Monster" and affirming that he is indeed a monster while the other rappers don't even have fangs? So funny to me.

KANYE really can do no wrong on this song when it comes to letting you know he is **that dude**. So much, in fact, that he's got women coming up to him trying to take his girl's spot.

Bride of Chucky is the fourth film in the *Child's Play* franchise, a series of movies whose main antagonist is a serial-killing Good Guy Doll. **NICKI**'s getting her shit off here, rapping in a whole different pitch and her capping it off by saying she's literally killing someone's career with ease makes it that much better. I don't think I need to tell you who wins here, but I have been doing so the entire chapter so who am I to switch things up now? **THE POINT GOES TO NICKI.**

★ ★ ★ ★ ★ ROUND 5 ★ ★ ★ ★ ★

JAY-Z: This is the end of his verse, and all you really need to know is that Jay-Z sniffs before rapping that he smells a massacre.

———————— **VS.** ————————

KANYE WEST: Ye closes his verse by declaring that he is from the future, so the present for him is actually the past. He follows that up with a reminder that his presence, his sheer existence, is a present.

———————— **VS.** ————————

NICKI MINAJ: Near the end of her verse Nicki lets you know who she is, from her hair and her curves to her ambition and ability to turn heads, she is the one. Not the two.

RESULTS: Why is **JAY-Z** so funny? Did he seriously have to sniff before saying he smelled a massacre? Anyway, I like the way he closes out his verse.

I would be filthy rich if I got a single dollar for each instance I have seen or heard someone say that their presence was a present over the years. The other line is just as fire, because a lot of **KANYE**'s career has been marked by him truly being ahead of his time. If anything I wish he had the foresight to not do some of the stuff he's done in recent years. But I digress. A great closer.

NICKI mentioning her pink wig and ability to think big, her "thick ass" and propensity to make cash is amazing. The rhyme scheme? The performance? The cadence? The word selection? This right here is a master class. **A POINT FOR NICKI.**

TOTAL POINTS FOR NICKI MINAJ: 5
NICKI'S THE OBVIOUS WINNER HERE.

"Monster" helped cement Nicki's position as a rap force to be reckoned with before her debut album even dropped. And it *still* rings off today. But you simply cannot be surprised. A lot has happened since then too. Record-breaking releases and big brand deals with the likes of Maxim and *Call of Duty*. The formation of her own record label, Heavy On It. The achievement of her first No. 1 on the Billboard Hot 100 with the track "Super Freaky Girl." There's also the beefs with other ladies in rap, including Lil' Kim, Remy Ma, and Cardi B, and discussions around the power of her fan base, the Barbz, on the internet. So much.

What I do know for sure, though, is that I'll always have the memory of hearing her verse on "Monster" for the first time and seeing everyone, everywhere, rap it. In fact, I bet if you were to open your window and start blasting "Monster" right now, there would be a crowd of people outside rapping every single word. I'm not advising you to do that, though. I don't know what the noise ordinances are where you live and I want no parts in getting you jammed up for playing music too loud.

Nicki Minaj Lyric(s) Libs

I don't know anyone else on this planet who can rhyme "gangsta" with "Sri Lanka," but that's what makes Nicki so damn good. There are a few Nicki lyrics with specific words **bolded**. Try your best to come up with two lines making those words rhyme, and tweet me your best lyrics!

I get the thumbs up like I'm hailin' a **yellow cab**
My flow nuts like M&M's in the **yellow bag**

_____ **yellow cab**

_____ **yellow bag**

—"Up Out My Face (Remix)" by Mariah Carey ft. Nicki Minaj

I'm hotter than, a hundred **degrees**
A lot of bread, no **sesame seeds**

_____ **degrees**

_____ **sesame seeds**

—"Lil' Freak" by Usher ft. Nicki Minaj

Yo, I'm in that big boy, bitches can't **rent this**
I floss every day, but I ain't a **dentist**

_____ **rent this**

_____ **dentist**

—"Truffle Butter" by Nicki Minaj ft. Lil Wayne and Drake

I was on the plane with **Dwayne**
You can call me Whitley, I go to **Hillman**

_____ **Dwayne**

_____ **Hillman**

—"Itty Bitty Piggy" by Nicki Minaj

"PRINT / RADIO"

Interlude

DANYEL SMITH, THE FIRST BLACK PERSON AND FIRST WOMAN TO BE EDITOR IN CHIEF AT *VIBE*, AND MANY, MANY OTHER THINGS

There are a lot of women I look up to, but there aren't a lot I look up to whose book I reread three times while writing my own. In fact, Danyel is the only one. Her book *Shine Bright: A Very Personal History of Black Women in Pop* is exceptional, and another notch on her belt of incredible accomplishments that include creating and hosting the NAACP Award–nominated podcast *Black Girl Songbook*, cofounding the hardcover culture magazine *HRDCVR*, writing for publications like the *New York Times, Teen Vogue,* and the *New Yorker,* to name a few, being editor of *Billboard* and editor at large at *Time*, and holding court as the first woman and first Black person to be editor in chief at *Vibe*, described by its legendary founder, Quincy Jones, as "a *Rolling Stone* for the hip-hop generation." But that's not even half of it, for me.

Danyel's work, words, and sheer existence have influenced a whole host of journalists and writers, myself included. Not only do tweets praising her previous pieces and covers she oversaw at *Vibe* make the rounds on the internet more than a couple of times a week, but you can find her applauding and resharing the work of younger writers as well. In fact, when Danyel joined us for an activation over at *The Gumbo* ahead of the release of her book I was so excited. I remember seeing the inquiry in my email and wanting to pinch myself because it didn't feel real. But it *was* real, and for young Black women who love to write about music, Danyel is one of our icons.

Danyel is from Oakland, California, a fact that is crucial to understanding her story and her work. In *Shine Bright* she recounts listening to Game 7 of the 1972 World Series on the radio with her grandfather, and how the Oakland Athletics' victory was the first time she felt like "a part of a hometown." On an episode of *Black Girl Songbook*, she talks about picking blackberries in her great-grand-parents' backyard in Oakland. When she joined *The Gumbo* for a Twitter Q&A in 2022, she said that while she wanted to be a journalist for as long as she could remember, it was the sounds of artists from her hometown like MC Hammer, Too $hort, En Vogue, Tony! Toni! Toné!, and Digital Underground that inspired her to enter into music journalism. In 1989, Lee Hildebrand assigned Danyel Smith her first paid story—a 1,500-word review of Natalie Cole's show at the Paramount Theatre in Oakland for the *East Bay Express.*

Soon after that, Smith held roles as the music editor at *SF Weekly*, a weekly columnist for the *San Francisco Bay Guardian*, a monthly columnist at *Spin*, and then as the R&B editor at *Billboard* in 1993. It was Bill Adler, journalist, archivist, record executive, founding publicist at Def Jam, and basically anything else you can think of, who recommended Danyel Smith for the job at *Billboard*. It was just the beginning.

In 1994 Danyel started at *Vibe* as music editor and was there until 1996. She took a year off to go back to school at Northwestern University, returning to *Vibe* in 1997 and getting promoted to editor in chief, a position she held until leaving in 1999. In 2006 she returned to *Vibe* as editor in chief again, as well as Vibe Media Group's chief content officer, overseeing the print issues and the website until 2009. When asked about what it was like holding a history-making role as editor in chief in 2021, she told *Vibe.com*:

> *I didn't really have any other model for Black woman editor in chief, really. For me, it was Susan [L.] Taylor of* Essence *and Cynthia Horner of* Right On! *I didn't even know them at the time, but if I didn't have [their Editor's Note] photos, I wouldn't know that I was supposed to have a photo on mine. So I love* Vibe. *If it was not for Vibe, if it was not for Quincy Jones launching Vibe, I would not be sitting right here talking to you right now.*

That's the thing about being the first at something: there isn't really a model or example for what to do. It's a heavy title that comes with just as many accolades as it does challenges, a fact that's made clear throughout this book.

Danyel has the kind of resume that, if I had it, I would get it printed on a blanket to sleep under every night. That's just me, though. At the time of me writing this, Danyel just announced that she's now a contributing writer at the *New York Times Magazine*. Not to mention that her Rolodex of interviewees is a who's who of musical GOATs, including Janet Jackson, Whitney Houston, and Beyoncé.

Any and every thing that Danyel Smith touches is a master class on how to tell a story. Despite having grown up with Ciara's music soundtracking my life, I could not have articulated her impact better than Danyel did in an episode of *Black Girl Songbook* where she celebrated Ciara's standing as the "First Lady of Crunk & B." There's also her November 1997 cover story for *Vibe* featuring the one and only Janet Jackson. There's a point in the interview when Danyel asks her if she's feeling competitive with her brother Michael, to which Janet says "yes." The two women start talking about guilt and family issues in a conversation that's so honest I truly don't believe any woman other than Danyel could have done the interview. And if you have not read her *ESPN The Magazine* story on Whitney Houston's national anthem performance at Super Bowl XXV, just know it's one of the best things ever written, period. It's powerful. Poetic. And places you right there with her. Three of the many things that make Danyel's work so great.

As Smith said in her book, "so many Black women and so much of Black women's work is undervalued and strategically un-remembered. We cannot sit quietly while everyone dresses like us and sings like us and writes like us and just kind of steals us from ourselves." That last part is one of the reasons I wrote this book. Danyel just gets it. And that's why I try to read every article and listen to every podcast she drops.

Now that I think about it, the same goes for the work in these next few chapters.

Interlude

HONEY, THE FIRST MAGAZINE TO SPEAK TO BLACK WOMEN OF THE HIP-HOP GENERATION

*J*uly 28, 1998. The way the cover shoot for the preview issue of *Honey* magazine came together feels like something out of a movie. Jonathan Mannion, a photographer and film director known for his iconic photos of some of the biggest names in music like Jay-Z, Aaliyah, and DMX, to name a few, shot Ms. Lauryn Hill just a few weeks before the release of her debut album, *The Miseducation of Lauryn Hill*. Getting her to the shoot was the result of pure persistence and determination. *Honey* magazine cofounders Kierna Mayo and Joicelyn Dingle knew they wanted Lauryn for the cover, so when Mayo wasn't getting a "yes" from Hill's then-manager Jason Jackson, Dingle decided to call Lauryn's mother's house to get the star to do the shoot. Yes y'all, her mother's house! Joicelyn used to work for Spike Lee doing merchandising for his 40 Acres and A Mule production company, and she connected with Lauryn when the Fugees did an autograph signing at the storefront. And guess what? When she made that call it worked! Despite being six months pregnant and having multiple shoots already scheduled for the same day, Hill agreed to do the cover for *Honey*'s preview issue.

Hill arrived at the *Honey* shoot a few hours behind schedule, but stuck to her word, and once she got there it was ON. The honeycomb backdrop was fashioned out of metallic mesh background laid on top of a gold fabric was crafted by a set designer hired by Mannion and the necklace worn by Lauryn included a silver bee that Mayo put there herself. When it was time to shoot, Mannion noticed that Hill was giving some of her best looks to a full-length mirror that was off camera. To combat this, Mannion grabbed the mirror and placed it directly under his chin to make her comfortable. And the rest, as y'all would say, was history.

But if the cover shoot itself needs a YouTube video, then the story of how the magazine came to be needs an entire docuseries. And like, ASAP. Kierna Mayo and Joicelyn Dingle set out to create a magazine unlike anything that had ever hit newsstands before.

There were hip-hop magazines and there were magazines for Black women, but there was not yet a magazine that spoke to the intersection of the two. *Honey* emerged as "the first magazine of its kind," as noted by Kierna and Joicelyn in their welcome letter in the preview issue, with the goal to create "a fearless entertainment, fashion and lifestyle magazine for young, urban women." Kierna and Joicelyn got into the use of the word *urban* on an episode of Kierna's podcast *Culturati*, where they noted that the word not only "included everyone who liked Black things," but also "flagged that there were Black and brown people around but didn't scare advertisers." Nonetheless, the goal was and remained clear: the magazine centered Black women and their voices, and was for, as Joicelyn put it, "any woman or femme-identifying person that felt that hip-hop vibe."

And felt that vibe they did. Kierna and Joicelyn shopped the magazine and their business plan around for years, with the goal of maintaining ownership and authority over the creativity. The offer finally came from Harris Publications, who told them they were already thinking about doing a magazine like *Honey*. Yeah . . . sure.

Moreover, they told them they didn't need to bring their lawyers or their business plan to the meeting. Hmmm . . .

Unfortunately, I'm sure you have an idea about what happened next. Harris allowed the ladies to maintain their positions as editorial director and editor in chief, but they were not going to have any vested stake in the magazine. In short, they lost ownership of *Honey*. That's the difficulty in starting your own thing, which Kierna and Joicelyn spoke about during that episode of Kierna's *Culturati* podcast. You need money to make things come to life, and the ladies wanted to deliver a quality product because the women who would buy it deserved and expected that. As Joicelyn said, "I didn't want to staple the magazine together, I wanted perfect binding. I wanted a beautiful thing, a beautiful book to present to these women."

Honey would go on to feature work by some of the biggest names in hip-hop journalism and media, like Joan Morgan, Mimi Valdes, Karen Good Marable, and Kierna Mayo herself, as well as landing Left Eye, Mary J. Blige, and Lil' Kim as cover stars. In total, only four issues (not including the Lauryn Hill preview issue) hit newsstands before Harris Publications sold the magazine to Vanguarde Media, headed up by the company's chairman and CEO, Keith Clinkscales, whom they had pitched the magazine to years earlier when he still worked at *Vibe*.

Because the ladies didn't have ownership, there was nothing they could do about the sale. And when Clinkscales presented them with probationary positions that meant they would relinquish their titles and rendered the fact that they founded *Honey* irrelevant, they walked away. They were pushed out of the magazine they created. I didn't know the full story of what happened until I listened to part 2 of Kierna's *Culturati* podcast episode, "The History of Honey Magazine," where she spoke with Clinkscales directly. Both parts of the episodes are on YouTube and I encourage you to listen to them. I can't sum it all up here but it's a story on ownership, equity, and the importance of community. And what I want you to remember is this: *Honey* was a first-of-its-kind publication that influenced the print and media industries thereafter.

I have the premiere issue of the magazine right in front of me. And I have to say, wow. Imagine having to do all of the editorial work and then throw in photo shoots and commissioning writers and planning out the design and literally everything else you have to do to create a magazine. They *did that*. They colored in empty cultural spaces with entire worldviews on women and hip-hop culture, complete with articles and interviews and everything in between.

Here are some of my favorite articles, ads, and really cool moments that appeared in the magazine's premiere issue, which featured Left Eye on the cover. It's the best way to highlight *Honey*'s impact.

Page 1 (The Cover)

The cover for this issue, the Spring 1999 premiere issue, features Lisa "Left Eye" Lopes in Nicole Miller swimwear and an appropriative Native American headdress—put a pin in this part, because we're going to get back to this cover later on in the chapter. In bold letters overlaying her image it reads: "POWER: The 55 Hottest Women in Music, Fashion & Film." Those women? The cover star Left Eye, of course, Ms. Lauryn Hill, Mariah Carey, Jada Pinkett Smith, Fiona Apple, Tyra Banks, and more. The cover also promises to showcase spring fashion looks as well as "New Beauty," citing "lovely lipsticks" and "spiky hair."

Pages 2–10

I love old advertisements, and pages 2 to 10 are full of them. In order, there's a Clairol ad that features a Black woman with short hair dyed by Clairol Textures & Tones 6-G Honey Blonde (a color I've rocked before), a Nike ad that affirms "a hero can be anyone who inspires you" alongside a picture of a woman holding a baby, an ad for the Mecca clothing line, an ad for Skechers that transports me right back to my childhood, and lastly an ad for Lady Enyce that features a woman lying on what seems like an endless sea of bananas. Yes, bananas.

Pages 14 and 15

There's an ad for Nicole Renée's self-titled, self-produced debut album. Since I was not familiar with her music, I streamed the album. The whole thing clocks in at 58:52, and there is some heat on here! My personal faves are "Sound of Love," "Strawberry," "Ain't Nothin' Changed," "Ugh! (God)," and "The Boy Next Door." As a matter of fact, I listened to this album while I wrote the rest of this chapter. Shout-out to Nicole Renée. Page 15 is a picture of a Black woman in a pea coat. It's an ad for Spiewak, "Outwear for real people since 1904." There are a lot more ads in the book that I'm not going to highlight, but you should know that a majority of them feature Black women. Intentional.

Page 16

This page highlights the DaMeditorial, a letter from editorial director Joicelyn Dingle and editor in chief Kierna Mayo—the DaM standing for their last names. You can practically feel the passion and commitment to the magazine jumping off the page. They define the word honey as "A sweet, sticky substance made by honeybees from the nectar of flowers and used as food, Sweetness, and my favorite definition, darling; dear, our readers." I love it. They go on to tell us that the magazine the reader is about to experience has been in the air a long time, which we've already discussed. They assert that "there is a real need for *Honey*—a fresh publication dedicated to the inspiration, style, and entertainment of young women with urban lifestyles. No other magazine is speaking directly to us. We knew we wanted our first issue to focus on the one subject *not* associated with women like us often enough." Whew. I love it. They also add, "There's a female side to everything, so *what* if we like sneakers and DMX. We also love spring's new pretty pink and Faith's jazzy sophomore album. And for this exact reason—that *real* honeys are quite complex—we have created a magazine which combines several layers of our compelling lives." So true. So necessary. And so important. Let's keep reading.

Page 22

Okay, this is definitely my other favorite page so far! Notes from the contributors! I love getting to hear them speak about their contributions to the issue and their careers at-large, specifically Vanessa Evelyn's approach to doing Lisa Bonet's makeup, photographer Mfon Essien finding comfort in wearing white Ts after a breast cancer diagnosis and a single-mastectomy, writer Tonya Pendleton reminiscing about the first time she heard Lil' Kim's debut album, Lou Freeman's assertion that she is no southern belle and her awe at photographing Left Eye for the cover, and asha bandele detailing the "life-affirming" trip to Cuba to interview Assata Shakur, which appears in this issue.

Pages 52–58

This story right here? One of my favorite articles in a hip-hop magazine, period. The article is titled "When and Where I Enter: The Lil' Kim Story," by Lil' Kim as told to Tonya Pendleton. The article was written while Kim was working on her sophomore album, *The Notorious Kim*, and finds the Queen Bee opening up like never before. In one part of the piece she talks about living out of the trunk of her mother's car and then moving in with her dad when her mom lost custody. From there she details how her father left for New Jersey after remarrying, and how much of her time thereafter was spent staying out on the street and with different friends. She says:

> *I started staying with guy friends, and that's how the stories came about on* Hard Core. *I lived that life in the street after that. I dealt with drugs, 'cause I didn't know what to do at that time. At that time, I had to do whatever I had to do to survive.*

Kim had always been open and honest, whether she was getting real about what she wanted in the bedroom on tracks like "We Don't Need It" or going toe-to-toe with detractors on *The Rolanda Watts Show*. But this extra bit of vulnerability and her willingness to tell a story by prefacing with "This is the first time I'm mentioning this" shows that there was an extra bit of care and comfortability provided by a magazine that was crafted with women like her in mind.

Pages 76 and 77

My favorite part about going to the hair salon as a kid was looking through all of the hair magazines. They were always filled with beautiful Black women with their hair done in all types of styles. That's essentially what these two pages are, with a special spotlight placed on the short, spiky cut. There's information on how to best take care of your hair depending on its texture and whether or not it's been processed, as well as products like combs and hairspray handpicked by the *Honey* ladies. There's also a section reminding the reader to tip their stylist 15 to 20 percent. They had the whole hair breakdown, y'all.

Page 117

dream hampton! With all that dream has done and worked on, I love that piece is all about travel. She talks about the importance of traveling, and how taking the trips with what you have at the time can provide you with "priceless" life education. dream is the GOAT.

The Honey Huddle: Gems from My Conversations with *Honey*'s Cofounders

I talked to Kierna Mayo and Joicelyn Dingle about the creation of their baby *Honey*, the importance of community, and the importance of looking toward the future.

Kierna Mayo on prepping the preview issue:

I remember the months leading up to [the preview issue] feeling like, "we outside." Literally . . . So Brooklyn summer is happening, but also we, unlike so many media entities, we just did not have any kind of real staff or support. So I say that to say what I remember the most is that we were doing everything. The small things, the big things, we were our own assistants, we were making cold calls, a lot of cold calls. Remember, before you have something to show, you have nothing to show. No one had even conceived of the possibility of a thing outside of *Essence*. We still sounded crazy coming to you, asking you for your time, your model, your makeup, your whatever. So there was a lot of selling. That's what I remember in those months.

Kierna Mayo on the Left Eye cover:

I struggle with that cover of *Honey*, having Left Eye in the indigenous headdress. We got pushback in real time which I didn't handle well. And we also made space in our version of *Honey* for Native American girls' stories. So we felt like we were doing right. We clearly mishandled this; we clearly appropriated and didn't handle the visual element of Left Eye moment correctly. But the spiritual and kind of like, moment in the culture that we were able to capture with Left Eye was really special. Of course, none of us knew what her fate was going to be. . . . So I appreciate this moment right now. I've actually never articulated how much regret I've had about that cover. Although so much of the meeting of Left Eye was such a highlight for me.

Joicelyn Dingle on one of her favorite *Honey* moments:

So one of the most exciting moments for me with *Honey*, was the very first day that we saw the preview issue. And that was at "A Great Day in Hip-Hop. We had no idea we would be receiving it that day. It was so symbolic. When the publisher gave it to us he was like, "I have something for you." And meanwhile we're watching Fat Joe come in. They're all just right there, Busta Rhymes, Missy, Da Brat, it was a lot to take in. . . . So they gave us a few and I gave one to Pete Rock. And he was like, "What is this?" Now, remember the conversation we had about urban and Black? So he's like, "What is this?" I said, "Oh, it's a new magazine for urban women." And he says, "So is this for Black women?" I said, "Well, it's for urban women." He's like, "No, is this for Black women?" I said, "Yes, yes, yes." [laughs] Made that whole argument crazy once again. But I had to mention that because, you know, to have all of those hip-hop artists gathered on that day and getting that in our hands, it was overwhelming.

Kierna Mayo on the use of the word *urban* to market *Honey*:

Oh, it was not easy, as you heard us talk about out on the podcast a little bit. And I think, you know, we all are a little bit revisionist in how we come back in time and like look at something, but I distinctly remember it being uncomfortable, like it was never a good fit. "Urban" or any of the ways in which we talk around Blackness, because that's what was happening. We were always talking around Blackness, even hip-hop itself. But what we had learned through the exportation of hip-hop, like we're taking it from the hood and bringing it upward and out to the entire country and ultimately the globe, was that to sell hip-hop you did have to kind of contort around Blackness in those early days, but arguably even now when you're selling to advertisers, when you're selling to whole institutions that don't know you, don't get you, just want the next hot thing. . . . So I conceded that we probably couldn't do this just talking about, "we're making a Black girl magazine."

The other piece about *urban* and why we use that language. You know, it had been used in hip-hop media, so *Vibe* was always already using this language. *The Source* was already using [it], which advertisers were already kind of sensitive to this. So it was already a thing. But there was another piece that was what we struggled with, certainly myself. I also wanted this to be an invitation to all women who felt aligned and adjacent to the spirit of Black women in hip-hop. The term *urban* when I was wrestling with it and trying to make it make sense, even though I kind of understood that this was a dance around Blackness, in some ways, I made it make sense because I felt it was also an invitation to other people of color who may have not been Black per se. And maybe to some extent, even white girls who felt like hip-hop was speaking to them in some way. What I knew and what I have said since that time to now was that Black women were at center, meaning that everybody else had to get in where they fit in.

Joicelyn Dingle on doing a *Honey* documentary:

Oh my God, yeah. We've already done some shooting. But now, I'm trying to get the funding for it. . . . I want to make sure we get everybody in there. Especially people that we worked with, the celebrities. You know Beyoncé, we shot her. But we also, when we left *Honey*, we shot her for our cover for *Like Pepper*, which was the name of the new thing that we were doing with this company called Urban Box Office. But at that time, nobody knew how to monetize. We were all making a lot of money and nobody knew how to monetize the Internet in 2000. . . . That company went under after like two years or so. But yeah, that was great. That would have been that was going to be our little comeback, *Like Pepper*. And we shot Beyoncé for the cover.

Kierna Mayo on *Honey*'s legacy:

The legacy of *Honey* is sex positivity. And the legacy of *Honey* is Black womanist theory, Black feminist theory. The legacy of *Honey* is a new kind of intersectionality that is fully embraced. So a natural sister can wear her wig the next day and still be respected and loved by the same people. Right? And we don't always have to choose for external reasons. The choices that we make are more and more internal.

Joicelyn Dingle on *Honey*'s legacy:

I really want us to be remembered for going outside of the rules. When you're talking about an industry with a tradition in it, when we're talking about publishing, I want us to be remembered for being fearless because *Essence* wouldn't have even put any rappers on the cover before we did. They didn't even put Mary J. Blige on there until we said we were going to. So I really want us to be remembered for being fearless, for being authentic to who we are, you know. And when I say being fearless, we shot women for this issue—a gay couple. That hadn't been done, at least not two Black people. And I want us to be remembered for, you know, loving. Loving black women with all of our hearts to the point of creating something that took so long! [laughs]

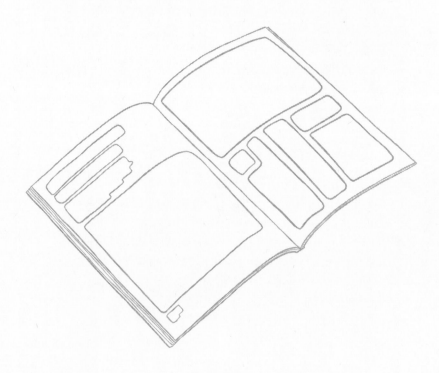

KIM OSORIO, THE FIRST WOMAN EDITOR IN CHIEF AT *THE SOURCE* MAGAZINE

Kim Osorio was raised in the Castle Hill section of the Bronx and hip-hop was embedded in her life from the jump. In her book *Straight from the Source: An Expose from the Former Editor-in-Chief of the Hip-Hop Bible*, she details buying a Sugarhill Gang vinyl around the age of "five or six," learning how to break-dance in the fifth grade to Chaka Khan's "I Feel for You," and having her first "one-on-one" fistfight with a girl who thought she was messing with her man around the time Naughty by Nature's "O.P.P." was out. She took a couple of internships at a distribution company and record label, freelanced at outlets like *Vibe*, *Billboard*, *One World*, and *The Source*, and even obtained her law degree before securing a job at *The Source*, affectionately known as "The Bible of Hip-Hop." However, Kim wrote that her law degree and lack of a formal journalism background made her "just an aspiring journalist to the *Source* team." Nonetheless Osorio became the magazine's editor in chief in 2002, the first woman to hold the position.

The significance of *The Source*, especially in the 1990s and early 2000s, can't be overstated. The magazine began as a newsletter in the summer of 1988, launched by friends and Harvard undergraduates David Mays and Jonathan Shecter. In 1990 the publication moved to New York City, where its impact and circulation grew—according to the *New York Times* the magazine had a circulation of 476,000 in 2003. The magazine also went through a few personnel changes over the years that included the departure of Shecter and the entry of rapper Raymond "Benzino" Scott as *The Source*'s co-owner. He held this position alongside Dave for years.

Here are some important things to know about *The Source* at its peak before we keep going. The magazine:

- Had some of the biggest names in hip-hop on its cover: Lil' Kim, Foxy Brown, Trina, Snoop Dogg, Lil Wayne, Wu-Tang Clan, Jay-Z, Mary J. Blige, LL Cool J, the list goes on and on.
- Hosted its wildly popular eponymous awards show.
- Had its finger on the pulse with its "Unsigned Hype" column, which put readers onto the hottest rappers without record deals—DMX, Biggie, Common, and Eminem all appeared in the column before they got signed.
- Had a five-mic rating system in the "Record Report" section that was the most coveted review an album could get at the time. *Passion of the Weiss* noted that in thirty-two years only fifteen albums got the five-mic rating upon their initial release.

When Kim got the role as editor in chief it was a big fucking deal. She was *leading* the editorial at the "Bible of Hip-Hop," and with her in charge *The Source* had three of its best-selling issues ever: the September 2002 Roc-A-Fella issue, the October 2002 Murder Inc. issue, and the October 2003 50 Cent issue. But Kim didn't officially get the title and the money that went along with the role until she was eight months into the job. And that's just one part of the story.

According to Kim's book *Straight from the Source*, some of the things she experienced working at the magazine and for Mays and Benzino included being told by a man in the office that Dave and Benzino thought she was too "weak-minded," hearing that Benzino and Mays were gossiping about her sleeping with rappers, and Benzino asking her to stay with him at a hotel and questioning her about her sex life. "It's not that I was ashamed to tell Ray whom I had been with," Osorio wrote. "It was that I knew exactly what he wanted to know and more importantly, I knew that he would use it against me."

Host and reporter Sidney Madden also described the culture that Kim said she encountered at the magazine on an episode of NPR Music's *Louder Than a Riot* podcast: "[Men] tacked pictures of porn to their cubicles and even watched porn in the office."

Osorio sent a complaint to HR in February 2005 and after not hearing anything for two weeks, she said she got a call from Mays and Benzino asking her to retract her statement. She refused. Then they fired her—Kim said it was a retaliatory discharge, Mays and Benzino said it was because of her "poor performance."[*] Kim sued *The Source*, Mays, and Benzino, alleging sexual harassment, retaliation, defamation, gender discrimination, and maintaining a hostile work environment. Mays and Benzino responded to the suit via All-HipHop.com, denying the claims while also mentioning her sex life in their statements.

On October 23, 2006, the jury found that Osorio was retaliated against when she was subsequently fired after filing the complaint with HR, and that Benzino defamed her in an interview. The sexual harassment, gender discrimination, and maintaining a hostile work environment claims were dismissed. In her book she wrote that she was awarded $7.5 million in damages, which according to NPR is "one of the largest judgments in the history of the state of New York." But it's the dismissal of the other claims that really sticks with me, because in my opinion it represents the persistence of a culture that leaves women feeling unsafe, uncomfortable, and unheard.

Kim became the executive editor at BET.com in 2005 and served as on-air talent for BET News briefs and *The Black Carpet*. She also served as the vice president of content at GlobalGrind.com, notched

---

* Mays and Benzino's purported reason for firing Osorio was detailed in a 2006 *Washington Post* article titled "Hip-Hop Editor Wins Suit Over Her Firing."

writing credits on TV series like *Million Dollar Listing New York*, *The BET Life of . . .* , *Notarized: The Top 100 Songs of 2011*, and some of the *Love & Hip Hop* reunion episodes, and executive produced on a bunch of shows, including *Growing Up Hip Hop* and *Black Ink Crew: Chicago*. She briefly returned to *The Source*—which was now under new ownership—as editor in chief in 2012. In 2021 Foxy Brown announced that Osorio was writing her memoir.

I had the privilege of hearing Osorio speak at the *Fresh, Fly, and Fabulous: Fifty Years of Hip Hop Style* fashion symposium hosted by the Museum at FIT in February 2023.* She sat with the exhibition's co-curator Elena Romero and former editor in chief of *Vibe* Emil Wilbekin for a conversation about hip-hop fashion in magazines, and I was awestruck listening to her talk about how she brought some of *The Source*'s biggest issues to life.**

There's so much we can learn from Kim, but I'll wrap this chapter up with her lawyer's words at the trial. He summed it up perfectly:

> *The eyes of a hip-hop music industry are upon you. You have a great opportunity here . . . to impose standards on that industry, and standards on other parts of the music industry. You have a chance to teach them something about dignity. You have a chance to teach them something about respect.*

Hopefully the industry will listen and learn.

---

* Shout-out to Elena Romero and Elizabeth Way, who curated the exhibition!

** I'm a Roc-A-Fella baby, so I naturally freaked out when she started talking about making that cover happen.

ANGIE MARTINEZ, THE FIRST LATINA HIP-HOP "VOICE" IN THE RADIO HALL OF FAME

I have an important story to share with you, about something that Angie Martinez experienced at work, years before she would be known as "The Voice of New York" and be the first Latina Hip-Hop "Voice" inducted into the Radio Hall of Fame.

Angie Martinez's mom, who also worked in radio, found out that the then-dance station Hot 97 was hiring interns. Angie had already interned at Miami radio station Power 96, and after an interview with the program director, Angie got the job. She hustled from the very beginning, writing in her memoir *My Voice*, "I did everything, whatever they needed me to do—running to get coffee, office work, errands. . . . Whatever anyone asked, I was on it. Pretty soon everyone knew if they needed something, they could ask me. 'We'll get Angie to get it. She'll do it.' I was that kid at the station."

That kid at the station also took it upon herself to learn as much as she could from all of the different departments, and it was only a matter of time before she got hired to work on the Hot 97 street team part-time. One of Angie's responsibilities in her new role was to take the Hot 97 van and drive one of the radio personalities, Deborah Rath, from Manhattan down to Six Flags Great Adventure in Jackson, New Jersey, for an event. Then after she drove back up to Manhattan she was supposed to drop the van off in a lot in Midtown. That's a *hike*, y'all. Like, truly so far. But no matter what, Angie *had* to put that van back in the lot before she went home. No ifs, ands, or buts.

Angie was basically running on E, though. She would go to school, then work, then back to school, and back to work. That was the cycle. And because she had another event to go to the morning after the drive to and from Six Flags, Angie decided to take the van home to the Upper West Side with her. That way she could nap a bit and be ready to go the next morning. But when she went outside the next morning there was a ticket right on the windshield. Shit.

Her employer found out that she broke the rules, and after being written up and sent home she was called in a few days later to speak with the promotions director, the marketing director, and the general manager. As she recounts in her memoir, they spoke for ten or fifteen minutes, "going back and forth about how this is not acceptable; it's against the rules; we've fired other people for this; what are we supposed to do; we're gonna have to let her go."

Angie interjected and asked to speak, and general manager Judy Ellis said okay. Here's a bit of what she said: "First of all, I've been working here now a pretty long time and I do whatever anybody asks at any time, and I don't want any credit for that. But I do think that the least I deserve is that if something goes wrong, somebody would ask me what happened." Whew.

And guess what they did, y'all? They asked her what happened. And she told them. About the two events she had to do back-to-back. About the long drive she had to make to take Deborah to and from Six Flags. How she only had four hours to get to the next event when she got back to the city. How she simply wanted to take a nap so she could show up on point like she always was. And guess what? Angie got to keep her job at the station, where she would rise in the ranks over the years and during its change from dance radio to hip-hop and become "The Voice of New York."

This is my favorite Angie Martinez story. Because besides her keeping her job, of course, Angie did something that I clung to the first time I read it, the same thing that she pointed out when she told it in her memoir: she used her voice. A voice that would run the airwaves for over two decades, from Hot 97 and currently at 105.1. A voice that would lead to a Radio Hall of Fame induction in 2020. A voice that gave and continues to give us some of the best interviews in hip-hop history.

There are the interviews with Tupac—which has never been released in its entirety—and Biggie at the height of the East Coast–West Coast rivalry. There's every single one of her interviews with Jay-Z. An interview with Barack Obama. A discussion with Michelle Obama. Kanye. Nicki. Lil' Kim. Rihanna. Mariah Carey. You can name practically anyone in and around hip-hop and rest assured that Angie's probably talked to them.

When it comes to her Radio Hall of Fame induction, Angie told REVOLT, "I think about the way in which hip hop has affected the world and changed the world culturally. If I think about my personal life, I mean, it gave me a career, a whole career, put me in the Radio Hall of Fame." Moreover, when she talked about the induction during an episode of *Drink Champs*, she said this moment helped her realize the importance of the achievement:

I went to a school, a broadcasting school. Black and brown kids in there. I look up at the wall, it's all the hall of famers. And there ain't nobody up there that look like me. And that was the day I was like oh, I get it.

And I get it, too. Angie wasn't just getting a piece of hardware, she was representing for her culture on all fronts, hence the title of this chapter. It's only right that a space designed to honor "those who have contributed to the development of the radio medium throughout its history in the United States" has Angie Martinez in its ranks. With all of the accolades I mentioned earlier, I hope it's pretty clear why. But if for some reason it's not clear, here are five of my favorite Angie Martinez moments to convince you. The key word here is *my*. But hopefully they'll be equally as important to *you* when you're done reading. (P.S.: Yes, they're all women. You know the title of the book!)

Mary J. Blige talks to Angie Martinez about the Burger King controversy (2012)

In 2012 Mary agreed to do a Burger King commercial singing about the chain's new crispy chicken snack wraps to the tune of her song "Don't Mind." Mary had hoped it would be a great branding opportunity and since she was a kid had wanted to create an iconic jingle for a fast-food company. But when the advertisement was released Blige was criticized for playing into stereotypes. In an initial statement to CNN, Blige said the ad was unfinished, and while Burger King apologized to Mary and pulled the commercial citing licensing issues, the people did not let up on Mary.

Quick aside, though. Angie and Mary go way way back. Like, they've been tight since practically the beginning of their respective careers. So when Angie was facing eviction from her apartment back in the day, she called up her friend Mary. Mary told Angie to come pick her up from the studio, and they drove to a check-cashing spot where Mary got the money. Angie kept her apartment and Mary never asked for the money back.

Mary hadn't publicly spoken about what happened with Burger King until she sat down with Angie on Hot 97. There she spoke about how the ad was not what she thought it would be, the severity of the backlash, and ultimately, how hurt she was. Mary had given so much to so many people for so long at that point—and to this day—and as Angie put it in her book, "it's shocking to see how one questionable move could make people flip on you."

I'm also reminded of how often people forget that those celebrities they love are people just like them. Yes, Mary has been super transparent in her music. Yes, she's been a vessel for a lot of people's healing. But, no, that doesn't make her the archetype of a "strong Black woman" who's not deserving of grace. That's why it was important—and I'm sure I'll say it a few more times throughout the rest of this chapter—for Mary to have a safe place to express that hurt and disappointment. So who better to interview her than her friend and powerhouse radio personality, Angie Martinez?

I don't think it mattered who was a part of the ad, because whoever it was would have been handled with the same kind of care, grace, and objectiveness that Angie gave Mary. And I think that's why I love this interview so much: it's a reminder to still respect the people who have been nothing but giving, even if they do something *you* may not like. I am so glad I wasn't on Twitter at the time because I would not have been here for it!

Foxy Brown stops by Hot 97 for an interview about her hearing loss (2006)

The last time Foxy Brown paid a visit to Angie Martinez's show was in the summer of 2005 to premiere her single "Come Fly with Me," featuring Sizzla. Accompanied by her friend and then-boss Jay-Z, Foxy talked about the new track, her plans for a video (never released), her process in the studio, and more. Near the end of that interview they started taking calls from listeners, but as she recounts to Angie in the 2006 interview, she remembers telling Jay-Z that she couldn't hear the callers.

While recording her album *Black Roses*[*] Foxy began noticing the onset of what would be diagnosed as "severe and sudden sensorineural hearing loss in both ears." At a press conference in December 2005 the rapper said she hadn't heard anyone else's voice in more than six months and that surgery was planned for the top of the following year.

The surgery was a success, and Foxy started recording and performing again. She gave Angie Martinez the exclusive interview in 2006 once she felt better, revealing that "the hearing was going on your show. You just held me down with such dignity and class and respect." The conversation was personal, honest, and eye-opening. Foxy opened up about her disability, the five-hour-long surgery, the device placed in her skull to help her with her hearing moving forward, her Gucci-covered hearing piece, and how her hearing loss unfairly and negatively impacted her business relationships. It was a powerful moment in hip-hop history for Foxy to go up to Hot 97 and open up about her disability, and shows the care that Angie took in respecting and protecting her experience.

Angie Martinez interviews Lil' Kim on the set of the Ladies Night remix of "Not Tonight" (1997)

Imagine you're on the set of a music video for a song that you're on, and then you're also interviewing the artists on the track and in the video as well. Pretty iconic if you ask me.

Angie Martinez spits the first verse on "Not Tonight (Ladies Night Remix)," proclaiming herself to be the "rookie on this all-star team." Angie was the rookie. The song was a remix to a track off of Lil' Kim's classic debut album, *Hard Core*, and Kim was already a star at the top of her game. Its features were no small feat, either. We're talking about

---

[*] *Black Roses* remains unreleased, making 2001's *Broken Silence* her most recent album. But I'm always anxiously awaiting new Foxy music. It doesn't even have to be a whole project. I'll take a verse, an ad-lib, anything she's willing to give.

Missy Elliott, Left Eye, and Da Brat here. Three hip-hop history makers. When Angie was asked to be on the track, Lance "Un" Rivera—Biggie's former business partner and cofounder of Lil' Kim's label Undeas—told her that he liked how she sounded on "Heartbeat,"* a track by KRS-One that featured Redman and Angie. The thing about Angie's feature on "Heartbeat," though, is that KRS wrote her verse. For the Kim track she called a few of her friends in music for tips, wrote a bunch of lines, went to the studio, and rapped them, and Un chose the best bars. Before she knew it she was recording the video in West Palm Beach, Florida, and performing the song at the MTV Video Music Awards. By the time Grammy nominations rolled around the track was nominated for Best Rap Song by a Duo or Group. Yup, just like that.

To be honest, the content of the interview is cool, but it's not why this particular convo made my list. Nope. What I love is that when Angie is interviewing Kim during the shoot, I see two women who are excellent at their crafts showing a tremendous respect for one another. Lil' Kim was, well, Lil' Kim. She was at the top in hip-hop. And Angie was, well, Angie. She was at the top in radio. And they were just laughing and joking and hugging and having fun. It's just cool to see women in different spaces in hip-hop supporting and loving one another.

Aaliyah stops by Hot 97 for an interview (2001)

"**W**e're getting ready to do the video for 'Rock the Boat' this week with Hype [Williams]," Aaliyah told Angie Martinez at the top of their interview. It's a bit uncomfortable for me to listen to this interview knowing that she would pass away just a few days later. I vividly remember where I was when I heard or, to be more specific, saw the news. I was getting ready for breakfast at my aunt and uncle's house when my aunt turned on the news and literally stopped

---

* KRS-One's "Heartbeat" sampled Taana Gardner's 1981 track of the same name, and let me just say, it is such a good-ass song! Also, Taana is from New Jersey; Newark to be exact.

cooking. Aaliyah had died in a plane crash on her way back from shooting the video in the Bahamas.

Aaliyah meant a lot to me as a kid. I was only six years old when she passed away, but, as I'm sure you know, there are some musicians who are attached to the memories even from your earliest years. In 2001 I started cheerleading. We never did any competitions or even any tumbling or stunts. In fact, all we ever really did was dance. Nonetheless, our routines were fire. And while I can't remember my coach's name, she must have been a big fan of Aaliyah, because she played her music *a lot* at practice. So much so, in fact, that the routine we performed in front of our families at our showcase that year was choreographed to "Rock the Boat." Which brings me to the interview.

She and Angie giggle a lot about a bunch of different things, with Aaliyah even mentioning at one point that she likes to laugh and a sense of humor is very important to her. Beyond the discussions around the music and movies and projects Aaliyah had been planning to work on you could hear how cool, calm, and relaxed she was. It was a beautiful, fun moment that, to me, immortalized an iconic artist just days before her death. That's why I love it.

Angie Martinez interviews City Girls rapper JT on the *IRL* Podcast (2023)

tweeted this at 1:02 a.m. on February 10, 2023: "love this convo with @ThegirlJT and @angiemartinez so much!" Six minutes later JT quoted my tweet with a "Thank you!" I went to her feed and saw a bunch of people sharing the same sentiment, that they loved the conversation Angie and JT had on Martinez's podcast, *IRL*.

I think social media combined with our current expectations of celebrities makes a lot of people feel like they're owed some sort of access to a famous person's life. It's even more interesting when our musicians release songs that touch on personal issues, and people feel like they need *more*. They want to know about the artist's romantic relationships. They want to know about the artist's family. They want to know about the artist's financial situation. And more often than not when artists do let people in on their lives, the personal details they share aren't handled with care. Instead they become a trending topic or get spun into something negative.

That is why JT's sit-down with Angie is on this list. We know a lot about the City Girls on the music front. The rap duo of Yung Miami and JT first caught my attention when they appeared uncredited on Drake's "In My Feelings." And then when they dropped "Twerk" with Cardi B and "Act Up"? You couldn't tell me *anything* during the summer of 2018!

On the podcast JT talked about being indicted for credit card fraud a week after the City Girls dropped their first record. She ended up serving two years in prison, and told Angie that she still beats herself up over where she feels like the City Girls would be if none of that had ever happened. She talked about going to the halfway house after she was released, and how chatter on the internet about what they perceived to be her "absence" when she got home influenced her to post online, a decision that almost got her sent back to prison for violating the rules. She talked about living with her dad and stepmother as a kid because of her mother's drug use and prison stints at the time, and how not looking like her half siblings made her feel like an outcast in her own home. (When she moved out at thirteen she went between staying with family members and her friends' houses.) She also talked about being ready to start therapy, and how sometimes she's her own worst enemy. It's a really good conversation, and the reason why I was up watching it when I needed to be asleep.

Even more illuminating is that JT reached out to Angie herself via Instagram DM telling her she wanted to do the show. It was relatable and personal. And let me be clear, it was not something that was owed to us. But what was clear is that JT knew that "The Voice of New York" would provide her with a safe space to get real and vent.

"AWARDS/
CERTIFICATIONS"

Interlude

A VERY RANDOM THING I LEARNED ABOUT FOXY BROWN

Writing this book taught me the importance of meal prepping. The worst thing that happened during this process was that I would be in a groove and then my stomach would start growling and I would have nothing to eat. I would try to ignore it. *Finish this chapter and then go cook or order something*, I would say to myself in my head. But then I wouldn't be able to focus because I was so hungry. And because I was so hungry I would spend the next thirty minutes scrolling through different apps trying to figure out what to order or I would walk to the kitchen to see what I could cook. Then after that there was of course another thirty minutes spent waiting on the food to get there or be ready. And after *that* I spent another thirty minutes eating the food. Anyway, after doing this a million times I decided to look up the favorite foods of some women in hip-hop. In my mind I thought I was doing some super-intense research that would help with the book, but in reality I just wanted to know if we had anything in common when it came to our palates. That's how I found out Foxy

Brown celebrated her sophomore album, *Chyna Doll*, debuting at No. 1 on the Billboard 200 chart with fried flounder, macaroni and cheese, yams, potato salad, and corn muffins with strawberry butter.

In a 1999 article published in the *New York Times* headlined "A NIGHT OUT WITH: Foxy Brown; Chyna Doll's Victory Lap In a Hip-Hop Caravan," David Kirby wrote about the evening he spent with the Brooklyn-bred rapper in Harlem. It was a snowy Sunday night, and Brown had just become the second woman rapper to have an album to top the Billboard 200.* Harlem was the perfect place for Brown to revel in the moment, telling Kirby that the neighborhood is like a second home for her. When she was a kid she took the subway to Harlem to attend church on Sundays. As a teenager Foxy and her friends would hang out in abandoned buildings in the neighborhood. And on this night in particular Foxy was back for dinner at Well's Famous Home of Chicken & Waffles on Adam Clayton Powell Jr. Boulevard.

Not only did Harlem feel like a second home to Foxy, but its residents also made sure that she felt the love too. A hundred-foot-long *Chyna Doll* billboard was put up next to the legendary Apollo Theatre. Fans yelled that they loved her from their car, blasting her music as they rode by. And at the restaurant she chose for dinner, the manager told the rapper they needed her new CD to play at the establishment.

It was lofty praise for Foxy, who had only just made her solo debut a few years earlier as a featured artist on LL Cool J's "I Shot Ya (Remix)." She was only sixteen years old when she wrote her verse, and lines like "I gets down, fuckin' with Brown, Fox, extra keys to the drop" made it clear she was a skilled rapper who would be around for a while. Her appearances on "Touch Me, Tease Me" by Case and "Ain't No Nigga" by Jay-Z in 1996 further cemented this fact, and in that same year she dropped her debut album, *Ill Na Na*.

---

* Ms. Lauryn Hill was the first with *The Miseducation of Lauryn Hill*.

When *Chyna Doll* dropped in 1999, *Entertainment Weekly* noted that it created "a beguiling fantasy life of limos and champagne" while also hinting at "how painful maintaining the fantasy can be." On "Hot Spot" she rhymes "Big ballin bitch, I want all of this shit / Six AMG's* with the spoiler kit." On "My Life" she raps, "My girls ain't the same, guess it's cuz the fame / Bitches smile in my face and throw dirt on my name." And on my all-time favorite Foxy Brown song, "I Can't," she talks about leaving a dude she can't trust for someone who will be honest and show his love with gifts: "The next nigga copin' me bags straight from Dior / Prada shoes, that's the bomb straight outta Milan." From lyrics about love and pain to luxury and fame, Foxy kept it real and raw through and through. The album going to the top of the charts—and later being certified platinum—was just the icing on the cake. (I wonder if she had cake that night.)

The next few chapters talk more about some ladies in rap and their historic award wins and *Billboard* certifications. These next few chapters are also the last few chapters of the book. I won't get too emotional, but I'm really glad that you made it here. Unless, of course, you skipped around, in which case I'm still glad you made it but am now more curious about which chapter you chose to start on and why.

In any case, let's keep reading!

Interlude

---

* AMG is short for Mercedes-AMG, a special "luxury performance" brand.

SALT-N-PEPA WERE THE FIRST ALL-WOMAN RAP ACT TO HAVE AN ALBUM GO GOLD AND PLATINUM

There's an episode of *Everybody Hates Chris* that's pretty much ingrained in my mind. I watched the show a lot as a kid and the premise is quite hilarious: the main character, Chris—played by the one and only Tyler James Williams[*]—and his friend Greg decide to join the wrestling team so they can get a varsity jacket and, as a result, gain respect, perks, and in his words "the only thing he really cared about": girls. The part that hooked me was a subplot where Chris's brother Drew hatches a plan to put together a girl group, make a video, and hopefully land them a spot on TV. He initially rebuffs his younger sister Tonya's request to join the group, but when she auditions for the group her performance is too good to deny her a spot on the roster. The song she chose to perform? Salt-N-Pepa's "Push It."

I remember that episode of *Everybody Hates Chris* so vividly because of all of the references to women rappers. But more than anything I remember how happy Tonya was to dress up like Salt,

---

[*] Tyler currently plays Gregory Eddie on *Abbott Elementary*, which cemented itself after its first season as one of my favorite shows ever. Shout-out to Quinta!

Pepa, and Spinderella, women who used their music and their sound to quite literally "push it." "It" being the boundaries, the limits, and everything women in hip-hop faced.

Salt-N-Pepa's careers are filled with a lot of "firsts"—they boycotted the 31st Annual Grammy Awards with their fellow nominees when they were nominated in the first-ever rap category after learning the category wouldn't be televised and made history at the 37th Annual Grammys alongside Queen Latifah as the first women rappers to win a Grammy—Queen Latifah won an award the same night later on in the ceremony. But the "first" I'm going to talk about in this chapter is how Salt-N-Pepa became the first all-woman rap act to achieve gold and then platinum album status.

A bit of backstory first.

Cheryl "Salt" James and Sandra "Pepa" Denton met during their first year at Queensborough Community College, with Salt telling *The Guardian* in 2017 that they were "polar opposites." But you know what they say, opposites attract, and the ladies became the best of friends, skipping class together to hang in the lunchroom and play cards and working together as part-time telephone operators at Sears. Salt's boyfriend at the time was producer Hurby "Luv Bug" Azor, who also worked at Sears* with them, and he had an idea to put a group together. Salt used to perform songs for her family in Brooklyn, and Pepa spit a few lines for Hurby one day at work when he asked her if she could rap. Soon after the audition the ladies, rapping under the name Super Nature, recorded the 1985 track "The Show Stoppa (Is Stupid Fresh)," a response to Doug E. Fresh and Slick Rick's classic song "The Show."

For the ladies to have their first foray into rap be an answer to two extremely popular, well-established rappers like Doug E. Fresh and Slick Rick was bold. Like really, really bold. But it was this

---

* Guess who else worked at this Sears at the same time as Salt-N-Pepa and Hurby? Martin Lawrence and Kid 'N Play. I know that their shifts were lit!

boldness that not only got them played on the radio, but kick-started a decades-long career that would cement them as pioneers in rap.

The group changed their name to Salt-N-Pepa after the lyrics "Right now I'm gonna show you how it's supposed to be / 'Cause we, the salt and pepper MCs" from their song "The Show Stoppa (Is Stupid Fresh)." The ladies also signed a deal with Next Plateau Records and recruited a third member, Latoya Hanson, the original Spinderella. In 1986 they dropped their debut album, *Hot, Cool & Vicious*. Shortly after its release Hanson left the group and was replaced by Deidra Roper, the new Spinderella.

"Push It" was not originally on their debut album. In fact, the song was initially recorded to simply be the B-side—the secondary and often less important track on the reverse side of vinyl single releases—to a remix of the *Hot, Cool & Vicious* track "Tramp." Salt told *Vibe* in 2010, "the funny thing about 'Push It' is we really didn't care for the record at all. Coming out of hip-hop, we were always a poppy kind of act. And so a lot of rappers used to question our credibility. . . . Hurby did the production on 'Push It' so when I first heard it I was like, 'Ah shoot . . . we are really going to hear it now.'" They really did hear it. In fact, a bunch of people did.

"Push It," the track that was recorded in the bathroom of the song's coproducer, Fresh Gordon, was taking off on the other side of the country. The late San Francisco DJ Cameron Paul started playing the B-side in the club and remixed the record for his label Mixx It. The song became a hit, and Paul's version was purchased by Next Plateau, who released it as an A-side and then placed it on a reissued version of their debut album, *Hot, Cool & Vicious*.* The success of the track boosted the sales of the album, which was certified gold on January 8, 1988, and then platinum on March 23, 1988. "Push It" went platinum the following year.

~~~~~~~~~~

* I learned this from an interview Cameron Paul did with Jarrell Mason for WUAG-FM/NJS4E. Wild how much information is out there on the internet.

The years that followed only brought the group more success, more gold and platinum singles and albums, and more autonomy. Hurby wrote and produced most of Salt-N-Pepa's first four albums, and it was through their desire to break out from under Hurby's control that listeners got songs like 1993's "Shoop," the first track that the ladies wrote and produced without him. Salt-N-Pepa's last album, 1997's *Brand New*, marked the first time they put out an album without any songwriting or production from Hurby. And with a career that includes a Lifetime Achievement Award from the Recording Academy, a star on the Hollywood Walk of Fame, and one of the best-selling albums among women rappers with *Very Necessary*, there's no denying the impact that the women have had on hip-hop as a whole.

But as a Salt-N-Pepa fan I can't help but go back to the late 1980s, when they made history with their debut album. The significance in *Hot, Cool & Vicious* going gold and platinum for me doesn't just lie in the numbers, but also in the fact that those numbers are representative of a number of people who listened to and were influenced by their music. I can show you this influence better than I can tell you, so here is a breakdown, by way of a chart.

The *Hot, Cool & Vicious* Influence Chart

"I'LL TAKE YOUR MAN"

The track was written by Hurby, and Pep told *Rolling Stone*, "He was a great writer. He wrote well for girls [laughs]. I do like performing 'I'll Take Your Man,' because that was a hard song. And that was [a] very bold, in-your-face song."

Speaking on the song in the same interview, Salt noted, "By the time it was time to record 'I'll Take Your Man,' I had found my voice, we had found *our* voice, and was way more confident."

"I'll Take Your Man" is actually my favorite song on the album for these very reasons. It's a braggadocious, bold, and direct song that places women at the center, and while we know Hurby was writing the lyrics at this point in their careers, there is not a doubt in my mind that no one could have performed what he gave them better than they did. You can hear the conviction in their voices.

I'm certain Salt-N-Pepa could take someone's man with pure ease if they wanted to.

"I'll Take Ya Man '97" by Mia X

When Salt-N-Pepa were interviewed by New Orleans publication *Off-Beat Magazine* during their stop in the Big Easy on their 1999 Greatest Hits tour, the writer let the group know that "New Orleans' own hottest lady of rap, Mia X," had done a remake of their song "I'll Take Your Man."

"I didn't hear about that, I think that's awesome—I'm flattered anytime someone does something like that," Salt exclaimed.

Mia's version of the song adds a special kind of bounce to the beat that screams New Orleans, and also builds upon the braggadocio of Salt-N-Pepa in a way that makes it all her own.

Salt-N-Pepa told listeners that they would "take your man, your fiancé, your husband," with Mia X adding in "the niggas you sweating and all your fuck friends."

"Take Yo Man" by City Girls

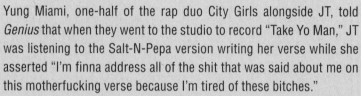

Yung Miami, one-half of the rap duo City Girls alongside JT, told *Genius* that when they went to the studio to record "Take Yo Man," JT was listening to the Salt-N-Pepa version writing her verse while she asserted "I'm finna address all of the shit that was said about me on this motherfucking verse because I'm tired of these bitches."

Whereas Salt-N-Pepa opened their song by proclaiming that they "came to out-rap you," and Yung Miami and JT upped the ante by letting the haters know that if they kept trying them they could not only "out-fuck" them, but that they would also, as the song title says, "take yo man" too.

The Salt-N-Pepa and City Girls versions showcase just how multidimensional women are. Salt-N-Pepa placed their powerful lyrics at the center of the potential heist, while the City Girls asserted their sexuality could result in someone's man getting taken. But both affirmed that the women could do exactly what the men do in their raps: boast in their raps, take charge, and talk openly about sex.

"PUSH IT"

"Push It" is an important song in Salt-N-Pepa's discography for all of the reasons I said earlier, and more. There are two things about "Push It" that stand out for me. First, the song is fun. I know that seems like a very simple explanation, but it really is just a super fun track.

Two, the video. Watching the women dance and perform together in those matching outfits is everything.

The song that took the world by storm and helped the group make history still has an impact on music today.

"Body" by Megan Thee Stallion

The repetition of "Body-ody-ody-ody-ody-ody-ody-ody/Ody-ody-ody-ody-ody-ody-ody" on Megan Thee Stallion's single reminds me of the "Ah, push it—push it good" that's repeated on the Salt-N-Pepa chorus. But that's not where the connections end.

Pepa told the *Guardian,* "For 30 years, we have been telling people that 'Push It' isn't about sex, but no one ever believes us. . . . It's about pushing it on the dance floor." And while Megan's "Body" is indeed about, well, body, what fans see in the video and when the track gets played outside highlights just how important the dance floor is to Meg as well.

"Body" is one of the more fun rap songs to come out in recent years, because it really is a call to not only celebrate your body but also push it on the dance floor.

"Good Love" by City Girls featuring Usher

Yes, another City Girls song. But honestly, who's going to stop me?

JT and Yung Miami take viewers to the famous Cascade skating rink in Atlanta for a function that makes you want to jump through the screen.

The influence of "Push It" is all throughout the video, from the matching outfits to the dance moves to the pure unbridled joy emanating from the people in the background.

When I first heard "Good Love" and then watched the video I knew it was fun.

"MY MIC SOUNDS NICE"

"I'll Take Your Man" is my favorite song on *Hot, Cool & Vicious,* but this joint right here is a very close second. In fact I almost fell off of the couch when the ladies performed it as a part of the "Hip-Hop 50 Medley" at the Grammys in 2023.

It's the way the beat, which samples Grover Washington Jr.'s "Mister Magic," is so smooth, and lyrics like "'Cause this is the year all men fear / Female MCs is movin' up here" feel like a prophetic declaration of what we now know is true: women were coming to stake their claim in the rap world.

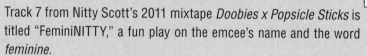

"FeminiNITTY" by Nitty Scott

Track 7 from Nitty Scott's 2011 mixtape *Doobies x Popsicle Sticks* is titled "FeminiNITTY," a fun play on the emcee's name and the word *feminine*.

She opens the songs by rapping the same words Salt-N-Pepa did on their cut, before making it clear that she's just not a pretty face, but also a problem on the mic.

When she rhymes "I could sit with the ladies / I could post with the boys," it's clear she not only heard what Salt-N-Pepa said in the 1980s on "My Mic Sounds Nice," but internalized it too.

Ava Duvernay's documentary *My Mic Sounds Nice: A Truth About Women and Hip Hop*

Ava DuVernay's 2010 BET documentary, *My Mic Sounds Nice: A Truth About Women in Hip Hop*, nodded to Salt-N-Pepa's song in its title and examined the history and impact of women in hip-hop.

It's no surprise that DuVernay's doc goes by this name. With appearances from artists including MC Lyte, Missy Elliott, Eve, Roxanne Shanté, Yo-Yo, and of course, Salt-N-Pepa, each minute reminds you that women have been in hip-hop from the very beginning making history and shaping the culture as a whole.

The full doc is on YouTube as I write this, but outside of that I'm not sure where else you can watch it. If it's still there by the time you get to this part of the book, I urge you to set aside some time to watch a production that affirms the mics of women do indeed sound nice.

"TRAMP"

The January 17, 1994, issue of *New York* magazine features an article titled "How Salt-N-Pepa Turned Rap on Its Head." Writer Dinitia Smith noted, "In Salt-N-Pepa raps, the women are in control. In their hit single 'Tramp,' it is the man who is the tramp."

Lines like "So I dissed him, I said, 'You's a sucker! / Get your dirty mind out the gutter'" and "You ain't gettin' paid, you ain't knockin' boots" flip the script on the overwhelming amount of rap songs by men that typically abhor women who choose to not only have sex freely and as frequently as they like, but simply choose to have sex, period.

On "Tramp" Salt-N-Pepa are in charge, commanding authority in a genre that attempts to often only afford that power to men.

"Tramp" by Foxy Brown

Track 15 on Foxy Brown's sophomore album, *Chyna Doll*, which debuted at the top of the *Billboard* 200 is a hard-hitting remake of the Salt-N-Pepa song.

Foxy's "Tramp" is both an affirmation that she, and all women who rap, can be in control, and a reminder that "broke niggas" have to step their game up before even thinking about getting close to her.

She was open, honest, and fearless, exuding the same characteristics that Salt-N-Pepa did on their song.

"No Scrubs" by TLC

I don't think about "Tramp" without thinking about "No Scrubs" almost immediately.

In an article for the *Washington Post* called "A Hit That Bashes Single Guys' Nerve," Lonnae O'Neal Parker called TLC's "No Scrubs" "a reaction to twenty years of hip-hop misogyny."

When Lisa "Left Eye" Lopes rapped "I don't find it surprisin' if you don't have the Gs (Gs) / To please me and bounce from here to the coast of overseas" she was doing what Salt-N-Pepa were doing on "Tramp," affirming a woman's right to take charge and have the type of man they want.

Of course you could connect "No Scrubs" to a host of songs throughout history, but when I hear Left Eye rap with so much power and conviction I hear the legacy of Salt-N-Pepa.

DA BRAT, THE FIRST SOLO WOMAN RAPPER TO HAVE A PLATINUM ALBUM

When I'm not in the mood to go anywhere or see anyone or do anything, one of my favorite things to do is order some food, sit down on the couch, kick my feet up, put YouTube on the TV, and watch old live performances. Late-night television, variety shows, music countdown shows—you name it. If the show had an artist perform it's guaranteed that I will go back and watch it! That being said, I do have a show I really really love to watch old clips of, and that's *All That*. *All That* was the sketch comedy series that literally defined my childhood. I mean, who didn't love seeing Kenan Thompson performing "Everyday French with Pierre Escargot," laughing at Lori Beth Denberg as "The Loud Librarian," or watching Amanda Bynes give advice with "Ask Ashley"? It was a perfect show, made all the more so by closing out each episode with a performance. One night I came across a video of Da Brat performing "Give It 2 You," the third single from her debut album, *Funkdafied*. *Funkdafied*, released in 1994, sold over one million copies and made her the first solo woman rapper to have a platinum album. I don't know if you've ever watched Da Brat perform "Give It 2 You" on *All That*, but you should.

There is something to be said about Da Brat pushing one million records right out of the gate. In fact, there is something that *should* be said about Da Brat pushing one million records right out of the gate. Alexandra Berenson, then head of A&R for record club Vinyl Me, Please, talked about the album on the company's blog in 2019:

> *It's not easy to sell over a million copies of an album; if it was, more male rappers would have done it. Plus, it's hard to sell over a million copies of an album when you're a woman, when you're a woman doing rap music, and when you're a woman doing rap music in 1994. To think how incredible that is! You have to pay tribute to that.*

With that in mind I've decided to pay tribute to Da Brat's platinum-selling, history-making album. I'm going to pick lines from songs on the album and tell you why they're the best and what they represent in the grand scheme of Brat's history-making moment. Very simple.

1. The song: "May Da Funk Be Wit 'Cha"

The line: *Now back from the 6-0-6-4-4 full of indo*

Why I think it's the best: 60644 is an area code in Chicago, and Chicago is where Da Brat was born and raised. It's the best line on the song for two reasons. One, Da Brat was inspired by MC Lyte and played all kinds of instruments growing up: baritone horn, trombone, drums, tuba, and trumpet. From there she started rapping, and when Kris Kross had a contest during their show in Chicago, Brat stepped up to the mic. She won and went back to her seat, but the group sent their bodyguard to find her. Soon after that she met Jermaine Dupri, and two weeks later she had the paperwork to become the newest So So Def signee.

Two, oftentimes when people talk about rap they talk about the East Coast, West Coast, and the South, and they should, but the Midwest should be repped just as much because so many different regions have made rap and hip-hop as a whole what they are today. Yes, So So Def is based in Atlanta, but Da Brat shouting out her hometown was a reminder that rap's impact comes from all over.

2. The song: "Da Shit Ya Can't Fuc Wit"

The line: *Settin' them swole, steady, going gold / Whatever we release, whatever we unfold*

Why I think it's the best: Da Brat used this song, the first on the album, to let it be known that she was going to do numbers whenever she dropped because she just had it like that. It's an even better line when you learn that Jermaine Dupri didn't even want a woman rapper on his label at first.

"[Kriss Kross] saw her while they were on tour, and they came to me and said, 'We got this female rapper you should check out.' And when they did it, I didn't want no female rapper," Dupri told *Complex* in 2013. "But I thought that since they said I should check her out . . . I'm like, what does she do that made them want me to look at her? So I at least decided to give it a listen." Thankfully he listened and gave her that paperwork I mentioned, because Da Brat's success helped contribute to So So Def's success. She wasn't just gold, she was going platinum. So yeah, talk your shit Da Brat.

3. The song: "Fire It Up"

The line: *One o'clock is the time to raise / Take a shower brush my teeth and correct my braids*

Why I think it's the best: I literally did this when I woke up today. Showered, brushed my teeth, and fixed my knotless braids. In fact, I'm sure that a lot of people reading this line did as well. If you didn't, that's okay.

I love this line because she was rapping about her personal style. "I had my pants backward, cut a hole in my baseball cap, stuck my ponytail through it—I wanted to be the third member of Kris Kross," she told *HipHopDX* in 2021. "So I'm grateful that I had a producer like Jermaine Dupri who did not try to change me. . . ." Da Brat rocked baggy jeans, oversized, shirts and her hair in braids. She was true to who she was and relatable because of it.

That's why when Da Brat's look changed around the release of her third album in 2000, a lot of people were shocked. It was noticeably different—tighter clothes and more stereotypically "feminine." But during an appearance on *Tamron Hall*, Brat asserted that the change was something she did all on her own.

"I would not let anybody change me or put me in anything tight until I felt it was safe, or I felt like it," she told Tamron. "Now, I did make most of my own decisions, really the majority of them. When it came to dressing, [Jermaine Dupri] never tried to change me. I stayed with my pants to the back and my big clothes for as long as I wanted to, and I felt like, 'Oh all these girls giving body, let me show I got something to work with too.' So, that's what that was all about."

Even if they weren't telling her to change straight to her face, the opinions of men played a large role in what sold and what didn't. Still do.

"Men still run the labels and they probably will forever, and if they have to create you, they will," she told *Variety* in 2020. "So it's still tough for female MCs, producers and writers if you don't have the support of a major male artist backing you—or if you're not super-duper sexy and have some big titties and a nice ass and can twerk. You can't go in there looking [tough] like I did [back in the day] and be like: 'I'm a rapper.' They're going to say, 'Let's get you out of those tomboy clothes and dress you up in a teddy.' But that changes who you are—and then your rhymes start changing because you look different. Then you're not so relatable because you're not being yourself anymore. Now you're somebody else."

Da Brat didn't abandon her tomboy style entirely, and I guess that's why I love this line. Just a relatable Da Brat rocking what she wanted.

4. The song: "Give It 2 You"

The line: It's me, the O.G. funk bandit

Why I think it's the best: Aside from this being one of my favorite songs ever—the LP version and all of the remixes—this line represents the G-funk sound Da Brat was putting down. In the 2019 documentary *Power, Influence and Hip-Hop: The Remarkable Rise of So So Def*, Snoop Dogg said, "One of the main strengths that JD [Dupri] has as a producer is to craft music to the artist's voice, to the artist's style."

Elsewhere in the doc Jermaine talked about how difficult it was to figure out a sound for Da Brat, saying he made "at least ten different records trying to" and "couldn't find it for the longest." But when he finally found it? He gave Da Brat a G-funk sound, the smoothed-out rap subgenre from the West Coast, and it was so well done everybody took notice. In a piece about *Funkdafied* written by Michael Penn II for Vinyl Me, Please, he said that "[Da Brat] fixates on the funk and never loses the groove; there's a palpable weight to every time she commands the listener's attention." That's why she's the OG funk bandit!

5. The song: "Funkdafied"

The line: I'm on a roll in control like Janet, dammit[*]

Why I think it's the best: Janet Jackson is a top-tier, god-level artist, and her third studio album, *Control*, topped the Billboard 200 chart and produced hits like "What Have You Done for Me Lately," "Control," "When I Think of You," "Nasty," and "Let's Wait Awhile." It's a great line to use in reference to your

---

[*] Honorary mention for when she raps "And freak this duet just like Ashford and Simpson." If you're not familiar with Ashford and Simpson, they were a husband-and-wife songwriting, production, and recording duo made up of Valerie Simpson and the late Nickolas Ashford. They wrote some of Motown's biggest hits, like "Ain't No Mountain High Enough," "You're All I Need to Get By," "Ain't Nothing Like the Real Thing," and "Reach Out and Touch (Somebody's Hand)." They also wrote Chaka Khan's "I'm Every Woman," which is a damn banger. And their song "Found a Cure" is excellent.

musical career, especially when you were in control like Da Brat was when *Funkdafied* dropped. She had control of the charts and her image.

The other part of that line that I really love is the "I'm on a roll" part. If you're not familiar with this phrase, it means to have a period of success. This song was obviously recorded before the album made history, but to hear Da Brat essentially predict her achievements is so cool.

Since the release of *Funkadafied* Da Brat has dropped three more albums, the last of which was *Limelite, Luv & Niteclubz* in 2003, and appeared on songs by Mariah Carey, Kelly Rowland, and Dem Franchize Boyz—"I Think They Like Me" is a hit! She took on new roles that included radio host and executive producer and cast member on the We TV reality show *Growing Up Hip Hop*. In 2022 she married her partner, Judy, and the following year she announced that she was pregnant after struggling with fibroids and being told she couldn't carry a child.

When Da Brat appeared on *The Mo'Nique Show* in 2011, she revealed what Jermaine Dupri told her when she made *Funkdafied*: "Okay, look Brat. I'ma tell you now—female rappers pretty much only go gold. So if it doesn't do whatever, don't be disappointed."

No disappointment necessary, JD.

MS. LAURYN HILL, THE FIRST WOMAN TO WIN FIVE GRAMMYS IN A SINGLE NIGHT

The funny thing about writing this book is that there's always a sign that pops up to tell me I should be working on whatever it is I'm planning to write about at that moment. Right now I'm on a plane, a lovely American Airlines flight, to be more precise, that thankfully took off not too long after we were originally scheduled to depart the East Coast in spite of a snowstorm. I'm fresh off enjoying a cranberry apple juice and a tray of grapes, crackers, and cheese, the last of which my gastroenterologist would not be too pleased to hear about me eating. I took a nap when I first got on the plane, and now that I'm wide awake I've decided to crack open my laptop and knock out another chapter. That is, not before I check my iPhone for some magical notification that may have popped up despite me not having Wi-Fi on this flight. I open the phone and there is obviously nothing there. I do the swipe-left maneuver that shows you your activity, the date, the temperature, health notes with advice like "how to priori-tize your sleep," and a random photo from your camera roll. Now you won't believe what fricking photo is there, in fact it's actually ridiculous that this photo is there because before I opened my phone I told myself this would be the chapter I would write. Right there on the screen is a photo I saved to my camera roll on February 24, 2019, at 11:20 a.m. And that photo is of the one and only Ms. Lauryn Hill holding her three Grammys at the 41st Annual Grammy Awards. Those Grammys, and more specifically that night, represent some "firsts" achieved by the legend and her classic album *The Miseducation of Lauryn Hill*, her solo debut and only studio album, released on August 25, 1998. So who would I be to not talk about Hill's record-breaking night at the Grammys? I'd be a nut, that's who I'd be! And nobody likes to be a nut.

Raised in South Orange, New Jersey, by a musical family, Lauryn was destined to be a star from her childhood. At the age of thirteen she performed on *It's Showtime at the Apollo*'s amateur night. In high school she founded the gospel choir and led the cheerleading team. At the age of seventeen she played the recurring role of Kira Johnson on the CBS soap opera *As the World Turns*. And when her senior year rolled around she costarred alongside Whoopi Goldberg in 1993's *Sister Act 2: Back in the Habit*.

In high school Lauryn met Fugees member Pras and formed a trio called Tyme with him and a mutual friend. When the friend left the group, Pras's cousin Wyclef Jean joined them and that's how the Fugees came to be.

A year after *Sister Act 2*, the Fugees released their debut album, *Blunted on Reality*. It was nowhere near as big or successful as its follow-up, *The Score*, but that didn't stop *Rolling Stone* (and other critics) from saying that "Hill, whose rich, sensuous alto is the Fugees' most conspicuous selling point, should leave the guys behind and go solo."

"I'd intended to be in the group forever, until I found myself in circumstances where I felt the inner desire to express myself, freely and openly without any constraint," Hill said in a 2000 interview. "Without anybody saying 'hey, you can't say that! That's not fly, you can't say that' . . . The only way I could've done that was in doing a solo release."

Here are some quick facts about that solo release, just so you can understand how BIG *Miseducation* was (and remains):

- *Miseducation* debuted at No. 1 the Billboard 200 chart—the first time a woman rapper had an album in that spot.
- The album was certified 3x platinum on November 4, 1998, just three months after it was released.
- The album's first-week sales were the highest for a woman in any genre at the time.*
- Everyone fricking loved it. *EW* gave it an "A," praising Lauryn's ability to make an "album of often-astonishing power, strength, and feeling." *XXL* said the album "not only verifies Lauryn Hill as the most exciting voice of a young, progressive hip-hop nation, it raises the standards for it." *Newsday* called it "an ambitious, sprawling and superb recording." I could keep going, but you get the gist.
- Artists from all genres of music have sung its praises— Maxwell, TLC, Kelly Rowland, Cyndi Lauper, and Jay-Z, who said with *Miseducation* Lauryn "made something that's going to stand the test of time."
- It was nominated for ten awards at the Grammys and Hill took home five golden gramophones: for Best R&B Album, Best R&B Song, Best Female R&B Vocal Performance, Best New Artist, and the big kahuna, Album of the Year. She was the first woman to win five awards at the ceremony and the first rapper to take home the coveted Album of the Year award.

* SoundScan didn't start tracking sales until 1991.

Now, I know you're probably wondering, How did she win R&B awards while also being the first rapper to win the big award? And you wouldn't be alone in that thought, because people have been debating whether or not *Miseducation* is a rap album or an R&B album since it dropped. Album cuts like "Ex-Factor," "When It Hurts So Bad," and "Nothing Even Matters" put Lauryn's singing skills on full display and certainly fit the R&B bill. Then there's the scathing diss track "Lost Ones" and the verses on "Doo Wop (That Thing)" that are most certainly rap.

The answer to your question is best answered by none other than Lauryn herself. In her 1998 cover story for *The Source*, Hill said, "I know this sounds crazy, but sometimes I treat rapping like singing, and other times I treat singing like rapping. But still, it's all done within the context of hip-hop." She's a rapper, she's a singer, the album is rap, the album is R&B, and it's all hip-hop. Got it? Cool. Back to the Grammys.

Lauryn's wins that night affirmed that hip-hop as a whole was award-worthy, but the fact that she also took home the most prestigious award in Album of the Year on top of it? *That* said her music, our music, was just as much of an art form as anyone else's. Of course, we don't need awards to tell us that, but the fact that Recording Academy members recognized *Miseducation*'s greatness makes me happy. It's one of the times they got it "right." With that in mind I always wondered, what if we as consumers could decide on the honors our favorite artists took home? Oftentimes an album or a song or an artist impacts listeners in ways that none of the categories can capture. And those specific points of impact best describe why a person wins—or should win—a Grammy in the first place!

So here are five more awards I would have given Ms. Lauryn Hill that night. All of them are totally made up. But all of them explain exactly why she won so many awards as well as Album of the Year.

Best Audible Middle Finger to Anyone Who Didn't Support a Woman's Right to do Whatever She Wants: "To Zion"

When Cardi B revealed she was pregnant during her 2018 *Saturday Night Live* performance there were two groups of people: those who were ecstatic for Cardi and her journey into motherhood, and those who thought she was making a big mistake by having a baby at that point in her career. The response was exactly what Lauryn had heard a little over two decades earlier when people learned she was pregnant with her first child, Zion.

On "To Zion" Lauryn croons "'Look at your career,' they said / 'Lauryn, baby use your head' / But instead I chose to use my heart." In this instance "they" represents the group of people who thought Lauryn was making a mistake by choosing to have a baby with her seminal solo album on the way. It wasn't the "right time" or the "best circumstances," to them.

But as Joan Morgan wrote her book *She Begat This: 20 Years of The Miseducation of Lauryn Hill*, "Black women rarely get credit for the strength it takes to choose motherhood in the face of both stigma and what the rest of society considers imperfect circumstances."

In a society where men are the ones who decide what's appropriate and what's not, choosing "your way" instead of the "right way" directly goes against that idea. With "To Zion," Lauryn affirmed your right to choose parenting on your terms. Why *wouldn't* that be awarded?

Best Diss Song: "Lost Ones"

"It's funny how money change a situation / Miscommunication leads to complication." That's how Ms. Lauryn Hill opens "Lost Ones," the venomous track that's widely believed to be a diss at Wyclef Jean. Not only were the two former groupmates, but

Hill and Jean had dated for a period of time too. I don't need to tell you that things didn't necessarily end well.

The circumstances around how the song was initially released are part of what makes it so good. Joan Morgan tells the story in *She Begat This*, but I'm going to give you an abridged version.

Lauryn took "To Zion" to the then head of Sony Music and Entertainment, Tommy Mottola, and he was *not* feeling it. He wanted Lauryn's music to sound like the Fugees, and as Morgan said he "thought this new mélange of soul, reggae, and relatively little hip hop from one of rap's best emcees was too much of a departure from a proven formula." That's when Lauryn's team decided to take "Lost Ones" to Ruffhouse Records so it could be pressed for distribution to DJs and mix shows. The song hit the streets like wildfire! And it made people want *more* Lauryn, thus creating the space for *Miseducation* to come through and blaze the charts.

So when she raps, "Who you gon' scrimmage, like you the champion? / You might win some but you just lost one," it's a checkmate to Wyclef and Sony.

Best World Building on an Album: *The Miseducation of Lauryn Hill*

The thing that I love about the winner of that last award, "Lost Ones," is that it interpolates Jamaican dance hall artist Sister Nancy's "Bam Bam." In 2016, *Billboard* said the song was "a strong contender for the title of most sampled reggae song of all time," and listening to it once will explain why. It's a smooth, bass-heavy riddim perfectly paired with Sister Nancy's voice. It's the perfect sample, especially when you remember that pioneers Cindy and Kool Herc are Jamaican, and that hip-hop and reggae have a close-knit relationship.

The thing that I love about the album is that, as Morgan said, Lauryn "deliberately wrote herself into the discourse of diaspora, drew on the global nature of black music, and fashioned herself a citizen of the world."

When Lauryn invokes call-and-response patterns at the end of "To Zion," it's an element directly tied to the postslavery music that led to the formation of the blues. When Carlos Santana's guitar starts playing at the opening of the same song, listeners are exposed to his influence by the blues and African rhythms. "Doo Wop (That Thing)" literally names the genre it's inspired by, a kind of rhythm and blues born out of African American communities in the 1940s that relies on light instrumentation, ensemble singing, and group harmonies.

Lauryn and her collaborators incorporated the sounds of so many parts of the Black diaspora at every stop, and it sounds authentic, organic, and beautiful. Yes, she gets this award too.

Lauryn Hill makes history

Best Album Skits:
The Miseducation of Lauryn Hill

I don't know why there aren't awards for album skits, but this is my petition to make it a reality. *Miseducation* opens by placing listeners in a classroom, the sound of a school bell signaling the start of class. Ras Baraka, an educator, author, and politician who would later become the mayor of Newark, starts taking attendance. When he gets to "Lauryn Hill," he repeats her name a few times before it's clear to the listener that she's not in class.

The skits continue throughout the album, but my favorite one is placed right at the end of "To Zion," when Baraka asks the class how many of them have ever been in love. The girls and boys in the room start sharing their definition of the word, and it's an innocent, honest, and eye-opening conversation between children and an adult about the simplest thing we've ever complicated. "Willingness to do everything for that person," says one boy. "Love is not phony!" says one of the girls. When asked how you know you're in love, one of the girls says, "It's sometimes, like when they try to act funny in front of they [*sic*] boys, like when they get around say [*sic*] they love you. They can't love you. 'Cause love-love-love wouldn't do that."

The presence of the students on the album is storytelling at its finest, with the kids' commentary rounding out a listening experience built around this idea of Lauryn's "miseducation." So yes, she gets this award too. And the kids should as well!

Most Prophetic Song:
"The Miseducation of Lauryn Hill"

The last song on the original album release is so prophetic it's not even funny. On the chorus Lauryn croons, "But deep in my heart, the answer, it was in me / And I made up my mind to define my own destiny."

At the time that I'm writing this *Miseducation* remains Hill's only studio album. She released her live album *Unplugged No. 2.0* in 2002, and after that removed herself from the public. She's dropped a few singles since then and appeared as a featured artist on a handful of songs. There have been shows here and there, and naturally a lot of calls from people for another album. Through it all Lauryn has stood firm in her desire to not let the music industry dictate her worth.

The legacy of *Miseducation* doesn't exist without contention either. In 2001 Hill, her management team, and record label settled a lawsuit with a group of musicians who wanted songwriting and production on the album. As reported by *Rolling Stone*: "The four musicians claimed in the suit that they worked on arranging and producing all the cuts on Hill's Grammy-winning solo debut, *The Miseducation of Lauryn Hill*, and requested partial writing credit on thirteen of the fourteen original tracks on the album, with percentages specified in the suit."

The track they didn't ask for credit on? "To Zion."

The suit emphasizes the importance of proper credit, and also reminds me that an album isn't any less impactful because of collaboration. In 2014 *Miseducation* was added to the Library of Congress's National Recording Registry, which is an archive of recordings with cultural, aesthetic and historical significance, and in 2021 the album was certified diamond by the RIAA for selling ten million units, making her the first woman rapper to achieve this feat. The album still gets played because of its impact, and it won all of the Grammys it did because of its tremendous power. And if none of the categories she won even existed, the ones I proposed would do just fine.

CARDI B IS THE FIRST WOMAN RAPPER TO EARN THREE DIAMOND-CERTIFIED RECORDS

'm listening to "Tomorrow 2," a track by Memphis-bred rapper Glorilla that features Cardi B. I remember staying up late in September 2022 waiting for the song and video to drop. I kept rewatching the clip Cardi shared the day before on her Instagram, which had a snippet of the haunting song "Pink Soldiers" from *Squid Game* at the top of the video, over and over and over. If you watched *Squid Game* on Netflix then you know that whenever that song started playing, something major was about to happen. Something that was about to quite literally change the game. I guess I had this feeling that Cardi B's feature on the song was about to do the same thing, figuratively. And I was right, because it's that kind of impact that has defined Cardi B's career thus far—her major-label debut single, "Bodak Yellow," rose to the top of the Billboard Hot 100 chart, when her single "Up" hit No. 1 on the same chart it made her the first woman rapper to have five songs hit the No. 1 spot on the Hot 100, when she took home the Grammy for Best Rap Album at the sixty-first annual ceremony for her debut album, *Invasion of Privacy,* it marked the first time a woman won the award as a solo artist since the category was first awarded at the 1996 telecast,[*] and when "Bodak Yellow" was certified diamond by the RIAA in March 2021 for selling ten million units,[**] she was the first woman rapper to have a single earn the honor.[***] By the end of 2021 Cardi B would reach diamond status two more times, once for her assistance on Maroon 5's "Girls Like You," and again for her single "I Like It," featuring J Balvin and Bad Bunny. In total, Cardi B has three diamond-certified records, making her the first woman in rap to achieve this feat.

Before we go any further, I want to share some Cardi B facts to help you better understand the woman who notched three diamond-certified records:

Cardi B made $250 a week working the cash register at an Amish market in the Tribeca section of Manhattan. Her last job before becoming a stripper, Cardi B was fired from the Amish market for giving one of her coworkers a substantial discount. I love this fact, not because she got fired, but because she was looking out for her coworker.

When Cardi B started stripping she lied to her mom and told her she was making money from babysitting. It was one of the managers at the market who suggested she try a different career path, with

---

[*] Ms. Lauryn Hill was the first woman to win in the category when Fugees' *The Score* won in 1997.

[**] I know you're probably wondering what moving ten million units means in this streaming era. I got you! According to the RIAA website, a unit is defined as a permanent digital download or 150 on-demand audio and/or video streams.

[***] Nicki Minaj would be the second when her hit "Super Bass" reached diamond status in November 2021.

Cardi B telling the *FADER* in 2016, "He was like, 'You're so pretty, you got a nice body.' He told me to go across the street to New York Dolls, the strip club. That's when I started stripping." The funny videos she posted online during this time led to her being cast on the show in the next item.

She was a breakout star on VH1's *Love & Hip Hop: New York*. "Hey, America, washpoppin'? My name is Cardi B," she proclaimed in her debut on the show in 2015. "You might know me as that annoying dancer on social media that be talking hella crazy, with the long nails and the big ol' titties." Her infectious personality helped take her to the top.

She dropped two solo mixtapes before her debut album. *Gangsta Bitch Music, Vol. 1* in 2016 and *Gangsta Bitch Music, Vol. 2* in 2017. Those titles are true to Cardi.

Her debut album, *Invasion of Privacy*, premiered at the top of the Billboard 200. Every single song on the album charted on the Billboard Hot 100. And every single song was certified platinum.

She's kept it real about getting help. There's been a lot of talk around ghostwriting and the assistance that Cardi B has gotten from friend and frequent collaborator Pardison Fontaine. But make no mistake, "Pardison is not a ghostwriter, he's a cowriter," she said during a 2018 appearance on *The Breakfast Club*. "I credit him on all the songs that he been [*sic*] in. . . . I'm putting my people on, you know what I'm saying? Atlantic noticed his working skills and noticed his music, they signed him too." The sentiment I expressed in the Salt-N-Pepa chapter applies here as well: no one can perform Cardi's songs like Cardi.

She enjoyed English class in school. Some of her favorite books are *To Kill a Mockingbird* by Harper Lee, *Their Eyes Were Watching God* by Zora Neale Hurston, and *The Coldest Winter Ever* by Sister Souljah.

Cinderella is her favorite Disney princess. Cardi said this during a sit-down with Maurice DuBois for *CBS Sunday Morning*, and I think it's so fitting because her story is a true Cinderella story. She went from being a cashier at an Amish market to a superstar.

She's obsessed with the US presidents. Cardi knows a lot about America's heads of state, and has a particular affinity for the thirty-second POTUS, Franklin Delano Roosevelt. In a 2018 interview with *GQ* Cardi praised Roosevelt's New Deal and establishment of Social Security. When she was a guest on Netflix's *My Next Guest Needs No Introduction with David Letterman*, the former late-night host took Cardi B to Roosevelt's library and museum in Hyde Park, New York. She was so excited! I'm a history nerd myself, and she had the same kind of enthusiasm I did when I visited the National Museum of African American History and Culture for the first time.

She's a Libra. Probably my favorite fact of all because I too am a Libra. And not to be all horoscopey (if that's even a word), but Librans are known to be imaginative and diplomatic hard workers who love to collaborate. Other famous Libras? Serena Williams, Will Smith, and Lil Wayne.

The thing about all of the facts I just listed is that they're more than things we know about Cardi B. They're things we know *because* of Cardi B. She's been open, honest, and authentic from the moment she started posting videos on the internet, and it's that kind of genuineness that's made her music inescapable, replayable, and as a result, diamond.

We can start with "Bodak Yellow," Cardi's major-label debut single that dropped in the summer of 2017. I honestly cannot remember going anywhere and *not* hearing the song. I heard it at parties. On the radio. In the store. On TV shows. In commercials. And when I opened my social media apps—grade school teacher Erica Buddington taught her sixth graders at Capital Harlem School a geography version of the song that went viral. The J. White–produced beat was the perfect foundation for lyrics like "I'm the hottest in the street, know you prolly heard of me / Got a bag and fixed my teeth, hope you hoes know it ain't cheap." Cardi's realness permeated the entire song and resonated with the masses, so when it rose to the No. 1 spot on the Billboard Hot 100 it wasn't a surprise, at least not to me. You. Could. Not. Escape. It.

"Bodak Yellow" kicked off a historic run. She won a bunch of BET Hip-Hop awards, a Grammy for her debut album, became a host on the Netflix hip-hop competition series *Rhythm + Flow*, announced that she was pregnant on *SNL*, performed pregnant at Coachella, attended her first-ever Met Gala, signed a bunch of endorsement deals, cohosted *The Tonight Show*, and dropped more chart-topping hits.

"I Like It" was released as the fourth single from *Invasion of Privacy* in 2018. Sampling Latin boogaloo artist Pete Rodriguez's "I Like It Like That" and featuring Bad Bunny and J Balvin, the song was the perfect celebration of Cardi's Latin heritage and a certified smash.

She opened the song rapping "Now I like dollars, I like diamonds, I like stunting, I like shining," unknowingly foreshadowing the RIAA certification the song would get a few years later, while Bad Bunny and J Balvin spit verses about their success and lifestyles. When *Billboard* interviewed Cardi about the song after it hit No. 1, she said, "People say they don't understand the Spanish parts of the song but they still love it. It just goes to show you if a song is great and it makes people dance and makes people happy, it doesn't matter what language the music is in." She was right.

That same year Maroon 5 recruited Cardi B for the single version of "Girls Like You," which previously appeared on their album without her vocals. "She was in the honeymoon period of her moment," Maroon 5 lead singer Adam Levine told *Variety*. "She was just beginning to be that female artist that everybody was talking about, and I thought it was an important thing for her to be involved. I knew she would have an interesting take on what was being said, and she would do it in a way that you wouldn't necessarily have thought of." That's exactly what Cardi did.

She kicked off her verse on the love song reminiscing about her days dancing at the strip club and closed it out by rapping, "I need you right here 'cause every time you're far / I play with this kitty like you play wit' your guitar, ah." I certainly didn't have "hearing Cardi rap about masturbation on a Maroon 5 song" on my 2018 bingo card, but I did have some variation of "Cardi B's gonna be Cardi B wherever she goes" on it.

That authenticity contributed to what Shea Serrano described in his book *Hip-Hop (and Other Things)* as the "2018 Cardi B effect." Shea noted that Maroon 5, "one of the biggest and most successful bands of the modern era, went well over half a decade without scoring a number one hit. That's how hard it is to score one of those." He added that with the Cardi B–assisted "Girls Like You," the group not only notched a No. 1, but the song also "sold more copies by itself than their previous seven songs combined." It was a gigantic, inescapable song that would not have done the numbers it did without Cardi.

Now, a lack of accolades is not a measurement of greatness, *especially in rap.* A lot of the best emcees to ever do it don't have Grammys, diamond, platinum, or gold plaques, or even full albums. Also, we are in the streaming era, so comparing Cardi B's sales to that of her forerappers[*] can be a bit complicated. Being able to have song after song at your fingertips for a monthly subscription fee is different from going to the store to actually purchase the music, or even purchasing it on your phone. Going diamond is still not an easy feat. The last thing I want to make clear is that those first two things are more reflective of the business of hip-hop and not the early days of the culture, when it was about fun, freedom, and self-expression.

Cardi B did it all, while remaining true to the woman she was when we first met her. She didn't change the way she spoke. She didn't lie about needing help. She didn't listen to people who tried to shame her for choosing motherhood at the height of her rise. She didn't stop hustling. This ability to remain authentic is important, because it's the natural progression in the work done and heat taken by the women in all of hip-hop before Cardi B even made an Instagram account.

(And being able to say you went diamond three times is pretty damn cool, too.)

---

[*] Don't you just love making up words?

OUTRO: THANK-YOUS

I have to shout out my entire family: my mom, dad, sisters, uncles, aunties (blood and honorary), and cousins (play and real). I hit them up more times than I could count to ask them a question, show them a picture, ask them to read something, or ask if they remembered a specific artist or song. All of my inquiries were very random and they came at all hours of the day. They never once seemed annoyed and always made it a point to check in and ask me how it was going, a gesture that was especially helpful on those days when I would sit in front of my computer for hours and have nothing to write. I'm very lucky to have the family that I do.

Then there are my best friends, my high school crew, my college homies, and my friends I've made through work. They're amazing, and they made sure I took breaks and actually slept. Because in the beginning, on the days that I couldn't stop writing, the only time I took breaks was to use the bathroom and eat, lol. They got me out of that quick, and read so much of this book for me on more than one occasion. Thank you all for being the best friends I could have ever asked for.

Then there's the GOAT Sean Desmond from Twelve. I learned so much from you during this process, and I'm so thankful that I got to make my first book with you leading the charge. Every time we would talk I would tell you I couldn't believe I was writing a book and you would say, "You're doing it." You gave me the space to create the book I've always wanted to, the best edits I've ever gotten in my life, and put me on to the best restaurant in Brooklyn. And Zohal! My random calls and texts and emails with questions and concerns or sometimes just straight-up anxiety never went unanswered. You kept me motivated and calmed a bunch of those random worries that popped up along the way! Then there's Jim and Shreya, the art gurus! You both listened to every single idea I had and helped me get this amazing cover. Monet, you drew the book jacket of my dreams. Seriously, I look at the images every single day. You are amazing. Sara, thank you for being such a great artist. You've drawn so many things for me over the years but I'm still shocked at how quickly you can get an image done. The day I sent you the MC Lyte reference I swear you drew it in five minutes. You're a magician.

Shea Serrano! You have been so supportive of *The Gumbo* for so long and you were one of the first people I called when I found out this book was happening. You are a true icon. I've learned so much from you over the years and feel honored to know you. If y'all haven't watched *Primo* yet, get on it!

Thank you to all of the ladies in this book for all that you've done, as well as all the ladies who took time out of their days to talk to me to make some of these chapters happen. Ms. April, Ms. Joicelyn, and Ms. Kierna, y'all are my heroes.

Thank you to archive legend Syreeta for making these interviews happen, sending me PDFs of magazines when I needed to source something for the book, and giving me words of encouragement along the way. I appreciate you!

Thank you to my *Late Show* family! I wouldn't trade the love, advice, and support I've received from you for anything in this world.

And last but certainly not least, I have to thank all the women who have been involved with *The Gumbo*. Please know that if you have been to a party, written an article, created a mix, DJ'd at one of our events, showed up to one of our Digital Dinners, reposted something of ours in your story, or retweeted a tweet, I am so so so thankful for you. Brooklyn and Quin, y'all are the best team I could have ever asked to work with. I'm so thankful to know and learn from you both.

ABOUT THE AUTHOR

NADIRAH SIMMONS is a writer and digital content creator committed to preserving Black history, hip-hop history, and pop culture, and finding new ways to tell stories on TV and the internet. In 2018, Simmons was inspired to put her love of hip-hop, Black history, and Black woman-hood along with her producing and writing skills into practice. She created *The Gumbo*, an innovative space in media for the creative excellence and activism of Black women in hip-hop and a safe haven free of politics.